The Crime Novel

Double Indemnity: the anklet. (Courtesy Motion Picture Academy Library)

The Crime Novel

A Deviant Genre

by **Tony Hilfer**

**University of Texas Press,
Austin**

First Edition, 1990

Requests for permission to reproduce material from
this work should be sent to Permissions, University
of Texas Press, Box 7819, Austin, Texas
78713-7819.

∞ The paper used in this publication meets the
minimum requirements of American National
Standard for Information Sciences—Permanence of
Paper for Printed Library Materials, ANSI
Z39.48-1984.

Library of Congress Cataloging-in-Publication Data

Hilfer, Anthony Channell.
    The crime novel : a deviant genre / by Tony
Hilfer. — 1st ed.
        p.   cm.
    Includes bibliographical references.
    ISBN 0-292-71131-X (alk. paper). —
    ISBN 0-292-71136-0 (pbk. : alk. paper)
    1. Detective and mystery stories—History and
criticism.   2. Crime in literature.   3. Criminals
in literature.   I. Title.
    PN3448.D4H55   1990
    809.3'872—dc20   90-12278
                                                   CIP

To Tom Hilfer
"Look! We have come through!"

Contents

The Postman Always Rings Twice: Lana Turner's Cora, "the gap between desire and expression." (© 1946 Loew's Inc. Ren. 1973 Metro-Goldwyn-Mayer Inc.)

Acknowledgments

A COMPLETE LIST OF those who helped me think out, put into form, and complete this book would be as long as the book itself, so what follows is the *short* list.

Bernd Wachter, a West German scholar, sent me *Uber Patricia Highsmith*, a book until then unknown to me that I found highly useful. This was collegiality on the international level.

Barry Gifford, the originator of Black Lizard Press, which has republished many of the finest American crime novels, gave the second draft of my book an incisive reading. But I might never have gotten to this draft had it not been for John Cawelti's searching critique of an inflated first draft. Cawelti's criticism enabled this book to attain its present shape, though I alone am responsible for its flaws. Moreover, Cawelti's account of the difference between the English and American forms of the detective novel in *Adventure, Mystery, and Romance*, along with George Grella's two classic essays on the subject, were the necessary context for my distinctions between English and American types of the crime novel.

The Midwest Quarterly granted me permission to use part of my article, "'Not Really Such a Monster': Highsmith's Ripley as Thriller Protagonist and Protean Man," 25:4 (Summer 1984): 361–374, in chapter 6; Cornell University Press allowed my use of Sander Gilman's translation of Hugo Ball's "Schizophrenia" from Gilman's *Dif-*

ference and Pathology: Stereotypes of Sexuality, Race, and Madness, copyright © 1985 by Cornell University Press (Ithaca: Cornell University Press, 1985), pp. 228–229; Harvard University Press and the Trustees of Amherst College permitted me to quote from *The Poems of Emily Dickinson,* edited by Thomas H. Johnson (Cambridge, Mass.: The Belknap Press of Harvard University Press), copyright © 1951, 1955, 1979, 1983 by the President and Fellows of Harvard College; and Warner/Chappell granted permission to use portions of the lyric from "Devil or Angel" by Blanche Carter.

Janet Lorenz of the Academy of Motion Picture Arts and Sciences sent me the stills from *The Postman Always Rings Twice* and *Double Indemnity.* The Roger-Viollet Agency of Paris sent me the photograph of Georges Simenon. I owe thanks to Hal Boucher for generously permitting the use of his fine photograph of Margaret Millar, to Patricia Highsmith for the use of the two photographs of her, and to Alberta Thompson for the photograph of Jim Thompson. I also wish to thank Sharon Thompson Reed for her lovely description of her father, Jim Thompson, in our phone conversations.

The University Research Institute of the University of Texas helped pay for typing and photocopying with a number of small grants. More of my colleagues helped with this project than I have room to name, but I especially wish to thank Don Graham, Wick Wadlington, Joe Kruppa, Bill Scheick, and Bill Sutherland.

For their sensitivity and professionalism in the production of this book I thank Frankie Westbrook and Barbara Spielman of the University of Texas Press and my copy editor, Alison Tartt.

My father, Harry Hilfer, gave welcome moral and other support. I owe more than I can ever repay to the dedicatee of this book, my excellent son, Tom, whose contribution went well beyond typing some of the manuscript. We both are deeply indebted to Chet Sottile and the staff, Karen and the rest, at Teen and Family.

And of course there is the amazing Jane Koock.

Introduction

THE SUBJECT OF THIS book is an almost completely overlooked genre, the crime novel, which I see as oppositional to the detective story.[1] My first chapter will contrast the crime novel to the detective novel, pointing to how it extends, inverts, and generally plays off against the conventions of its better-known parental genre. As Alistair Fowler notes, "The value of the generic horizon is obvious from the difficulty that arises when it is missing,"[2] exactly the case with the crime novel.

In fact, one needs to know not only the genre but the types: "No work, however avant-garde, is intelligible without some context of familiar types."[3] These types or formulae are what I outline in chapter 1, primarily in terms of character type and theme. Chapters 2 to 5 then go on to develop typological variations on the themes of madness, alienation, sexual passion, and justice, showing a certain logic of possibilities for what writers can do with these themes.

Thus, I affirm the interest of the genre not by denying but by exploring its conventionality, agreeing with Fowler that convention and genre enable rather than limit literary creativity: "Far from inhibiting the author, genres are a positive support. They offer room as one might say for him to write in—a habitation of mediated definiteness; a proportioned mental space; a literary matrix by which to order his experience during composition. Claudio Guillén . . . suggests that genres operate as problem-solving models. Instead of a daunting void, they extend a provocatively definite invitation."[4]

What Italo Calvino describes as true of all literary works seems to me especially helpful for understanding crime novels: that is, they are "modelled on fixed structures and we might almost say on prefabricated elements—elements, however, that allow of an enormous number of combinations." Thus, "what can be constructed on the basis of these elementary processes can present unlimited combinations, permutations and transformations."[5] Unlike some current theories, Calvino's concept of "the literature machine" does not proclaim "no authors need apply": "Literature is a combinatorial game that pursues the possibilities implicit in its own material, independent of the personality of the poet. But it is a game that at a certain point is invested with an unexpected meaning, a meaning found not on the linguistic plane . . . but slipped in from another level, activating something that is of great concern to the author or his society."[6] I see crime novels as combinatorial games with just such unexpected meanings.

My approach then is synchronic, to explore the genre as a set of thematic possibilities, rather than diachronic, to trace its historical evolution and its reflections of social change. I believe the logic of the genre better defines it than its chronology. This may be the result of the crime novel's relative invisibility as a distinct genre. Not having a clear awareness of precedent, writers kept reinventing what could be done with a murder novel in which the protagonist is not a detective and the reader may know from the start whodunit. What these writers have in common is less a knowledge of each other than of the detective novel with its warehouse of conventions open to subtle alteration or complete inversion.

There are, it is true, national differences, a distinct English type of crime novel correlative to the conventions of the English detective novel and a distinct American type of crime novel correlative to the conventions of the American detective novel. Chapters 3 to 5 center on these distinctive forms. But the schizophrenic theme of chapter 2 is so innate to the crime novel's genius of inversion that it recurs in both national forms. And, to complicate matters further, some Americans write English-type crime novels, just as Ellery Queen and Rex Stout wrote detective novels in the English mode, while John Dickson Carr moved to England early in his career so as to be closer to the source of his inspiration. The crime novels of Margaret Millar and Patricia Highsmith get in between the English and American modes to create some original effects.

Georges Simenon, whose crime fiction is also a subject of chapter 6, is more obviously anomalous in that he is the only author I cover in this study, except for the Irish Flann O'Brien (chapter 5), who is not American or English. But then Simenon is an anomaly in French literature as well, writing in a dry, almost behaviorist style of the sort that post–World War II French critics were to call "le style Américain,"[7] though Simenon had come to it early and on his own. Simenon tracks the same ground that characterizes the American form, especially the concomitant themes of the pathological world, phenomenologically analyzed, and the alienated protagonist, respondent to this world.

It is possible that criticism may eventually demonstrate political and aesthetic flaws not only in given crime novels but even as intrinsic to the genre, built into its conventions. I hope not since my complicity with the form will be readily apparent as this book proceeds. My case rests on how the permutational possibilities of the types within the genre create a literary situation too rich to be critically sentenced to an imprisoning term. The authorial role, once more, is not to transcend the genre but to play out "particular variations on generic and modal conventions."[8] This may be by way of inverting or at least playing against certain conventions: "the defeating or reorienting of our expectations about a text's comformity to precedents becomes part of its meaning."[9] Many crime writers resemble the spy novelist John Le Carré in having "beaten the genre trap—not, though, by venturing outside . . . but by finding unexpected room within."[10]

The principle of the crime novel is that nothing succeeds like excess, even its conventions being oppositional to, sometimes even parodic of, the rational containment of the detective novel. National differences are heightened: the English crime novel ultimately accommodates society, though in a quirkily idiosyncratic fashion; the American crime novel tends toward alienation and nihilism. Some readers may find me guilty in my exploration of these differences of hunting with conservative English hounds while running with anarchistic American hares. This is a fair cop. Not only do I sympathize with both tendencies, but can point to no middle ground. To be more judicious would betray the deviancy of the genre.

In the course of this study I take help from wherever I can get it: Fowler on genre, Cawelti and Grella on the detective novel, Freud on the uncanny, Merleau-Ponty on the phenomenology of perception, and so on. All these perspectives were adopted after the fact as what a particular group of novels seemed to call for. I have not constructed a critical approach and used works of literature to illustrate it so much as answered to the novels themselves. I hope to demonstrate a far greater implicative power in crime fiction than any form of popular culture is supposed to have except when treated as symptom rather than symbol.[11] I use the epigraphs to the chapters to suggest certain of these implications. Chapter 6 concludes the book with a set of close readings of two novels each by the four writers who most brilliantly work out the possibilities of the genre: Georges Simenon, Margaret Millar, Patricia Highsmith, and Jim Thompson.

Finally, I must acknowledge various sins of omission.[12] There are excellent crime novels not even mentioned in this study because there was not enough room in a chapter for yet another fine work that fit the type, or the book did not fit any of my types (I by no means claim to have discovered every existing crime novel variation), or because I did not know the book existed. Nominations from readers are welcome.

I do know of Ruth Rendell, Elmore Leonard, Robert Merkin, and other first-rate contemporary crime novel writers, but it seemed to me more useful to establish the genre these writers work in than to review their reasonably well-known books. Moreover, the most interesting thing about these contemporaries is how they play about with current topical issues—i.e., U.S. intervention in Central America for Leonard—that would require a book in itself to properly examine.

For the same reason I do not include those canonized writers who anticipated the crime novel's conventions—Poe, Dickens, Dostoevsky—or avant-garde writers of metaphysical detective and crime novels—Robbe-Grillet, Queneau, Nabokov, Sciascia, Handke.[13] The present study is intended to explore rather than to exhaust critical possibilities.

The Crime Novel

1

The Crime Novel
Guilt and
Menace

Mr. Walker preached today on the govern-
ment of the thoughts. Thought I, what thun-
ders mutter in these commonplaces. Suppose
he had rolled back the cloud of ceremony and
decency and showed us how bad the smooth
plausible people we meet everyday in society
would be if they durst, nay how we should behave if we acted out our thoughts—not how
devils would do, but how good people that
hope to be saved would do if they dared—I
think it would shake us. These are the real
terrors.

RALPH WALDO EMERSON, *EMERSON IN HIS
JOURNALS*, ED. JOEL PORTE, ENTRY FOR NOV. 11,
1832

THE NOVEL IS IN ORIGIN an oppositional, even parodic form.[1]
Don Quixote is oppositional to the romance, Richardson's novels to
the cavalier ethos of Restoration drama and libertine poetry. And the
oppositions continue within the novel form, every *Pamela* inviting
a potential *Shamela*. Frederic Jameson tells us that "genre theory
must always in one way or another project a model of the co-
existence or tension between several generic modes or strands," that
"the play of structural norm and textual deviation . . . characterizes
such analysis at its best" because "the value of narrative models lies
in their capacity to register a given text's specific deviation from
them."[2] We shall find such variation in crime novels but within the
larger frame of what Alistair Fowler calls "antigenres," "antitheses
to existing genres." In Fowler's definition "an antigenre . . . is not
directed against a particular original. Moreover, it has a life of its
own that continues collaterally with the contrasting genre."[3] Deviation from the detective novel is the norm of the crime novel, providing cues to reader expectations and thus becoming the source of
rather more tortuous satisfactions than those of the detective novel.

To be sure, the crime novel has origins independent of and separate from those of the detective story in Godwin, Hogg, Poe, Collins,
Dickens, and Dostoevsky. Though some of the formula of the crime
novels are in these predecessors, they mainly derive from and are re-

inforced by playing off against the detective story. So I shall begin my extended definition of the crime novel by emphasizing features oppositional to the detective form.

Some of these features are described in Julian Symons's *Bloody Murder: From the Detective Story to the Crime Novel*. As Symons notes, character psychology and implicative setting are frequently essential in the crime novel whereas an ingenious puzzle may be dispensed with altogether. The reverse is true of the detective novel. Symons sees an important distinction in social attitude: that of the classical detective story is traditionalist and conservative but in the crime novel it is "often radical in the sense of questioning some aspect of law, justice, or the way society is run." While I agree with these distinctions, there is an important one that Symons does *not* make: he includes Hammett, Chandler, and Ross Macdonald as "serious crime novelists" when, in fact, they are serious detective novelists.[4] P. D. James, whose own detective novels are serious and intelligent, recognizes the absence of the detective as the definitive generic distinction: "The detective novel has a death at the heart, a death which is mysterious. At the end of the book we know what we didn't know to begin with, that is, who committed the murder, whereas in the crime novel we may know from the very beginning either who had done it or who is going to do it. Therefore, one of the prime interests in detective fiction is the solution of the mystery and why it happened. The prime interest in the crime novel may be the effect of this crime on the murderer himself. In detective fiction you certainly do have justice personified or at least represented by a detective. You obviously couldn't have a detective novel which didn't have a detective."[5] The distinction is crucial, for the central presence of the detective guarantees the rationality of the world and the integrity of the self. *But the central and defining feature of the crime novel is that in it self and world, guilt and innocence are problematic.* The world of the crime novel is *constituted* by what is problematic in it.

Consequently, the crime novel differs not only from the detective story but from popular art generally, if Abraham Kaplan is correct in asserting that "Popular Art depicts the world, not as it is, nor even as it might be, but as we would have it."[6] Crime novels do not necessarily depict the world as it is, but few depict the world as we would have it. Jacques Barzun even accuses crime novel readers of indulgence in guilty pleasures: "What we are in fact given . . . is 'stories of anxiety,' which cater for the contemporary wish to feel vaguely disturbed."[7]

The function of the detective hero is to guarantee the reader's ab-

solution from guilt. This is basic to the genre's form of wish fulfillment. In contrast, the reader of the crime novel is maneuvered into
various forms of complicity. The inversion of the detective story
reader's expectation is, in fact, so consistent as to become, for the
experienced crime novel reader, a new expectation. One approaches
the crime novel with an uneasy but perhaps, as Barzun asserts, a not
altogether unpleasurable anticipation of threat and guilt. Thus a detective in a crime novel can prove useful as a threat to the main character and/or as an agent for plot closure but can be the protagonist
only when doubling in the role of killer or falsely suspected, since
the traditional detective hero would prematurely foreclose the anxiety and guilt central to the crime novel. The protagonist of the crime
novel, then, will be the murderer (*The Talented Mr. Ripley*), a guilty
bystander (*The Lodger*), a falsely suspected (Cornell Woolrich), or
the victim (*Before the Fact*). The very adoption of such perspectives
is oppositional to detective story conventions, throwing them quite
out of kilter and keeping the problem of guilt and complicity, of
menace and victimization at the fore. Guilt is so pervasive in the
world of the crime novel that even the falsely suspected may begin
to doubt their innocence in the face of near universal conviction
(sometimes legal conviction) of their guilt, and even victims may be
in unconscious (or, worse yet, conscious) conspiracy with their murderers. The murderers in crime novels may not be caught; if they
are, they may well be the characters with whom we most identified.

Each of the four protagonist types of the crime novel leads to a
variation on the theme of guilt that thoroughly subverts the reassurances of the detective story.

1. *The killer as protagonist*. What is most reassuring about the
detective novel is its solution to the seemingly intrinsically murky
and problematic concern of its plot: that of guilt. The detective
genre works to divest guilt of its anxiety and ambiguity by trans-
forming it from the realm of psychology into that of logic. Guilt is
both denied for the self by being projected onto the criminal other
and is rationalized as a problem susceptible to rational solution. As
Brigid Brophy argues in a brilliant essay distinguishing between detective and crime novels, "The detective does the Ego's work: making
sense of the irrational and acquitting us of blood-guilt."[8] Concentra-
tion on the criminal would induce precisely the element of the irrational and anxious that the detective story is designed to outflank:
"if we become too concerned with the motives of the criminal, his
guilt is likely to seem increasingly ambiguous and difficult to define."[9] Thus, though the crucial scene in the classical detective
story is the detective's revelation of the murderer, what then follows

is that, far from dwelling on his reactions to exposure, the murderer "is positively rushed off-stage at the end." The detective novel generally mutes the theme of punishment, sometimes seems almost to overlook it.[10] What matters is the detective's revelation, not the murderer's punishment, for in this myth of rationality truth takes priority over justice.[11]

The detective novel, then, denies guilt, defending the ego against the rival impositions of id and superego: "the detective story does not pile . . . guilt onto its readers by seducing them into imaginatively participating and concurring in a murder. On the contrary: its form is carefully calculated to make participation impossible. By the very terms of the puzzle, the reader cannot follow the act of murder through the consciousness of the murderer."[12]

In contrast, crime novelists lessen or abolish that reassuring distance. And when the crime novel goes the opposite direction, emphasizing the otherness of the murderer, the uncanniness of this other in the role of protagonist or as a direct threat to him is threateningly magnified. Of a book in "the esoteric tradition of Patricia Highsmith," a reviewer comments: "It leaves you uncomfortably uncertain of what you feel, whom you sympathize with."[13]

2. *The guilty bystander as protagonist.* Though there are few protagonists in this category, the structural slot is important as yet another bar to the exemption of the reader. As W. H. Auden argues in "The Guilty Vicarage," the role of the detective is less to prove the guilt of the murderer than the innocence of all other characters. The murderer is a scapegoat whose expulsion redeems the Edenic community and reassures the reader of the externality of guilt to world and self. In John Cawelti's summation, "the detective intervenes and proves that the general suspicion is false. He proves the social order is not responsible for the crime because it was the act of a particular individual with his own private motives. . . . It is not the confrontation between detective and criminal so much as the detective's rescue of false suspects . . . that constitutes the dramatic nexus of the classical formula."[14]

The crime novel formula of a bystander who from motives of venality, fear, weakness, or vicarious participation fails to reveal the murderer spreads rather than limits guilt. If the bystander is an ordinary person, the implication of the universality of guilt widens a fortiori whereas an extraordinary protagonist may be more appealing for us to identify with, worse yet. Moreover, the reader's role is discomfitingly close to guilty bystander since we too witness crimes. By continuing to read we become accomplices after the fact.

3. *The falsely suspected as protagonist.* The detective's role is to

exculpate the falsely suspected. There are usually a number of false suspects since they also serve the plot function of diverting our suspicion from the actual killer.

But one type of crime novel has a single false suspect as protagonist. In Tzvetan Todorov's description, "a crime is committed in the first pages and all the evidence in the hands of the police points to a certain person (who is the main character). In order to prove his innocence, this person must himself find the real culprit, even if he risks his life in doing so. We might say that in this case, this character is at the same time the detective, the culprit (in the eyes of the police), and the victim (potential victim of the real murderers)."[15] I would add to this that sometimes such a protagonist cannot keep these roles straight, thus intensifying paranoia and making for an even more uneasy relationship to the reader. The ruling principle of the world such novels create is not clinical paranoia, where you wrongly suppose that "they" are out to get you, but structural paranoia, as in Kafka or many large organizations, where they really are, where the whole of what sociologists nicely call "the surround" oozes menace. If reality, as these sociologists argue, is a social construction,[16] the falsely suspected find themselves in a world where they are, by definition, guilty, although they did not, in fact, commit a crime.

Another variation is what James Sandoe calls "the puzzle of the vanishing lady": "You will recall the story of the girl and her mother who arrived in Paris one afternoon during the year of the Exposition, went to a crowded hotel and were assigned to different rooms, whereupon the mother vanished as completely as if she had never existed while all the world seemed bent upon denying to the frantic girl that she had ever existed."[17] Here the social existence, the memory, sometimes even the personal identity of the protagonist (that he/she is who he/she claims to be) is massively denied.

Frequently, such novels end in reassurance with the falsely suspected vindicated through the crucial help of a lover/defender who reaffirms the protagonist's truth (often at the point where the social definition of reality is beginning to give even this protagonist doubts). But these formulaic rescues are so contrived and rickety as almost to defeat their ostensible purpose; what the reader carries away from such novels (and a number of excellent films made from them) is not the tagged-on reassurance but the pervasive insecurity. And the protagonist just may *not* luck out.

4. *The victim as protagonist.* One of the most reliable conventions of the detective novel is the invulnerability of the hero.[18] We have as much assurance that the detective will survive the most ex-

treme peril as that Tom Jones will escape hanging and we share in his invulnerability. Moreover, the detective novel is as scrupulous about protecting us from identification with the victim as with the murderer. The victim is frequently the most loathsome character in a detective novel, thus freeing us from undue concern with the *death* of a *person* so that we can concentrate on the *solution* to a *puzzle.*

The victim as protagonist, then, represents a logical extreme of the crime novel, forcing the reader to track the process of a character toward his or her own murder, a murder to which the character unconsciously, or even consciously, assents. Though victim-protagonists are rare, the theme of an at least partial complicity on the part of the victim is a crime novel formula. F. Tennyson Jesse, the author of a classic crime novel to be discussed in chapter 5, invented the term "murderee," and Georges Simenon, a reader in criminology as well as medicine and psychology, asserts that "one of the branches least known to the general public is victimology, that is to say the responsibility of the victim in almost seventy percent of the crimes."[19] In actual fact such responsibility may be merely carelessness (not locking the door, etc.), but in the crime novels of Simenon and Highsmith, among others, the victim shares the crime with the perpetrator and the novel probes "the psychology of the self-appointed victim."[20]

The four protagonist types outlined above are the central conventions of the crime novel. *All* crime novel protagonists are variations on one or another of these types. There are also a number of recurrent themes around which chapters 2 to 5 are organized, though the privileging of these is necessarily somewhat arbitrary and themes of equal importance may have been overlooked. The themes selected are, however, recurrent and suggestive: doubling and schizophrenia in both English and American novels—instances of the crime novel's privileging of deviance. Two prototypically American themes are the fictional world as structurally pathological and fatal passion as a response to this pathology; the problem of justice is the central concern of the English form. Each of these allows its specific variation on the general structural motif of inverting detective story conventions.

In this chapter I have for the most part treated the detective novel as well as the crime novel as if each were all of a piece, disregarding national differences. These differences in the detective novel are well known, having been thoroughly explored by such critics as George Grella and John Cawelti.[21] As indicated above, there are similar differences in the crime novel, having to do with world perception, passion, and justice. But as I lead into two English crime writings that play on national differences, I need to distinguish the form of reassurance in the classical English detective novel from that of the tough American form because these are what the respective crime novels put into question.

It works like this: the English detective reassures us of an ultimate rationality, "a benevolent and knowable universe," "a world that can be interpreted by human reason, embodied in the superior intellect of the detective."[22] While there are puzzles solved by the American detective,[23] his real function is to validate the American myth of personal integrity, absolute individualism, and stoic self-control. His exemplary role is not to explain the world but to survive it.

The threat raised in the English novel is of an unexplainable world, the synechdoche for which is an unsolved crime. Until the crime is solved, everything seems awry. But this turns out to be because we were looking at it the wrong way: "the explanation as in the case of all good riddles requires not so much working one's way through a mass of evidence as being able to see the problem from a different angle. Once the new angle or perspective has been grasped, the solution is simple and obvious."[24] A wonderful example is William James's conundrum of the meaning of "Pas de lieu Rhone que nous." The French words here are immediately recognizable but stubbornly refuse to cohere into meaningful syntax. The perspective shift is from semantic meaning to phonetic sounds and thence back to meaning in a different language system: "Paddle your own canoe."[25] The detective's skill is precisely the ability to code "seemingly unrelated data into a coherent system of signs, a text identifying the malefactor."[26]

The modern anxiety of a world without symbolic depth, all signifiers with no signifieds,[27] is at an opposite pole from the detective novel in which all signifiers, in the detective's resolution, transparently reveal their significations. Consequently, to the degree the crime novel puts the signification process into doubt or even exploits the gap between socially accepted signification and ultimate reality, it subverts the reassurances of the detective novel.

The threat in the American detective novel is of the entrapment of self, its loss of control. The function of the femme fatale is to *fail* to sway the hero, thus highlighting his control over the self and, in a qualified way, the world. The world of the American detective is too corrupt to be tidily rationalized, but the detective retains at least the illusion of control by his sardonic knowingness. He distances himself from emotional engagement with others by his ability to reduce

them to a phrase: "The cheaper the Crook, the gaudier the patter."[28] Philip Marlowe, not so terse as Spade, is equally dismissive: "Human contact for Marlowe is a sterile process where his arid preconceptions about others are constantly reinforced. . . . Nothing surprises Marlowe because he projects only self-interested mechanical actions onto others."[29] The alienated posture of the tough detective becomes a reassurance about how to live, with style, in a job-centered, emotion-denying society. In contrast, the American crime novel protagonist will give all to love *or destroy himself by not so doing*, shatter into schizophrenia, and confront a world either stubbornly enigmatic or too corrupt to be borne.

The first of my two English crime writings, Colin McCabe's *The Face on the Cutting Room Floor* (1937), speaks to an English fascination with the recently emergent tough American style. Julian McLaren-Ross in *Memoirs of the Forties* recalls his aspiration "to create a completely English equivalent to the American vernacular used by such writers as Hemingway, Cain and O'Hara . . . ,"[30] and Julian Symons has recently commended the Hammett-Chandler type of crime story with its "specifically American language, racy, energetic, powerful and crude. . . ." Symons notes how "the American crime story has a liveliness, sense of place and feeling for bitterish comedy that its British counterpart generally lacks."[31] This interest in the tough American style with its odd mix of sentimentality and nihilism, its lyricism of disgust is central in McCabe's novel, praised by Symons as "The detective story to end detective stories."[32]

The author of this extraordinary work is Cameron McCabe, who is also its protagonist, first-person narrator, murderer, and murder victim. But how could he be the author when he dies, by murder, or, as another character claims, suicide, about four-fifths of the way through the novel? The novel is completed with an epilogue—in the form of an epitaph for McCabe—by another character, the newspaperman Muller, who not only comments, from a Marxist point of view, on its style and meaning, especially the meaning *of* the style, but defines the novel in terms of the detective story genre. He quotes from and argues with reviews of *The Face on the Cutting Room Floor* by such critics as C. Day Lewis and W. H. Auden, though the novel had not yet appeared for them to read, much less review. Finally, Muller himself commits the last murder of the book, thus proving the contention of McCabe's ghost, who haunts Muller's attempt at a rational explanation for the novel's vertiginous turns by denying that he was the murderer, and accusing, seriatim, various

other characters until he has run through most of the novel's drama-
tis personae, sardonically concluding, "And then everyone else killed
him" (236).

Though the name Cameron McCabe appears on both the cover
and the title page, the novel was actually the work of Ernst Julius
Borneman, a young German whose prominence in Berlin Socialist
activities had necessitated his flight to England. His distance from
the cultural assumptions of English and American detective fiction
and the newness of the English and American idiom to his ear gave
him purchase for a novel that foregrounds and defamiliarizes linguistic and moral convention.

Muller quotes "Torquemada" of the *Observer* as complaining
that McCabe "has learnt most of his trade in the United States" and
that "he has not yet quite decided which language to use," and notes
other reviewers' protests that "all characters talked that same half-
half language . . ." (209). McCabe's anomalous status as an American working in England who "used to be Scottish"—as Muller (and
Borneman) used to be German—is thus both thematic and oppor-
tunistic. Indeed, anomaly is the generative principle of this oddly
effective novel in which everything is either half-half or altogether
other. When McCabe says of a character, "The skin of his forehead
moved like the skin on boiling milk" (15), we recognize the generic
hard-boiled label. Later we have "I felt empty, no man ever felt empty
like that" (185). Of course, *every* tough protagonist feels empty like
that. Chapter 19 has a self-evident source, with passages like the following: "Things change and it's good they change, but it's bad when
you don't know what the change is for. It's also bad when they
change and afterwards there's nothing left by which to remember
how it was before" (95). Muller comments that "we have to forgive
him [McCabe] for the terrible Hemingwayish chapter nineteen . . ."
(211). But more interesting is Muller's theory of tough language as
an expression of late capitalist anomie as filtered through various
specific cultural influences: "McCabe is, even at the beginning of
his book a normal young man who shows the normal marks of his
background—the certain innate toughness of the 'dour Scotsman'
which found support and amplification in that modern America
which, ashamed of its pioneer toughness, produced a first reaction
towards a curiously sugary sentimentality and a second reaction towards a synthetic and romantic modern toughness which is typified
by writers like Hemingway, Hammett, Cain, McCoy, Fessier and, to
a certain extent, by the O'Hara of *Appointment in Samarra*" (199).
This style is a defense: "To hide the soft interior the thing produced a fine weatherproof shell of nonchalance. Nothing mattered,

nothing held any surprise, nothing caused embarrassment, nothing was good, nothing bad, everything was accepted as a matter of course" (200). Irony substitutes for political action: "McCabe, morally uprooted, is fascinated by everything unstable, uncertain, ambiguous, equivocal, multifarious. It is, therefore, not surprising to find him adopting a method of writing which has all these qualities" (204).

A recent work that goes "McCabe's" novel some better is the 1986 television play *The Singing Detective* by Dennis Potter, "the authentic wild man of British television."[33] Potter parodies the American style without disowning it, while subverting the melodramatic plots of the American form to explore the etiology of the paranoia and despair the plot usually rationalizes and masks. No less pyrotechnical than the McCabe book, "the disquieting potency of Potter's mixture comes from the emotional rawness underlying all the technical haute cuisine."[34]

The play begins on a "misty, moody, highly atmospheric 'thrillerish' winter's evening in London, 1945," a type of setting reinforced by a typical point of view: an offscreen, "side-of-the-mouth style" voice-over: "And so the man went down the hole [to a basement nightclub], like Alice. But there were no bunny rabbits down there. It wasn't that sort of hole. It was a rathole" (2). We seem to be securely in the world of film thriller but soon find that we are in a different sort of hole, a hospital ward where a patient, a thriller *writer* named Philip Marlow, is undergoing treatment of "a ragingly acute psoriasis, which looks as though boiling oil has been thrown over him" (3) and composing the novel *The Singing Detective*, from which the preceding scene derived. Thriller and hospital scenes alternate with the experiences of the child Philip, trying to solve the mysteries of self and others. The hospital registrar's comment illuminates the interrelationship of these timescapes: "It must be hellishly ticklish to work out a plot in a detective story, I should think. I suppose you have to scatter clues all over the place" (44). Childhood and hospital are clues to the psychological meanings of thriller conventions.

The old and young Philip are, in effect, Philip tough and Philip tender. Marlow's self-described "paperback-soiled, mid-Atlantic, little side-of-the-mouth quips" (100) are character armor originating in the insecurities and betrayals of the displaced Yorkshire lad:

MRS. MARLOW: He didn't want to come. I don't think Philip likes the idea of London.
AUNT EMILY: Oh, he'll change his tune. It's the best place there is, Philip.

PHILIP: (*Fiercely*) Chunt like whum though, be it!
MARY: (*Puzzled*) What—? What's he say?
MRS. MARLOW: He says it's not like home.
PHILIP: There yunt no place like the Forest! Where cast thou go up
   here? Where be the trees? Where be the oaks? The elms. Where
   the beech, you tell I that! (128–129)

Neither Yorkshire idiom nor the raw emotion expressed in it are ne-
gotiable in London and Philip has already realized the necessity of
concealment:

AUNT EMILY: We shan't be able to understand a word he says.
PHILIP: (*Suddenly fierce*) I byunt going to talk much! I byunt going
   to talk at all! I be going to kip my mouth shut! (128)

Or better yet, in side-of-the-mouth-style voice-overs that give the illusion of a speaker emotionally in control, arbiter of a world created
in his image. As Marlow observes, "Of course I talk to myself. It's
more civilized than the conversations I *used* to have" (132). Emotion
is best left to those melancholic popular songs, allusive to the action, that are almost as much a convention in thrillers as the voice-
over: "Banality with a beat" (196). "I've Got You under My Skin"
pervades the first hospital scene. The mid-Atlantic style by dis-
counting desire makes it affordable, as when Marlow attempts to
damp down his excitement at Nurse Mill's forthcoming grease job
on him with a bit of "Chandleresquerie": "I had on my best pyjamas,
the ones with red stripes and blue forget-me-nots. I was all dressed
up and talcumed under the armpits. A million dollars was about to
call. I was ready for it" (15). (This, of course, parodies the first para-
graph of *The Big Sleep*.) Later, asked his religious belief by the registrar, he replies, "Malthusianism" (40).
   Marlow's writing is clearly a desperate attempt to maintain control, allowing him to revise or delete his wife, Nicola, and her lover.
Indeed, the lover almost catches on, anxiously commenting: "He
seems to *know* too much. He's got hold of too many details. Where's
it coming from? How does he get it? What's his game?" (146). He
almost sees his part in the game: "It's as though—as though— (*with
difficulty*) Nicola. I know this sounds crazy. I feel almost as though
he had made all this up" (147). Marlow's language *graphically* controls them:

   I have this awful—I have this awful dash he stops himself comma
   and all but shudders full stop
NICOLA: Darling dash question mark
   They look at each other. Weirdly, almost frighteningly, they seem

> to have no idea of what they have just said, which is delivered in a
> totally straightforward manner. (149–150)

"Paper Doll" is a recurrent background tune in the play and Marlow
conflates all treacherous women into one, his own creation.

But that Marlow can solve his misery on a word processor seems
doubtful, especially when the processor, unbidden, blips out the
letters "*H-e-l-p*" (76). Marlow's word-association sessions with the
psychiatrist seem self-accusatory as he gives "Liar" for "Writer,"
"Prison" for "Sentence" (176), and the sequence Woman-Fuck-Dirt-
Death (177). If he is imprisoned in his sentences, perhaps he chose
the wrong genre. As he complains, his mother should have named
him Christopher. The prisoner of his self-made Hell, he quotes the
other Marlowe:

> Hell hath no limits nor is it circumscribed
> In one self place, where we are is Hell
> And where Hell is, there must we ever be. (22–23)

The staff psychiatrist suggests that Marlow wants to be in Hell;
like his Americanized tough style, it is an excellent hiding place
(97). This gets to Marlow, being essentially an external confirmation
of the argument he has been having with himself, and he begins a
painful emergence from his illness and toward a relation, however
compromised, with his wife. Nicola may be a double-crossing bitch,
but she is not half as bad as his tough detective novel version of her.
Though a bit compromised and shopworn, she is, to echo one of the
pop songs, his baby.

The point of the play is not to deny the reality of misery; Potter,
who suffers from the same skin illness as his protagonist, is not
known for his uplift. But while basing *The Singing Detective* on the
force and even, to a degree, the authenticity of the tough perception
of life, a perception that clearly appeals to him, Potter plays out the
limitations of the code. It is ultimately a dead end, figured in images
of disgust notably meaner than Philip Marlowe's harshest efforts:

> NICOLA: You've been ill too long. You've been stuck with your own
>   thoughts too long. That's all it is.
> MARLOW (*Suddenly*): I want to sleep with you again.
> She blinks. Then—
> NICOLA: Philip?
> MARLOW: With a big mirror alongside.
> NICOLA: Listen to me—
> MARLOW (*Cutting in*): So I can turn my head while I'm doing it and
>   leer at myself. And so that when it starts shooting up in me and

spurting out I can twist to one side coming off your hot and sticky loins and *spit* straight at my own face. (197)

After this, hasn't Potter earned the ending in which Marlow and Nicola walk down "the corridor to freedom" out of *The Singing Detective* to the tune of Vera Lynn singing "We'll Meet Again" (248–249)?

These works, separated by forty-nine years, testify to a continuing English fascination with the emotional and philosophical resonances of the American detective novel form coupled with an acute critique of its pervasive misogyny. Both deconstruct detective story into crime story, exposing their protagonists' complicity with by far the most criminal aspect of the American detective form: its convictions of style, convictions that implicitly justify misogyny and alienation. Thus both works curve back into the English convention of accommodation with social reality and repudiation of American postures of alienation.

2

Deviant Impulses Incest and Doubling

A victim of dismemberment, completely
   possessed
I am—what do you call it—schizophrenic.
You want me to vanish from the scene,
In order that you forget your own appearance.
I will press your words
Into the sonnet's dark measure
My acid arsenic
Has measured the blood in you to the heart.
From the day's light and custom's
   permanence
Protect yourselves with a secure wall
From my madness and jarring craziness

But suddenly sadness will overcome you.
A subterranean shudder will seize you
And you will be destroyed in the swinging of
   my flag.   HUGO BALL, "SCHIZOPHRENIA"

Je est un autre
   ARTHUR RIMBAUD, *UNE SAISON EN ENFER*

CRIME FICTION IS post-Freudian, the influences on it including not only writers such as Poe and Dostoevsky who invite Freudian analysis but also Freud himself. In "Some Notes on Miss L." Nathanael West enjoins that "Psychology has nothing to do with reality nor should it be used as motivation. The novelist is no longer a psychologist. Psychology can become something more important. The great body of case histories can be used in this way ancient writers used their myths. Freud is your Bullfinch. You cannot learn from him."[1] Crime writers do in fact use psychology as motivation but also as a warehouse of archetypes, a Bullfinch's *Mythology* or Ovid's *Metamorphoses*, "the kind of mythology that might emerge if Oedipus, endowed with Freudian knowledge about himself, still saw fit to enact his myth."[2] Freudian and other psychiatric concepts work less to explain motives than to provide conventions and effects. Their use enables the crime writer to engage us in the nervous center of the genre where an uncomfortable identification merges into recognition of an appalling otherness, an otherness that is a dangerous potential for the self, its carnival mirror image.

Freudian mythology is especially evident in a recurrent structural pattern of substitutions: victim for victim, criminal for victim, individual for image, self for other. Freud explains this repetition-com-

pulsion in *Beyond the Pleasure Principle:* "The patient cannot remember the whole of what is repressed in him, and what he cannot
remember may be precisely the essential part of it. . . . He is obliged
to *repeat* the repressed material as a contemporary experience instead of . . . remembering it as something belonging to the past."[3]
Those subject to the compulsion appear at first as if victims of fate:
"The impression they give is of being pursued by a malignant fate or
possessed by some 'daemonic' power; but psycho-analysis has always taken the view that their fate is for the most part arranged by
themselves and determined by early infantile influences." An instance is "the lover each of whose love affairs with a woman passes
through the same phases and reaches the same conclusion."[4] In "A
Special Type of Object-Choice" Freud analyzes how "passionate at-
tachments of this kind are repeated many times over with all the
same peculiarities—each an exact replica of the others—in the lives
of those who belong to this [compulsive] type: indeed, in consequence of external conditions, such as changes in residence and environment, the loved objects may be so often replaced by others that
it comes in the end to a long chain of such experience being
formed."[5] This is because each actual woman is only yet another
copy of the "maternal prototype": "If the love-objects chosen by our
type are above everything mother-surrogates, then the formation of
a long series of them . . . becomes comprehensible as well. We learn
through other examples which psycho-analysis has brought to light
that the pressing desire in the unconscious for some irreplaceable
thing often resolves itself in an endless series in actuality—endless
for the very reason that the satisfaction longed for is in spite of all
never found in any surrogate."[6] Repetition is a basic instinct and
"The theory of the instincts is so to say our mythology. Instincts are
mythical entities. . . . "[7] The permutational possibilities of the myth
of repetition are enunciated in the title of John T. Irwin's Freudian
study of William Faulkner: *Doubling and Incest/Repetition and Revenge.* In the crime novels in this chapter, incest is a motif in some,
and doubling, repetition, and revenge in all.

The novel that carries such themes to (or perhaps beyond) their
limit, screaming Freud in every line, is Horace McCoy's *Kiss Tomorrow Goodbye* (1948). Yet this gross, bizarre, heavy-handed, preten-
tious, naive, weird, sick psychological extravaganza, both over motivated and curiously unmotivated, has the virtues of its extremities.
It seems to me more interesting if less credible than McCoy's better-
known *They Shoot Horses, Don't They?* (1935). There is a genuine
pathology in the later book, to which the reader has a complicated

relation. A first-person killer narrative, the novel invites the reader in second-person address into its protagonist's skewed scene, the-world-according-to-the-killer:

> This is how it is when you wake up in the morning of the morning you have waited a lifetime for: there is no waking state. You are at once wide awake, so wide awake that it seems you have slipped all the opiatic degrees of waking, that you have had none of the sense-impressions as your soul again returns to your body from wherever it has been; you open your eyes and you are completely awake, as if you had not been asleep at all. That is how it was with me. (81)

The speaker, "Ralph Cotter" (one of several aliases, but we are never told his real name), is an east Tennessee mountain boy who despite his Phi Beta Kappa college education has become a career criminal. A prison farm is the setting of his morning song. The morning is to be that of his escape and his morning consciousness merges two competing aspects of self that run throughout the novel: memory, nostalgic but ultimately destructive, and desire, anticipative of heightened life but corrupted with pathological hatred. At first, the narrator allows the process of morning to carry him back to rural Tennessee memories that will eventually prove his undoing: "I was always awake to greet these fragments, hungrily smelling what little freshness they had left by the time they got back to me, smelling them frugally, in careful precious sniffs, letting them dig in the vaults of my memory, letting them uncover early morning sounds of a lifetime ago: Blue jays and woodpeckers and countless other birds . . . " (81). The anticipation the day brings is not only of his planned escape from prison but of revenge on the "sickly sodomist" who is his cellmate, the protagonist "feeling a fine fast exhilaration that to-day was the day that I was going to kill him, that I was finally going to kill him" (82).

This interplay between memory and desire runs throughout the novel, oddly mediated by its olfactory imagery. For standing against the apparently regenerative powers of morning and the past is the stink of the presence of others, seventy-two unwashed bunkmates: "a pillar of stink the like of which you cannot conceive; majestic, nonpareil, transcendental . . . " (81). But in the schematized Freudian logic of the novel the apparent contrast is revealed as identity: the smell of childhood is localized in the Huele de Noches bushes Ralph associates with the funeral of his grandmother, and his grandmother is associated with the family outhouse in a bizarre blend of Freudian notions of anality, incest, and regression. In a childhood incident Ralph was accompanying his grandmother, whom he thought

his mother, to the outhouse, but frightened by the overheard violence of horses mating, he seeks refuge under her capacious black
skirt. This becomes a game, especially useful for hiding from his
grandfather's punishments, thus literalizing both aspects of the Oedipus complex, the desire for mother and the fear of father, the death
wish for a return to the womb and the pregenital association of anality with sexuality.

Though haunted by fragments of remembrance of the grandmother throughout, the protagonist is resisting full recognition of
what is, in fact, the novel's primal scene, its origin. *Kiss Tomorrow
Goodbye*, the very title of which initiates the foreclosure of the
novel's temporality, is an exaggerated instance of what Peter Brooks
argues for all narrative: it starts at the end. Plot is "a kind of diver-
gence or deviance," its tension "maintained as an ever more complicated postponement or *détour* leading back to the goal of quies-
cence" (103). Plot temporarily retards a movement toward ending
and origin, death and primal scene; the end of plot is to kiss tomorrow goodbye.

The inevitable conclusion of McCoy's plot is detoured by the two
main actions of Ralph's criminal aggressions and sexual entangle-
ments. Both these circle back to the beginning/ending by way of a
pattern of repetitions entrapping Ralph in Freudian seriality. Ralph
projects the anal component of his fixation into a universal hostility
especially directed toward men as potential sibling rivals (in the
fashion of Freud's *Totem and Taboo*): all other men become shit to
him and he regrets that "now I'd never know . . . how it felt to kill
all the people I didn't like" (312). Ralph's escape from the prison
farm is engineered by Holiday, the sister of a prisoner, Toko, incapable of getting away on his own. But Ralph calculatedly murders
Toko, blaming it on a guard. Ralph's own brother, we find, was killed
in an *apparent* accident and the substitutionary logic is clear: both
brothers were putative rivals for the possession of a woman, the
grandmother, Holiday. Ralph kills Toko so as to substitute for him,
thus contriving a situation in which Holiday can substitute for the
grandmother in a reconstructed family romance.

Though Holiday as a repetition of the grandmother is dangerous,
she seems less a threat to Ralph because as a criminal, promiscuous
woman she ideally fits into the mechanism Freud described as "the
most prevalent form of degradation in erotic life," that is, seeking
out women who deflect Oedipal guilt by "evoking no reminder of
the incestuous persons forbidden to it."[8] Ralph fears Margaret, the
rich girl who physically resembles the grandmother, evokes in his
memory the odor of Huele de Noches, and offers him financial sanc-

tuary. In Brooks's terms, Margaret represents "the fear . . . of the im-
proper end": "The possibility of short-circuit can, of course, be represented in all manner of threats to the protagonist or to any of the
functional logics that demand completion; it most commonly takes
the form of temptation to the mistaken erotic object choice, who
may be of the 'Belle Dame sans merci' variety, or may be the too perfect and hence annihilatory bride. Throughout the Romantic tradition, it is perhaps most notably the image of incest . . . that hovers as
the sign of a passion interdicted because its fulfillment would be too
perfect, a discharge indistinguishable from death, the very cessation
of narrative movement."[9]

The return of the repressed is gradual, it being what the plot
retards. But eventually we come out at the memory of the outhouse and the quasi-incestuous relation with the grandmother.
Ralph meets Margaret at her club and as they walk out into the
night air he flashes back to the past, experiencing the Uncanny,
which, Freud tells us, "occurs either when repressed infantile complexes have been revived by some impression, or when the primitive
beliefs we have surmounted seem once more to be confirmed."[10]
With McCoy's usual overdetermination both these causes come into
play as Ralph's *final* repressed memory of the grandmother surfaces:
at the age of seven Ralph saw his grandfather castrate a ram. Later he
played the skirt game once too often with his grandmother and when
she threatened to have the grandfather do to him as he did to the
ram, he killed her; Ralph's identification of Margaret with the grandmother converts her into "this girl, this ghost, Alecto, the unceasing
pursuer, born of a single drop of the God-blood Uranus ripped upon
the earth . . . " (310). He projects Margaret as a figure of fate and she
does take his gun from him, thus symbolically fulfilling the grandmother's threat, but Margaret *means* only to protect him from the
person *she* sees as most dangerous to him: himself. But she is real
for him only as a symbol:

> She tightened her fingers around mine. "Please, let me try to help
> you," she said.
> "I killed you once," I said. "Do not make me kill you again . . . "
> She turned loose my hand.
> I walked into the darkness. . . . (311)

He flees to Holiday. Having constructed Margaret as a surrogate of
the grandmother, he has constructed Holiday as a surrogate to Margaret. But Holiday *now* knows of his murder of Toko and is waiting
for him with a gun: "She just smiled. She was Tisiphone. Tisiphone,
Alecto . . . and where was the third? Wasn't there a third?" (313).

Megaera is the third of the Erinyes, the Furies, who were born of the blood of Uranus which fell on Gaea when Cronos emasculated him. The Erinyes, "personified pangs of conscience after breaking a taboo," had as their original function the revenge of "injuries inflicted only on a mother,"[11] hence their pursuit of Orestes. Ralph's furies are his grandmother, Margaret, and Holiday, triple forms of fate constructed by his guilt. Holiday, for Ralph a mere surrogate for a surrogate, kills him not because she is Tisiphone but because she is Toko's sister, an aspect of her identity Ralph has overlooked. But she does finally give him what, until then, he had not known he wanted: "There was another flash of fire and my eyes went out and now I could see nothing. I could see nothing and feel nothing, but I had a vestige of awareness left that made me know I was pulling my knees up and pushing my chin down to meet them, and that at last I was safe and secure in the blackness of the womb from which I had never emerged . . . " (314). Thus, in an ultimate Freudian cliché, Ralph's murders do in fact bring him home.

What are we to make of all this? I have not imposed Freud on McCoy's text nor even tried to use Freud to interpret it. McCoy's protagonist is given to brooding on Oedipus: "Myths and memory retreat before intellect. Oedipus is dead. . . . " (301, McCoy's ellipsis). And when an acute companion picks up on his compulsions, he responds, "Don't try to psychoanalyze me. I can do a much better job of that than you can. . . . " (195, McCoy's ellipsis). The Freudian overtones are obviously and abundantly intended by McCoy. And they are not more extreme than those which Irwin finds in Faulkner or Brooks in everyone. Of course, Faulkner's characters' psychic dilemmas are affecting because on any number of levels they are more real and immediate, his world more credible. McCoy's play on psychoanalysis is *delirious*, as if a fictional version of Freud based on Disney's version of classical music, a fantasia of the unconscious, with Freudian motifs doing a dance of the crocodiles to the music of "A Night on Bear Mountain."

The novel's energies are in excess of and unmotivated by the plot. The protagonist's sexual reductiveness, contempt, and fear, his extreme misanthropy and brutality seem less revelations of a character than symptoms of some rather exotic disease. Yet McCoy's pop primitivism is what is most alive in his writing, and his book is at its best when it allows the escape of a certain raw pathology from the confinement of plot and characterization.

The substitutionary logic of incestuous desire is nicely played on in Margaret Millar's *Beyond This Point Are Monsters* (1970). In the conclusion of this novel Mrs. Osborne's advertisement promising money and legal exemption for anyone who knows "the where-abouts" (164) of her son, Robert, turns up his killer, Felipe. We discover that Robert was accidentally killed in a fight caused by Felipe's blackmail attempt. Felipe had seen Robert return from the field where his father is found dead from a supposed accident and throw a bloody two-by-four into the reservoir. Robert has evidently taken a more direct method with his alcoholic and abusive father than the genteel fashion favored by his mother: "She'd maneuver him into the living room . . . close the doors and windows and pull the drapes. Then the arguing would start. If things get too loud she'd sit down at that piano of hers and start playing to cover them up, a piece of good firm chords like 'March of the Toreadors.' She couldn't admit they quarreled any more than she could admit that he drank" (72–73).

We wonder about Mrs. Osborne's motives at this point. Extremely possessive of her son, she has reconstructed his room in her own house, keeping his clothes and his spare glasses there. She has even decorated it with his framed copies of medieval maps with their archaic captions: "Another said simply, 'Beyond this point are monsters.' The phrase appealed to Robert. He printed a sign and taped it outside his door: BEYOND THIS POINT ARE MONSTERS" (120). It cannot help but occur to the reader that Mrs. Osborne has trapped Felipe for revenge, an expectable convention in this type of plot. Moreover, Mrs. Osborne reveals that it was she who murdered her husband, Robert merely dutifully covering her tracks, and we know that the murderer in conventional thrillers likes to confess her last murder to the intended victim of the next one. This is exactly what does not happen. After her revelation, she instructs Felipe to open her safe and take his money. When he finds it too dark to see the combination, she suggests he's short-sighted and makes him put on Robert's glasses. She tells him there is no reason to rush: "She reached out and touched the top of his head very gently. 'We haven't seen each other for such a long time, son'" (175). Clearly, Felipe is not to die but neither is he to leave. The stunning last line of the novel is "During the night one of the neighbors woke to the sound of a piano and went to sleep again" (175). We now know the full meaning of the sign on Robert's door.

So far we have seen a son substituting for a mother and a mother substituting for a son; for the sake of symmetry we need a father substituting for a daughter and a daughter for a father, which Marc Behm logically enough combines in a single book, *The Eye of the Beholder* (1980). Behm's plot is as fully bizarre as McCoy's, but the writing is controlled, even cool, and the schematic psychology implied, rather than overstated. In contrast to Millar, however, Behm's book, like McCoy's, is a sort of surrealistic cartoon. Behm plays Freudian motifs for what might be called off-laughs in a creepy, not quite parodic, not quite funny offspin of sixties black humor. The novel does have a detective, indeed "The Eye" is the only name we are given for him. Fittingly, the villain is a beautiful, treacherous femme fatale. How the Eye discovers this is by spying on her through a window as she commits a murder and what he does about it is to shadow her through a series of identities she assumes in the course of committing roughly (I lost count) twenty-six more murders, intervening after the fact a few times only to conceal evidence and to anonymously warn her of potential danger.

Behm manages to make this unorthodox approach to detective work seem almost natural by his offhand treatment of it. There is, of course, a psychological explanation. The Eye has a daughter, Maggie, now twenty-four, whom he has not seen for the twenty-three years since his wife disappeared with her, years later sending him a class photo of fifteen nine-year-olds with the comment "I bet you don't even recognize her, you prick" (2). At first he favors one or another of the schoolgirls, "But he no longer had any preferences. He knew them all by heart now and he loved every one of them" (3). He is certain, beyond all reason, that someday he will find the door to the classroom, enter, call a name, "and out of the multitude would rise his lost child" (3). Obviously the murderess, who turns out to be one year older than the lost girl, becomes his surrogate daughter.

The Eye's protection remains anonymous; he never makes himself known to the killer. Indeed, in an apparent accident he causes the death of the one man she did actually love. Ostensibly he was trying to save this man, only realizing after the fact that she was not planning to kill him. But she made him the exception because as an older man he was clearly a father-surrogate, and we may suspect the Eye does not need this competition. Eventually, despite the Eye's best efforts, her luck runs out and the novel concludes with an especially outré scene of pathos:

> On the last night of his life, the Eye dreamed of the corridor. He found the door, and it was unlocked. He opened it and stepped into the photograph.
> And there he was!
> The fifteen lovely faces turned to him, alive and miraculous and startled.
> He stood before them, absolutely certain that he was awake and that everything else, the whole long, long saga of his longing, had been a dream.
> Maggie? he asked.

> But he died before his lost daughter could answer him. And they
> buried him beneath the oak trees beside his inviolate grave. (183)

This bit of pop sentimentality should be either comic or unacceptable, and it is part of the *offishness* of this novel and its genre that
it somehow works to deliver a sickly sweet throb of illegitimate
emotion.

The doublings examined to this point have been external, or at
least externalized, protagonists projecting their mother, son, and
daughter imagos at appropriate targets, those who in some way or
another fit the fantasy. But all this, of course, comes actually from
within, and the logic of doubling as well as its economics should
eventuate in the splitting of the protagonist into two selves, the apparent self of social roles and the actual self of murderous compulsiveness. Even, after all, in the most orthodox mystery-detective
novel, the criminal, however sane, must be duplicitous simply in
order to avoid detection—that is, the revelation that he is the sort of
self that would commit this particular crime. But this is rarely ex-
trapolated into a psychological significance. In the crime novel such
structural duplicity is radicalized to the point where the criminal
may look with horror and loathing at the outcome of his uncontrollable impulses or these impulses may form themselves into a
second self, quite unknown to the social one who may, in fact, be
not only as shocked but as mystified as everyone else at the actions
of his/her unknown shadow.

The novelists' usual term for such doubling is "schizophrenia," as
defined in a citation from *Black's Medical Dictionary* at the beginning of Patrick Hamilton's *Hangover Square* (1941): "a cleavage of
the mental functions, associated with assumption by affected person
of a second personality" (v). Though no longer a received medical
definition, having been replaced by "multiple personality," "schizophrenia" is still the novelistic and popular use, and the one I shall
employ in this chapter. Some of the novelists' schizophrenics may
be schizophrenic in the psychiatrists' meaning as well. But the novelists are responding to what is primarily a literary, generic problem:
how to externalize that otherness in the self which commits terrible, unacknowledgeable acts?

Moreover, in contrast to the normative values of psychiatry, the
interest of the crime novel's presentation of the schizophrenic protagonist is in its paradoxical merger of sympathy, irrationality, and
logic: the schizophrenic protagonist must be in some way justified.
The illness becomes an adaptation to a given world, enabling a more
active, exotic, energetic self or at least a more perceptive, knowing

self. Of the selves the crime novelist protagonist splits into, it is the crazy one who is more authentic.

Such is the case with Hamilton's *Hangover Square or The Man with Two Minds: A Story of Darkest Earl's Court in the Year 1939* (1941). Hamilton's full title signifies his combination of psychological analysis and sociological specification. The protagonist, George Harvey Bone, is the best of a sorry lot of would-be actresses, fascists, and parasites who camp out in Earl's Court lodgings while centering their lives around pubs and parties, complacently unaware of the personal (murder) and national (the war) catastrophe inexorably building toward eruption. Bone's difference is his perception of the emptiness of life in darkest Earl's Court, his presentiment of international disaster, his relative personal and political decency. But Bone has negotiated his personal Munich, a shabby compromise in which he has "created a negative personality and found a place of sorts" (57) as butt of condescension and giver of small loans. The sane Bone plays "his usual role of hysterical dupe" (304) to the venal pseudo-actress Netta, who puts him into "the class of men who desired her, who sought her favours, and to whom she intended to give no favours" (56), instead "spasmodically and lovelessly" granting them to the fascist sympathizer, Peter, whom she finds stimulating because of his cruelty and violence. Clearly the life of the *sane* Bone is abject, aimless, and dead. But occasionally there is a "click" in his mind, and a Bone quite unknown to the sane emerges. This *insane* Bone recognizes the deadness of his world and his self:

> A silent film without music—he could have found no better way of describing the weird world in which he now moved. He looked at passing objects and people, but now they had no colour, vitality, meaning—he was mentally deaf to them. They moved like automatons, without volition of their own. He could hear what they said, he could understand their words, he could answer them, even; but he did this automatically, without having to think of what they said or what he was saying in return. Therefore, though they spoke it was as though they had not spoken, as though they had moved their lips but remained silent. They had no valid existence; they were not creatures experiencing pleasure or pain. There was, in fact, no sensation, no pleasure or pain at all in this world: there was only himself—his dreary numbed, dead self. (5–6)

This dead self is characteristic of what psychiatrists *now* call schizophrenia: "Blunted, flat, or inappropriate affect."[12] Yet how "inappropriate" are Bone's "feelings of emptiness and nothingness,"[13] a classic symptom of schizophrenia, to the Earl's Court crowd? If "living at the periphery of life"[14] is a schizophrenic symptom, darkest Earl's Court is a schizophrenic world. Bone lives at the periphery *of* this periphery. But the *insane* Bone has a sense of purpose lacking in the sane one: "There was no sensation, but there was something to be done. . . . He could not think of it at first but it would come . . . " (5–6). This aim is to murder Netta (later Peter is included).

The title of Hamilton's novel comes from a quip about the aftereffects of the everyday round of "drinks, smokes, and Netta": "Taking a little stroll around Hangover Square" (26, 24). Bone's intended violence introduces a purpose, however perverse, to Netta's hung-over world: "Living in a vacuum, with practically no vision of the future, and practically no awareness of the past, she bothered very little about anything—least of all about George, who oddly enough, and unknown to both of them, at certain seasons directed his mind exclusively to the problem of killing her by violence" (161–162). Bone's *insane* perception seems to implicate not only the Earl's Court crowd but the prewar world: "As he walked along the crowded street in the rain he was again beset by that nasty feeling of being in a dream, of only being able to keep himself active and conscious by an effort of will, by concentrating mentally on his plans, and obeying its demands. Again he couldn't understand what all these people, none of them about to kill anybody, were up to, what they were getting at. They had no reality or motive" (238). Bone commits his futile murder of Netta and Peter on September 3, 1939, as England emerges from its prolonged hangover to a new world of motive, reality, and violence.

John Franklin Bardin's extraordinary novel *The Devil Take the Blue Tail Fly* (1948) is like *Hangover Square* in its naturalization and, to a degree, justification of a schizophrenic consciousness. Though Bardin provides an elaborate etiology for his protagonist's illness, this is less compelling than the narrative swirls that put us inside her experiences, her fantasies, her confusions of past and present terrors (another version of seriality) and force us to try to distinguish reality from fantasy, past from present. Frequently we find we have been taking the one for the other, thus participating in the character's disorientation.

This character is Ellen Purcell, a performer on the harpsichord, married to a popular conductor, Basil. At the beginning of the novel she is preparing to leave a mental institution and resume "normal" life. From the beginning there are signs that all is not well. Basil means well toward her, but there is a major, finally fatal gap of sympathy and perception, besides which Basil, we discover, is in love with another woman. The dawning realization of her husband's affair is part of what forces Ellen inexorably back into the serial pattern of sexual betrayals that began with her father's vicious puritanism, a thin mask for his repressed incestuous desire and sexual jealousy. This pattern had climaxed in an act of violence toward her first lover, Jim, a folk singer who casually seduced her, incorporated her into his act, and cheated on her. One cause of her illness is an incompletely repressed memory of finding herself in a hotel room with his dead body. As it happens, she didn't quite kill him and he reappears, after her return from the institution, to sexually blackmail her. He forces her into a hotel room where she awakens covered with blood. This time it is real. And, of course, we expect her husband's eventual death, less than a murder but more than an accident.

Ellen, or rather her alter ego, Nelle, kills one man (twice, in fact) and causes the death of another, but she is the victim—not victimizer—of four dominating men in her life: her father, Jim, Basil, and her psychiatrist. They have betrayed her, the first three sexually but all four, and more important, ontologically, denying the reality of her alienated perceptions as they deny the reality of her music. When Ellen returns home from the institution, the key to her harpsichord is missing. Though Bardin leaves us in the dark about what really happened (thus equivalent to Ellen's anxious uncertainty), we suspect, as she does, that her husband has concealed it. He identifies her playing with her illness and indeed the two seem closely related. The question, however, is which Ellen is the more valid, the sane or the musical one? As Ellen drifts back toward madness, her schizophrenic separation of affect from behavior is an apt response to the false and empty social scene which values her not for her music but the factitious celebrity of it. Her mechanical responses to the monstrous celebrity hunter, Mrs. Smythe, exactly fit the occasion: "'What a lovely dress, Mrs. Smythe—and what a lovely party! And now you say kind things to me as well. I'm really overwhelmed!' As she said these polite words, made this fitting response, she noticed with cold amazement that they proceeded in proper sequence, made sense, and seemed to meet Mrs. Smythe's approval" (55). And her observation of the critic who she knows will write a preprogrammed review of her performance sees accurately his automatism: "He wet his lips and, as if its action were controlled by a mechanism, his hand skittered up to his head, patted and smoothed his clay-colored hair. She was amused to see a droplet of perspiration forming on his brow and, while she waited for him to speak again, she chose to speculate as to which side of his nose it would streak down eventually" (532). Schizophrenia, in the current psychiatric meaning, seems the natural response to a world in which feeling is never consonant with words. Ellen's music is more real than Mrs. Smythe, who can "know nothing of music, of my world of sound, of what it means to set tones down in space and time so that they relate, so that you can build on them other tones, inject into them rhythm, give them weight and meaning, construct with them a reality" (550). The musical self has the reality lacking in the social self.[15]

Ellen's husband is a musician too, a conductor, but, as she knows and he doesn't, a fake one. He is to music as Mrs. Smythe is to the social scene: they drain reality out of whatever they conduct. But Basil's greatest crime is that, in conspiracy with her psychiatrist, he has betrayed her music by allowing talent-destroying shock treatments. To rob Ellen of music is to rob her of self: "she depended upon it . . . for without it she did not know herself. Outside its orbit she was a bundle of sensations, a walking fear, an appetite, a lawless creature. But when this sound existed, she understood, her life had meaning, order, morality. This was her end, she was its means" (577).

In an excruciating irony, the treatments rid Ellen of her talent but not of her disease, embodied in her murderous mirror image, Nelle. Significantly, Nelle begins one of her encroachments upon Ellen just after Basil suggests that she give no more concerts. And, although music is Ellen's most vital and authentic self, Nelle also has a claim, which she asserts against the psychiatrist's rationalization of her. She sees herself as Ellen's "better part" and Ellen as *her* invention. As Ellen's unsocialized self, Nelle knows who Ellen's enemies are and how to take direct action against them. She shows Ellen how to outflank her father's hypocritical puritanism by coming on to him, facing him threateningly with his illicit desire. Nelle is Ellen's recognition of the reality of her relationships.

Bardin's novel resembles his image of Ellen's dream: "But of course, in the dream . . . these events, that had taken months to occur, had slipped into one another in a night, fitting together one inside the other like a Chinese puzzle" (539). The novel is a Chinese puzzle, a false-bottomed box. But it denies us the euphoria of some playfully self-reflected fictions because it convinces us that Ellen's box, though lacking in a firm foundation, has real walls.

Bardin's Chinese-puzzle novel frequently mystifies the reader about the status in reality of a given scene: whether it is current reality, memory, or dream. Reality in the sense of authenticity and the reality of the emotional life as represented by music and rage is the theme of the novel. But in neither Bardin's nor Hamilton's novel is there any mystification about the identity of the schizophrenic killer. The question in Hamilton's novel is not even so much whether Bone will kill Netta and Peter as when. It is more confirmation than surprise when Nelle brings about the death of Ellen's husband. But one of the possibilities of the schizophrenic convention is to mystify the identity of the second self, to build toward a revelation of it as the combined peripety and recognition scene of the novel. The difference between this revelation and that of the conventional mystery novel is that the identity of the murderer has been as unknown to himself/herself as anyone else.

So with the most vicious of these schizophrenic selves, "Evelyn Merrick" in Margaret Millar's *Beast in View* (1955). The mad "Evelyn" with her self-projection of a beauty calling for immortalization and her crystal ball by which she predicts disasters to others (which, in fact, with some help, occur) is more intense and vivid than the drab and envious person who imagined her into murderous being. This novel too plays with point of view and when reread, with the puzzle of identity solved, reveals a continuous irony based on the gap between pathetic actuality and murderously romantic fantasy.

Revelation is delayed by the elaboration of a plot situation that seems to promise a conventional wish fulfillment. The terrified Helen Clarvoe begs her lawyer, Paul Blackshear, to protect her from the malevolent Evelyn Merrick, who has been persecuting her with vile accusations and threats. Paul, though put off by Helen's coldness and unattractiveness, has a wry recognition of his proper role: "Behind her wall of money, behind her iron bars, Miss Clarvoe was the maiden in distress, crying out, reluctantly and awkwardly, for help. Blackshear made a wry grimace as he pictured himself in the role of the equally reluctant rescuer, a tired, detached, balding knight in Harris tweeds" (17). A lonely widower of fifty, Paul is "struck by the sudden realization that he was in his way as badly off as Miss Clarvoe" (31). Perhaps Helen, with her old-fashioned clothes and close-cropped hair, is the ugly duckling, a potential swan to the man who can awaken her. But before this rather stereotyped transformation and fulfillment can be accomplished, Helen must get past the blocking figure of Evelyn Merrick: "Outside, on the busy street, Evelyn Merrick was waiting for her" (130).

The novel seems to be a contest between Paul Blackshear and Evelyn Merrick that will eventuate in the rescue of Helen Clarvoe. But Evelyn's menace is genuine; she has a gift for discerning a potential victim's vulnerability and exploiting it to the hilt in envenomed telephone sorties. The novel opens with Helen Clarvoe responding to a voice that identifies itself as "a friend," an implicit taunt that Helen recognizes as such:

> "I have a great many friends," Miss Clarvoe lied. In the mirror above the telephone stand she saw her mouth repeating the lie, enjoying it, and she saw her head nod in quick affirmation—*This lie is true, yes this is a very true lie.* Only her eyes refused to be convinced. Embarrassed, they blinked and glanced away. (1)

Helen perceives the obvious madness of the voice, but Evelyn throws Helen's accusation back at her: "Mad? Oh no, *I'm* not the one who's mad, it's you, Clarvoe. *You're* the one who can't remember. And I know why you can't remember. Because you're jealous, you've always been jealous of me, you're so jealous you've blacked me out" (3). There is some truth in Evelyn's accusation since the *real* Evelyn Merrick is a somewhat unhappy but perfectly sane young woman, and the homicidal multiple personality of the novel is Helen Clarvoe, who mimics the real Evelyn's voice so well that she fools even herself. The book uses misdirections of point of view to delay this revelation, but from early on Millar plants such moral and psychological clues as Helen's slip of the pen in a letter to her mother: "Dear Mother: it has been a long time since I've heard from you. I hope that all is hell with you" (10). "Evelyn" eventually makes this repressed wish come true. Earlier, Helen reflects that if she had not broken off the initial encounter quickly enough, it was because "her loneliness had compelled her to listen; even words of evil were better than no words at all" (5).

The key to Helen's madness is that even words of evil are better than no words at all. When Helen's father discovered she had been passing on Evelyn's academic triumphs as her own, he cruelly told her, "Your punishment, Helen, is being you, and having to live with yourself" (98). Helen believes this; it has become for her a parental doom internalized as self-fulfilling prophecy. Whereas "Evelyn" has her kicks, even to a more emotionally fulfilling relationship to Paul Blackshear: "Poor old bungling Blackshear, looking for her all over town, like a blind man feeling his way through a forest. One of these days I will pop out at him from behind a tree" (152). After she has "kidnapped" Helen (as, in a sense, she really has), "Evelyn" finds Mrs. Clarvoe's anxiety almost irresistibly amusing:

> "Evelyn? Answer me. *Answer me.*"
> "Well, you needn't shout," Evelyn said coldly. "I'm not deaf, you know. I have what you might call 20-20 hearing."

"Listen to me, please. Have you seen Helen? Have you talked to her?"
"Why?" she smiled to herself because she sounded so sober and earnest when all the time she was bursting with laughter. Had she seen Helen? What a marvellous joke. (152–153)

The novel's title itself equivocates. It alludes to the end of Dryden's "The Secular Masque," where Momus, addressing respectively Diana, Mars, and Venus, mocks their futility:

All, all of a piece throughout;
Thy Chase had a Beast in View;
Thy Wars brought nothing about;
Thy Lovers Were all untrue.
'Tis well an Old Age is out,
And time to begin a New.[16]

Blackshear was on the wrong chase in the wrong genre: even a reluctant knight does not expect the maiden to double as the dragon he means to rescue her from:

"Give me the knife, Helen."
In the mirror she could see Blackshear approaching, slowly and cautiously, a hunter with a beast in view. (201)

Though in this novel we are surely meant to side ultimately with Blackshear and "normal" reality, Helen's perspective on Blackshear is disturbing because not *altogether* false. The distinction between hunter/hunted becomes at the least blurred, if not reversed. In the conventional detective novel the reader is secured in his/her normality by the novel's firm presentation of deviance as the sign of the unacceptable other. In the crime novels of this chapter, deviance is never unequivocal and is sometimes even the sign of the authentic self, and whereas the plot drive of the detective novel is the reader's participation in the linear pursuit of the criminal, in the crime novel we get caught up in circular patterns of substitution wherein the categories of criminal/victim, guilty/innocent shift and slide, putting us into doubt about just what beast we have in view.

3

Ontological Insecurities Time and Space in the American Crime Novel

I saw a man upon the stair,
A little man who was not there,
He was not there again today;
Gee, I wish he'd go away.

QUOTED IN FREDRIC BROWN, *NIGHT OF THE JABBERWOCK*, WITH SLIGHT VARIATION FROM THE ORIGINAL BY HUGHES MEARNS

Me Miserable! Which way shall I fly
Infinite wrath and infinite despair?
Which way I fly is Hell; myself am Hell;
And, in the lowest deep, a lower deep
Still threatening to devour me opens wide
To which the Hell I suffer seems a Heaven.

WELL-KNOWN CRIME WRITER

THE CRIME NOVEL addict has a recurrent dream. He is *In a Lonely Place* with but a moment to *Ride the Pink Horse* because *The Big Clock* is counting down and he has a *Rendezvous in Black*. He runs down *Scarlet Street* to *Nightmare Alley*, only to find himself trapped at *The Dark Corner, Where the Sidewalk Ends*. All along he has been in *The Eighth Circle, The City of the Dead*, where there can be only one outcome to the race against time: *D.O.A.* At this point one may find *A Stranger in My Grave*.

Titles of crime novels and films evoke a time that is at best almost too late (*Deadline at Dawn*), a space that is rarely more than a temporary refuge from terror. Favored words are "black" (*The Bride Wore Black, The Black Path of Fear*), "dark" (*The Dark Fantastic*), "night" (*The Night Has a Thousand Eyes, Night and the City*), variants on "street" (*Street of the Lost, Sunset Boulevard, Asphalt Jungle, The Moon in the Gutter*), variants on "dead" (*The Beast Must Die, I Married a Dead Man*), and "big," used to intensify some overwhelming situation (*The Big Combo, The Big Heat, The Big Knife*). Place names are ironic (*Providence*) or forthrightly bleak (*South Florida Book of the Dead*), and titles that sum up conditions are less than hopeful: *They Don't Dance Much, You Play the Black and the Red Comes Up*. Horace McCoy titles suggest a narrative that begins as well as ends in closure: *I Should Have Stayed Home*,

Kiss Tomorrow Goodbye, They Shoot Horses Don't They, No Pockets in a Shroud.

Of all these only *Night and the City,* set in a nightmare London composed all of angularities and shadows, has a setting other than American, but even this film has an American protagonist who seems to infect the landscape with his desire and doom. In the English detective and crime novel setting may be memorable and evocative—the fens have a particular dark appeal for detective writers—but novels in which the setting exudes negative, antagonistic force are rare: besides Hamilton's tale of darkest Earl's Court there is the locale of Symons's *The Progress of a Murder,* from which delinquency leaks as from a cracked sewer main, and the spiritually sordid world of Graham Greene's masterwork, *Brighton Rock.*

But as W. H. Auden demonstrates, the anagogical setting of the English detective novel is typically Edenic, the Great Good Place. For Auden, Raymond Chandler's Los Angeles is not an exception to the rule but a member of a different category: "Actually, whatever he may say, I think Mr. Chandler is interesting in writing, not detective stories, but serious studies of a criminal milieu, the Great Wrong Place, and his powerfully but extremely depressing books should be read and judged, not as escape literature, but as works of art."[1]

Auden's definition is wonderfully prescient and half wrong. "The Great Wrong Place" is a *typical* setting of American detective and crime novels and thus as conventional and mythical as "the Great Good Place." Contrary to Auden and to George Grella's completion of the outline of "the Great Wrong Place" in his justly celebrated essay, "Murder and the Mean Streets," the American detective novel is escapist and wish-fulfilling but in an American as opposed to English mode. If the English escape is into a dream of a (re)ordered society, the American escape is into the dream of the last just man whose integrity *is* his alienation. Grella's claim that "with their American penchant for dissolution, alienation, and despair, the hard-boiled novels, however tough or exciting on the surface, cannot justly be called wish fulfilling" misses the point that dissolution, alienation, and despair can be components of an American dream about absolute integrity, a moral separatism that updates a Puritan origin of the American self into an odd sort of glory: the Solipsist Justified. In fact, Grella demonstrates that the detective story is a version of the American "romance": "If the dominant American novel is . . . a romance, so is the American detective story, and for the same reasons. Where the English novel is notable for its mental, moral, and spiritual health, and as Richard Chase points out, 'gives the impression of absorbing all extremes into a normative view of life,' the American novel has a 'penchant for the marvelous, the sensational, the legendary, and in general, the heightened effect.' The American novel is 'less-interested in incarnation and reconciliation than in alienation and disorder.'"[2] This alienation and disorder is our wish since, as in Chandler's famous manifesto, mean streets call for the hero noble enough to survive them.[3] From Sam Spade to Dirty Harry, this is the individualist hero of our collective dream.

The Great Wrong Place suits the tough detective, giving him something to be tough about:

> The other part of me wanted to get out and stay out, but this was the part I never listened to. Because if I ever had I would have stayed in the town where I was born and worked in the hardware store and married the boss's daughter and had five kids and read the funny paper on Sunday morning and smacked their heads when they got out of line and squabbled with the wife about how much spending money they were to get and what programs they could have on the radio or TV set. I might even have got rich—small-town rich, an eight-room house, two cars in the garage, chicken every Sunday and the *Reader's Digest* on the living room table, the wife with a cast-iron permanent and me with a brain like a sack of Portland cement. You take it, friend. I'll take the big sordid dirty city. (*The Long Goodbye*, 204)

Chandler, in fact, knew that the toughness in his novels "was largely bluff" and responded to Auden's comment by emphasizing style over plot and theme: "How could I possibly care a button about the detective story as a form? All I'm looking for is an excuse for certain experiments in dramatic dialogue. To justify them I have to have plot and situation; but fundamentally I care almost nothing about either. All I really care about is what Errol Flynn calls 'the music,' the lines he has to speak."[4] This music has the energizing rhythm of disgust: "Down at the drugstore lunch counter I had time to inhale two cups of coffee and a melted-cheese sandwich with two slivers of ersatz bacon imbedded in it, like dead fish at the bottom of a drained pool. I was crazy. I liked it" (*The Little Sister*, 199). The Great Wrong Place is the best of all possible worlds for the American tough hero because what other one could offer such guilty pleasures as the mix of indignation and complicity in Marlowe's jeremiads?

This hero does feel frequently depressed, defeated: "The physical exhaustion at the end of the hard-boiled novel is a sign of *accidie*, which even the op [a Hammett hero] experiences: 'I felt tired, washed out.' . . ."[5] Some of Marlowe's most lyrical flights are inspired by this accidie: "I was a blank man. I had no face, no meaning, no personality, hardly a man. I didn't want to eat. I didn't even want to drink. I was the page from yesterday's calendar crumpled at the bottom of the waste basket" (*The Little Sister*, 99). But does not this prose savor its discontents? And it is part of a passage that ends with Marlowe being crazy enough to enjoy his new world cheese and bacon sandwich.

The greatest menace to the tough detective and perhaps his secret temptation is summed up in images of loss of control whether by physical immobilization, unconsciousness, the descent into subconsciousness, the stylistic flirtation with death, the ultimate "big sleep."

> A pool of darkness opened at my right and was far, far deeper than the blackest night.
> I dived into it. It had no bottom. (*Farewell, My Lovely*, 138)

So recurrent was this image that it was parodied in the Sam Spade radio series where the hero took his dive once an episode. But he will not drown. Marlowe emerges from the pool to a hallucinatory vision of smoke hanging in the air and dissociation from his body: "The throat felt sore but the fingers feeling it didn't feel anything. They might just as well have been a bunch of bananas. I looked at them. They looked like fingers. No good. Mail order fingers. They must have come with the badge and the truss. And the diploma" (140). But Marlowe, however sardonically he expresses it, still knows who he is and what to do:

> "Okay, Marlowe," I said between my teeth. "You're a tough guy. Six feet of iron man. One hundred and ninety pounds stripped and with your face washed. Hard muscles and no glass jaw. You can take it. You've been sapped twice, had your throat choked and been beaten half silly on the jaw with a gun barrel. You've been shot full of hop and kept under it until you're as crazy as two waltzing mice. And what does all that amount to? Routine. Now let's see you do something really tough, like putting your pants on." (143)

The irony does not keep the passage from being in fact part of the tough detective's routine. Intrinsic to his identity is that he "can take it."

Consequently, the Great Wrong Place of the detective novel is a Heaven compared to the Hell of the crime novel. In the latter, integrity, though possible, is problematic, while the threat to the protagonist's life and identity is more real. The usual categories of self-identity and self-evidence shimmer and blur, radically destabilizing the world and his relation to it. The character cannot be sure who's on first or what's on second; and sometimes the only certainty is that the umpire is wrong. A number of these novels touch on the motifs of schizophrenia, earlier examined, and criminal passion, the subject of the next chapter, but my emphasis here will be on their creation of an ontologically pathological world.

In these crime novels, the everyday world of normal perceptions loses its taken-for-granted secure status. In an ontologically pathological world, those under threat must become phenomenologically hyperacute. The crime novel presents a phenomenologically upside-down world, inverting or intensifying to the point of breakdown the normative structures of perception so brilliantly analyzed in Maurice Merleau-Ponty's *The Phenomenology of Perception*.

"Time," Merleau-Ponty observes, "is a setting to which one can gain access and which one can understand only by occupying a situation in it, and by grasping it in its entirety through the horizons of that situation."[6] But in the crime novel time grows exponentially desperate and horizons shrink to claustrophobic enclosure. In normal perception, Merleau-Ponty explains, "*I am given to myself,* which means that this situation is never hidden from me, it is never round about me as an alien necessity, and I am never in effect enclosed in it like an object in a box."[7] Precisely the contraries in this statement are definitive of the space of the crime novel. The mistake of the traditional theories of perception "is to introduce into perception itself intellectual operations and a critical examination of the senses, to which we in fact resort only when direct perception founders in ambiguity."[8] Since all appearances and occasions do inform against them, crime novel protagonists must interrogate their world. This situation is analogous to someone with impaired senses: "the patient substitutes for tactile recognition and perception, a laborious decoding of stimuli and deduction of objects." As with the schizophrenic, "everything is amazing, absurd, or unreal, because the impulse of existence toward things appears to itself in all its contingency and because the world can no longer be taken for granted."[9] Presences in the world become enigmatic, threatening: "A shadow passing or the creaking of branches have each a meaning: everywhere there are warnings with no one who issues them." When "life has become decentred," the sense of a "lived distance" becomes "both too small and too great: the majority of the events cease to count for me, while the nearest ones obsess me. They enshroud me like night and rob me of my individuality and freedom. I can literally no longer breathe; I am possessed." The decentered crime novel protagonist, like the schizophrenic, lives in a world where possibility seems to be shrinking to the vanishing point: "The shrinkage of lived space, which leaves no margin to the patient, leaves no room for chance."[10] In Ludwig Binswanger's words, we see in decentered perception "the freedom of letting 'world' occur . . . replaced by the unfreedom of being overwhelmed by a certain 'world-design.'"[11] The protagonist of the 1946 crime film *The Dark Corner* says, "I feel all dead inside. I'm backed up into a dark corner and I don't know who's hitting me."[12]

The gaze of the other no longer shares in constituting self and world but becomes competitive, displacing. Merleau-Ponty explains: "The affirmation of an alien consciousness standing over against mine would immediately make my experience into a private spectacle, since it would no longer be co-extensive with being. The *cogito* of another person strips my own *cogito* of all value, and causes me to lose the assurance which I enjoyed in my solitude of having access to the only being conceivable for me, being, that is, as it is aimed at and constituted by me." This, of course, is a pathological situation since "we have learned in individual perception not to conceive our prospective views as independent of each other; we know that they slip into each other and are brought together finally in the thing. In the same way we must learn to find the communication between one consciousness and another in one and the same world." But the crime novel literalizes terminal competition: "With the *cogito* begins that struggle between consciousnesses, each one of which, as Hegel says, seeks the death of the other."[13] The architect of the "frame up" creates a world of false appearances that incriminate the self. But to struggle with this other, for whom the self is a pawn in the game, the self must first discover who is hitting him or her.

It is Cornell Woolrich's distinction to have created one of the most consistently ontologically pathological worlds of any crime novelist, specialists in paranoid perception as they are. It is questionable whether this paranoia is clinical or structural, structural paranoia being defined as a response to a world where "they" really are out to get you and paranoia is, in effect, the reality principle.[14] Woolrich's creation is structurally paranoid through and through. Since his novels are variations on an obsessive theme, I shall explore them as all of a piece.

Certain Woolrich passages specify the outlines of his world:

And the rooms were dark. There was no laughing sound in them, no odor of cigarette smoke. I was alone, a lost, frightened thing straying around, my whole world crumbled away all around me like the shell of an egg. (*The Black Angel*, 19)

> I don't know what the game was. I only know its name; they call it
> life.
>   I'm not sure how it should be played. No one ever told me. No
> one ever tells anybody. I only know we must have played it wrong.
> We broke some rule or other along the way, and never knew it at the
> time.
>   I don't know what the stakes are. I only know we've forfeited
> them, they're not for us.
>   We've lost. That's all I know. We've lost, we've lost. (*I Married a
> Dead Man*, 7)

Time is what has to be raced against: "Oh, clock on the Paramount,
that I can't see from here, the night is nearly over and the bus has
nearly gone. Let me go home tonight" (*Deadline at Dawn*, 173).

"Home" in Woolrich is a kind of anti-matter, virtually invisible
but a logically necessary binary opposition to the real locale of his
narratives: Not-Home, Nowhere City, revealed through a phenomenologically elaborated image cluster of night, dark, and shadow.
Central to Woolrich's world is what Merleau-Ponty describes as "the
strange mode of existence enjoyed by the object behind our back.
The hysterical child who turns round 'to see if the world behind him
is still there,' suffers from no deficiency of images, but the perceived
world has lost for him that original structure which ensures that for
the normal person its hidden aspects are as indubitable as its visible
ones." Thus, "the distress felt by neuropaths in the night is caused
by the fact that it brings home to us our contingency, the uncaused
and tireless impulse which drives us to seek an anchorage and to sur-
mount ourselves in things, without any guarantee that we shall always find them."[15] Woolrich's Night is a presence, more convincingly characterized than any of the human characters in his stories:
"this wariness wasn't of the immediate stretch of sidewalk behind
them, of someone skulking up in back of him, it was more general,
more widespread, it was of the entire night behind him. On two di-
mensions: both the hours of it, and the island-wide depths of it"
(*Deadline at Dawn*, 14). Night, embodied otherness, has "the strange
mode of existence enjoyed by the object behind our back." Light
merely functions to heighten it: "Three anemic lightpoles widely
spaced down its seemingly endless length did nothing to dilute the
gloom; they only pointed it up by giving it contrast. As if saying: see,
this is what light is like—when there is any" (*Deadline at Dawn*,
15). In this world absence is the main presence; another being may
emerge as a sign within the dark, like the one first discerned as a
glowing "red mote" suspended in mid-air in *The Black Path of Fear*.
There is an extended description of the mote's movement in space
from which the protagonist derives certain deductions:

It gave itself away, the red pinpoint. It went up suddenly about two feet in a straight vertical line. Then it stopped again, froze there. I translated it. The smoker had risen. He was erect; he was full height now, where he had been seated or crouched or inclined before.

It was deftly done. There wasn't sound to go with it. He was trying to remain intangible, non-present to me. He didn't know he'd already given himself away. The red ember must have been an oversight; perhaps long incessant habit made him forget he was holding smoldering tobacco out before his face. (32)

The protagonist errs by reading into the sign an assumption that goes beyond the phenomenological evidence but is otherwise exact. He is transfixed by the phenomenon and personifies it in an emblem of mesmerizing terror: "I stared, hypnotized. I couldn't take my eyes off it. It was like a red bead of danger, a snake's eye fixed on me" (32). The protagonist then feels a knife pressed to his throat at which point, having established its dominance, the presence declares itself, flaring up from the darkness:

There was a swirl of air across my steaming face, as if an arm had swept up overhead. A second arm, not the one coiled behind the knife. Something snapped twig-like up there above eye-level, and a match-head creased by a thumb-nail fizzed and flared out like a rocket, blinding me with its suddenness.

Then it calmed to a steadier flame and came down close, between our two faces but a little offside, so that it didn't get in the way. The face in front of me slowly caught on in the back-shine, came through stronger, like something being developed on a photographic plate. (34)

Only then does the protagonist discover that "It was a woman" (35).

The figure emerging from darkness and absence may be the protagonist's savior, a kind of female guardian angel as with the prostitute, Midnight, the woman behind the cigarette, embodiment (through name and occupation) and dispeller of the dark who enables the protagonist's escape from a frame-up and his revenge upon those who murdered his beloved and framed him for it. In *The Black Curtain* (1941) the saving figure appears as a voice from above crying a name and as a face that isn't there:

At first, as he quickly corrected his angle of vision, brought it down window tier by window tier, all he found was a sudden blank spot, where a face had been amongst all the other faces. The center window, on the second tier, was where the hole was. But the face itself had gone before he could locate it, it was only its absence that registered. The surrounding ones quickly pressed in to fill the gap and then even that was gone.

He knew the cry had been meant for him, but that was by sheer instinct alone. It had been "thrown" directly at him, not to the right and not to the left; the intensity of vibration caught by his eardrum somehow told him that. (61)

The unit of the couple in Woolrich is intrinsically unstable; in his revenge novels the beloved is an ideal memory, motivating murder. In the other novels the couple exists only as threatened. An unthreatened life together is always a future projection functioning really to heighten present anxiety in the manner of a lightpole heightening the dark. Woolrich characters are to anxiety as the criminal lovers of chapter 4 are to passion: they *are* their anxiety, defined in contrast to a society either indifferent or hostile to them. In *The Black Curtain* the protagonist realizes that who has been stalking him is an embodiment of "organized society itself" (79). The couple seems almost produced by the indifference or hostility of the other: "But we only had eyes for one another, even after *they* were inside with him and the door was closed. We stood there, the two of us, in a frightened little world of our own with nobody else around" (21, my italics). Woolrich's lovers huddle together in the dark: "And when you felt that way, you needed your complement. You couldn't go on alone, you were too small, too helpless. Two helpless children in the dark" (*The Night Has a Thousand Eyes*, 286). Could such love survive security?

There are no characters in Woolrich except as conduits of mood. His protagonists are there for the purpose of ascribing and motivating the phenomenological descriptions. Some character must be feeling the thing and have a reason to do so, the plot having solely the function of providing the reason. Other characters provide solace and help or menace and obstruction. His hero and heroine could both be called "the boy" and "the girl": "His name was Johnny Marr, and he looked like—Johnny Marr. Like his given name sounded. Like any Johnny, anywhere, any time. Even people who had seen him hundreds of times couldn't have described him very clearly, he looked so much like the average, ran so true to form" (*Rendezvous in Black*, 2).

Woolrich's occasional happy endings are so unconvincing because his characters have no other ontological base than their anxiety. Paradise exists only insofar as it is lost. The small town, Glen Falls, Iowa, to which the couple in *Deadline at Dawn* yearns to regress, is out of Norman Rockwell, as a wishful daydream responding to the danger of New York. The protagonist of *I Married a Dead Man* (1948) comes out of a coma after a train wreck to find she is the object of mistaken identity. Through a series of incredible coincidences she is mistaken for a woman who died in the wreck with her husband. The man's family, who have never seen the wife, offer to share their peaceful home with her.

Inevitably, this world, a wish-fulfillment, cannot withstand the pervasive insecurity that caused it to be dreamt. The protagonist receives a series of letters, asking quintessentially decentering questions: "Who are you?" (99), "Where are you from?" (101), "What are you doing there?" (106). Her seemingly secure world "was for people in their own houses, not for you. And out there, nothing. Nothing that belonged to you or was for you" (102). Self begins to crack as well as world: "Somebody was walking along the quiet night sidewalk very close by. That was she. The trees were moving by her, slowly rearward. Somebody was climbing terraced flagstone steps. She could hear the gritty sound of the ascending tread. That was she. Somebody was standing before the door of the house now. She could see the darkling reflection in the glass opposite her. It moved as she moved. That was she" (151). Woolrich characters are most themselves when in states of self-distantiation and structurally paranoid anxiety.

It should by now be clear that paranoia is the name of the game in this type of crime novel. Some such novels have a fey quality, exploiting the odd and comic qualities of the inverted world, the through-the-looking-glass world, more than its dreadful aspects. In all these novels time is decentered. The narrative pace is either headlong (fast forward) or excruciatingly protracted (frame advance) as the protagonists scramble to stay a step ahead of the big clock or fear that they are about to be caught in its machinery. Sometimes these protagonists' perceptions are so contradicted by the seemingly irrefutable public version of reality that they cannot help but wonder whether they have been hallucinating their version of events. Two especially amusing performances are Joel Townsley Rogers's *The Red Right Hand* (1945) and Fredric Brown's *Night of the Jabberwock* (1949). Both have an eccentric narrator and an impossible situation involving "a little man who was not there." In fact, Hughes Mearns's poem is alluded to in one book and quoted in the other. And, of course, Brown's novel is an extended play on the Alice books, the solution to the mystery, indeed, depending on which Carroll novel encodes a vital clue. And, as in Carroll, space is privileged over time.

Though the novels have an urgency of narrative pace, they are notable for the spatial tilt their worlds take on until a shift of perspective can show their apparently absurd structure as illusory. In Ann

Chamberlain's *The Tall Dark Man* (1955) and Kenneth Fearing's *The Big Clock* (1946) the threat, however, is time, the protagonist in each running only hours, minutes, and finally seconds away from the hunter.

In the last part of *The Tall Dark Man* Sarah Lou Gross, the thirteen-year-old protagonist, sees a "red-rimmed clock" showing 7:25: "Sarah watched the long hand quiver, tense, leap forward. She thought how many clocks she had watched since three forty-five that afternoon, and how their pale expressionless faces would be always with her" (196). Just before school let out at 3:45, in last-period study hall, Sarah had looked out the window to the woods and become sole witness to an argument eventuating in a murder. Mesmerized, she watches a tall dark man drag the body of his victim into the woods, then return and scan the landscape with binoculars for possible witnesses, finally locating Sarah.

No one believes Sarah's story because she is the girl who cried wolf, a storyteller who fantasizes so vividly that she momentarily believes her own stories, as in her "evil story" about a classmate's father, Rowland Rath, who strikes her as a pedophile merely because of his name. The story gets out of hand and she must admit it was a fiction, as one part of herself knew even when she was telling it.

The upshot is that no one believes Sarah or likes her, though up until her witnessing of the murder she had rather cherished her isolation. Now, certain that "he would be waiting" (35), she is desperate for protection. The homeroom teacher, though not unsympathetic, does not believe her story and cannot give her a ride home because of a teacher's meeting, though she could have done so "any other afternoon" (43–44). Sarah, who has courted unpopularity, is for the first time aware of the danger of isolation. She is running short of alternatives and the building is emptying out.

School is a natural setting for a novel in which time is a presence because time there is so completely routinized. At 3:45 school is out, with school organizations meeting until 4:45. But by 4:42 Sarah has still not found a protector. She finally tries the principal's office, but her fears are dismissed as another tale and by now the 5:00 bell has rung. By 5:25 she is hiding in a booth in the girl's lavatory, hoping that by 6:00, when the lights go out, the tall man will suppose her to have eluded him.

While hidden, she begins, through overheard conversations, to see into the hidden life of the school, one which has previously escaped her, partly because of her own lack of interest. Chamberlain quite wonderfully conveys this: how teachers speak to and think about students, the modes and manners of popularity and unpopularity, the group dynamics of such as the Drama Club, whose late stay has in fact kept the lights on past 6:00. The Drama Club seems for a time Sarah's salvation as the members dramatically adopt her. But she makes the mistake of telling them about the tall man, and, less than half believing her, they seize the occasion for a mock chase around the school grounds, effectively abandoning her.

She somehow knows they won't catch him. She has even a peculiar sympathy with the tall man, who relates somehow to her other Sarah Gross, "her complete and mirrorlike twin" (175). Sarah's self-division is apparent throughout, but her situation on this one day has intensified it to the point where she feels the tall man as "a part of her, in fearsome projection . . . roaming the windy dark . . ." (96). And one of her selves yearns to become his murderee: "One of her, indeed, would rush willingly into the long arms of the stranger. Yes, stepping at last beyond the door, this one, would stand deliberately in the light, waiting for him to see her. With a cry of joy, she would recognize him in the dark. On light feet she would skim the earth and fly into his strong embrace, and he would enfold her and they would be there forever. Somewhere, against the black screen of the sky, rabbits and daisies would do a static dance" (176–177).

One of the strengths of the book is that the point of view remains firmly fixed on Sarah and her perception of her world, and refuses the usual explanatory rationalization. We never are told the motive or even the name of the tall man; there is no intrusive psychological explanation of Sarah's divided self or her feeling of kinship and attraction to the tall man. In the last scene set within the school, Sarah finally gets through to her mother on the telephone, only to be told, " 'Why do you always have to ruin things? Everything that pleases me and your father and that should please you. . . . Oh, I know why.' The voice, half-strangled with sobs, stumbled on. 'I knew you would do something. You always do'" (187). It is at this moment Sarah makes a cold clear decision to leave the sanctuary of the school. Here is material for several case histories, but they are left for the reader to extrapolate.

In the conclusion, Sarah makes it most of the way to her house by tagging along with people, but the tall man is indeed close behind her and the distance still too great. She saves herself by dashing into Rowland Rath's house, who, though the person most injured by her stories, believes her and calls the police. Mr. Rath informs her that the police just found the victim's body. The novel ends wonderfully:

"Then you do believe me." She clasped her hands ecstatically. "You know it isn't just another story. You know that it's the truth."

Rowland Rath placed his pink hands firmly on his knees. "Sarah,"
he said in his mild voice, "I would have believed you anyway." (215)

Is this ending entirely reassuring? Is it complete closure of at least
one theme in the story, Sarah's lies and the forgiveness and intuitive
awareness of her one victim? Or does it at least raise the question
that Rath believed her because at some purely latent level her accusation had an evanescent validity, that he too has a shadow self?
Earlier, explaining her lie about Rath to the homeroom teacher,
Sarah goes from his name to his manner: "I wrote it three times in
my notebook, thinking how like a villain he sounded. Rath, with
Rowland attached to it: How like a movie villain, sounding cruel.
Then I thought how cozy nice he is, how soft and squishy-sounding
he says 'How do you do' to me when he sees me home from school.
And about his pink face and his expression like one of my old dolls
with a silly grin" (42). Does the reader's mind move through these
impressions to the same association as Sarah's? If so, does this ever
so lightly conveyed intimation diminish or rather increase Rath's
saving role? Is it as one whose shadow self has been sublimated from
menace into compassionate intuitiveness?

In Kenneth Fearing's *The Big Clock* point of view fluctuates, always first-person but not the same: seven characters in all get at
least one shot at their version of events. But the dominant voice is
clearly that of George Stroud, whose point of view begins and ends
the novel and is that of eleven of its nineteen chapters. Indeed the
novel is about George's attempt to outrun and delay events, to put
his own falsifying construction upon them so as to head off other
characters from knowing where he was, when he was there, what he
saw, what he knows, and, in a sense, who he is.

George lives life and relates to time according to the principle of
whim. This is his weakness and his strength. He lacks the coldly
methodical egoism of his boss, Earl Janoth, and of Janoth's ruthless
right-hand man and only friend, Steve Hagen. Their mechanistic, ar-
mored personalities appear to put them in tune with the inexorable
personality of the big clock, and in George's mind the mechanistic
power of Janoth Enterprises merges into that of "the big clock,"
George's metaphor for the nature of things:

I told myself it was just a clock, a vast machine, and the machine
was blind. But I had not fully realized its crushing weight and power.
That was insane. The machine cannot be challenged. It both creates
and blots out, doing each with glacial impersonality. It measures
people in the same way that it measures money, and the growth of
trees, the life-span of mosquitoes and morals, the advance of time.

And when the hour strikes, on the big clock, that is indeed the hour, the day, the correct time. When it says a man is right, he is right, and when it finds him wrong, he is through, with no appeal. It is as deaf as it is blind.

Of course, I had asked for this. (145)

George asked for it by following the logic of his chancy relationship to time. Accidentally encountering Pauline Delos, Janoth's beautiful, mysterious mistress, and feeling a spark between them, George calculates the odds: "Why not? I knew the risks and the cost. And still, why not? Maybe the risks and the price were themselves at least some of the reasons why. The cost would be high; it would take some magnificent lying and acting; yet if I were willing to pay the price, why not? And the dangers would be greater still. Of them, I couldn't even guess" (37–38). It is a moment "snatched from the very teeth of the inner works" (45), a kind of defiance of the big clock. The next day George takes Pauline on a tour of Antique Row, where he discovers an unrecognized Louise Patterson painting and outbids for it "a big monolithic brunette, sloppily dressed and with a face like an arrested cyclone" (47). George is a collector of Pattersons, having several at home and one in his office.

But things start unraveling. As George drops off Pauline at her apartment building, he has a near encounter with Janoth, who looks right at him but at too great a distance to recognize him. This becomes crucial because Janoth proceeds to murder Pauline in a jealous rage and is persuaded by Hagen to avoid incrimination by finding and liquidating the man who had been with Pauline, who alone saw Janoth at the wrong place at the right time. Before the fatal termination of their quarrel Pauline had told Janoth about the Patterson and a few other highlights of her encounter but without revealing her lover's identity. Janoth and Hagen invent a cover story that allows them to use their own organization as a detective agency. To head this investigation they need a creative, quick-thinking person. Who better than George Stroud?

So George is hired to find the little man who *was* there, himself. And he perfectly grasps the real reason for the manhunt. He could go to the police only at the cost of his marriage. The alternative is to slow down, mislead, and generally sabotage the investigation, *playing for time*, as much Janoth's enemy as his own. The cards are stacked against George except for one thing. George knows the danger of the big clock whereas Janoth, a solipsistic idealist with an abstract sense of mission, is too much of a megalomaniac to recognize it exists. He overestimates his own centrality and is blind to the power of contingency.

George, in contrast, is a man nimble in time, a player with contingency, skating along the razor's edge. Lacking Janoth's idealism and grandiose moral vision, George's concern is with what he particularly values—his marriage and even the Louise Patterson painting, which for safety's sake he should destroy, it being a clue to his identity. George chooses not to find it expendable. As a rescuer of privileged moments from the big clock, George does what is right for him.

Despite George's roadblocks, the hunt begins to close in. It is a matter of time until someone notices the Louise Patterson painting in George's office; she has become an unlikely celebrity after Janoth's news magazine puffed her work in the hope it would lead to the witness. The hunt narrows down to the Janoth building and begins to move up the floors, with witnesses of the mystery man posted at all exits. George, coordinator of the hunt, shows his dedication by declaring he will not leave the building until the man is caught. At this moment, the point of view shifts to Louise Patterson, whom someone helpfully brings to George's office in the hope that she may provide some clue to the buyer of her painting. She is, in fact, the brunette George outbid and is ready to expose him. But in a coded way she asks him about the fate of the painting and he intimates that it is safe—so far. Recognizing the threat, she reflects that, even if a murderer, a collector of her paintings deserves consideration.

Besides, she too is a rebel against the big clock, more obviously so than George, whose outward propriety disguises his nonconformity. Communicating in whoops and shrieks, she cannot quite maintain her dignity with Mr. Klausmeyer, "the polite dignified worm" who is the corporation's emissary, even though she appreciates "how he gave my apartment a crazy atmosphere of respectability or something" (151). She considers him one of those "microscopic deities" (155) who are natural enemies to art. When he comments on her four children and asks after her husband, she gives way completely: "'I've never been married,' I said, again shrieking with laughter, against my will. God, I would learn to act refined, beginning tomorrow, if it was the last thing I ever did. 'They're all LOVE children, Mr. Klausmeyer'" (156). That she decides against exposing George is consistent.

Odd people outflank even ones in Fearing's world. Just as the search reaches George's floor, he learns that Janoth has been deposed from his publishing empire by a hostile takeover. George calls it off with seconds to spare. He then meets Louise Patterson at a bar, reassures her about the painting, and somewhat mortifies her by explaining that he is not a murderer since she had been feeling proud of her bravery in confronting one. George notices that "Yesterday she'd looked like something out of an album, but today she'd evidently taken some pains to put herself together. She was big, and dark, and alive" (172). George keeps her phone number on spec: "I would never call her, of course. It was enough, to be scorched by one serious, near-disaster. All the same, it was a nice, interesting number to have" (175). As he leaves the bar, he sees a newspaper headlining Janoth's suicide.

Woolrich was the master of an especially threatening variation on the theme of ontological insecurity, that in which the protagonist must overcome some form of amnesia so as to recover time and constitute innocence. The classic in this formula (now a staple of soap operas) is his *The Black Curtain* (1941), though John Franklin Bardin's *The Deadly Percheron* is also memorable. The questions of identity implicated in the formula are nicely forecast in *The Big Clock*, toward the end of which George tells a story, a parable really, to his daughter, George. (This is also his wife's name.) Earlier he has told her about a little girl who was upset by seeing another face mimicking her every time she looked in a mirror. The girl solves this by mimicking the face. It all depends on the point of view. The later story, which he tells on the phone, is about Claudia:

> "And here's what she did. One day she started to pick at a loose
> thread in her handkerchief, and it began to come away, and pretty
> soon she'd picked her handkerchief until it all disappeared and before
> she knew it she was pulling away at some yarn in her sweater, and
> then her dress, and she kept pulling and pulling and before long she
> got tangled with some hair on her head and after that she still kept
> pulling and pretty soon Claudia was just a heap of yarn lying on the
> floor."
> "So then what did she do? Hello?"
> "So then she just lay there on the floor and looked up at the chair
> where she'd been sitting, only of course it was empty by now. And
> she said, 'Where am I?'"
> Success. I got an unbelieving spray of laughter. "So then what did
> I do? Hello? Hello?"
> "Then you did nothing," I said. "Except you were always careful
> after that not to pull any loose threads. Not too far." (169–170)

George's affinity to the Patterson painting is a thread of his personality which he refused to pull. The way to fake out the face in the mirror is to redouble its mimicry, mimic it back.

In the amnesiac novel the protagonist's problem is being a heap of yarn lying on the floor that must be raveled up to full identity. This also involves discovering the identity of an unknown other who has somehow substituted a mimic face for one's own in the mirror. The crime novel protagonist lives *at best* in an ontologically insecure

world: "What is there to say, when they tell you you have committed a crime, and you and you alone know you haven't? Who is
there to hear you, and who is there to believe you?" (*Phantom Lady*,
63). The structure of the world appears not as rationally causative
but as deeply erroneous: "It isn't easy to die at all, but it's even
harder to die for a mistake. I'm not dying for something I've done,
but for a mistake. And that's the hardest way to die of all" (63).
There was a witness, someone who could put this character at the
right place at the right time to prove his innocence, but she cannot
be found and sometimes even he is uncertain of her real existence:
"Sometimes they've got me wondering myself if there really was
such a person, or, if she wasn't just a hallucination on my part, a
vagary of my own feverish imagination" (84). These doubts occur to
most well-framed protagonists, as if signs of an inverse providence,
one that validates false appearance, condemns the innocent, and delivers the guilty from detection. Though in the end the world *may*
turn right side up again.

This will not, however, happen in a type of crime novel where the
setting is effectually a kind of Hell, an irredeemably corrupt milieu
such as the world of James Ross's *They Don't Dance Much* (1940), a
novel described by Raymond Chandler as "a sleazy, corrupt completely believable story of a North Carolina town about the size of
Raleigh."[16] Ross's novel has a malignantly ironic symmetry. In its
plot, characters, and language this is a stripped-down novel, mini-
malist before the fashion. Ross's own summation is appropriately
terse:

> The book was written as the Depression was ending and as the stage
> was setting itself and the characters assembling for the presentation
> of World War II. Since then, this region of the South has lost much of
> its rural flavor. The roadhouses have long since disappeared. Human
> greed and the evils it generates haven't. Some reviewer said the novel
> was "Southern Gothic," suggesting a piece of fiction dealing in fan-
> tastic occurrences in an overdrawn setting. My memory is that my
> aim was to show the way it was and leave it to the reader to reach
> his own conclusions as to the point of it, or draw his own moral, if
> he needed one. (*They Don't Dance Much*, [i])

No one can complain that the morality of Ross's novel is overly
explicit. Such distinctions as the characters make tend toward the
pragmatic or ironic side, like Smut Milligan's explanation of why he
will rent his cabins to the respectable folks for an hour or two but
not to prostitutes: "It would get me closed up. . . . Another thing is
if I was to die and go to hell, it would create a bad situation. If I'd
made any money off whores, I couldn't hold up my head in hell"

(284). Early in the novel, the narrator, Jack, listens to the radio, "but it wasn't long before the only programs I could get were inspirational programs that told you how to get more out of life. I shut it off . . ." (45). Later, a character sings "Death Gonna Lay His Cold, Icy Hands on Me," but he is lying on the ground, drunk, at the time. The distinction between the nice folks and the best folks is that the best folks keep their messing around covert. Asked by a local boy about how to loosen up a reluctant girl, Jack reflects that he must be pretty dumb: "Everybody in town had had that girl except me, and now him" (42). In this materially grounded world, religious and social codes have become bad jokes.

Its narrator's voice is not so much cold as indifferent, anomic. Jack just doesn't care all that much about anything or anyone but himself, nor does anyone else in his world. As Bert Ford is being tortured to reveal where he has hidden money, he asks his tormentor, Smut Milligan, what he has against him. Smut replies with what seems to him obvious: "I ain't got a thing in the world against you, but I want your money" (115). (True, Bert may have made his money as a strikebreaker in Detroit, but Smut would not be one to hold this against him.) Jack is upset when Smut puts a coal to Bert's foot and he can "hear it frying in a minute," but it is more a physical than moral distress: "The smell of him burning made me a little sick. I reckon that was what fixed Bert too" (116). When Bert turns out to have lied about the location of the money, Smut tortures him in a way more horrifying than that noted above but with a dispassionate efficiency. It is the same with the man Smut frames for the murder: "I ain't got a thing in the world against him. He's a dope, but I like him all right. I just rather it would be him than me" (242). These characters are in Hobbes's state of nature; Smut, in particular, sees himself in "such a war as is of every man against every man." In the event, Smut, among others, dies in this war. Two characters, however, profit: the richest man in town by happenstance ends up with Bert Ford's money and Smut's roadhouse. And: "I drive back to Main Street. When I passed the Smathers furniture store and undertaking parlor LeRoy was standing in the front door. Things were beginning to break for him too" (293).

In a book so scrupulously flat in style, character, and plot, a point or moral could only be superfluous, adulterating a setting in which the reader beholds nothing that is not there and the nothing that is. I do not mean to suggest that this nothing takes any but the most material form. What most readers will carry away from the novel is, in fact, much its most material image. Bert Ford's body is a physical problem for Smut and Jack that they solve temporarily by dumping it in the container of an isolated beer still. Though ordinarily he would welcome it, Jack is upset about an impending warm front: it means the beer will work off sooner. In fact, the still owner has tasted it, though not, luckily, dipping too deep. So Jack and Smut volunteer to run off the beer while the still's custodian takes a trip to see his sister. Smut cannot retrieve the body until he strips and climbs into the container with it. They then burn Ford's body in the still furnace and run off the beer: "We put the cap over the container and got the cooling stand rigged up. Smut looked after the fire and I looked after changing the water in the cooling stand and catching the liquor. It took us most of the night. When we finished there was about fifty gallons of it and it looked like good liquor, but neither one of us had the stomach to taste it" (147). Ross's rather dreadful book approaches in its way Roland Barthes's ideal of "white writing," a writing as free as can be from moral presuppositions, cultural givens, and literary echoes. What is disturbing in the novel is how much its characters take for granted things we find dreadful. It is a book that consistently delivers nothing, adding nothing to it. There is one major rhetorical figure—in the title, *They Don't Dance Much*—but even this is about what isn't there.

An earlier novel, *You Play the Black and the Red Comes Up* (1938), takes the opposite route: from the title on, this book is all style, playing out the tonal possibilities of a naive first-person narrator undergoing desolating experiences. The book verged on parody to the point of putting off some of its contemporary reviewers.[17] In Edmund Wilson's classic essay on California writing, "The Boys in the Back Room," he described it as "a clever pastiche of Cain which is mainly as two-dimensional as a movie" and comments, "It is indicative of the degree to which this kind of writing has finally become formularized that it should have been possible for a visiting Englishman . . . to tell a story in the Hemingway-Cain vernacular almost without a slip."[18] For the author, writing under the pen name of Richard Hallas, was Eric Knight, who wrote *The Flying Yorkshireman* the same year, and, of course, *Lassie, Come Home* in 1940. But the book is not simply a parody nor was Knight precisely a visiting Englishman. Raymond Chandler was born in Chicago but spent his formative years in England. When he came to America to live, he heard the language as foreign, and such unfamiliarity foregrounded its literary possibilities. Knight emigrated to America in his teens,[19] surely to the same effect.

And the narrative voice in *You Play the Black and the Red Comes Up* sounds less like Cain, whose characters run the emotional gambit from the A of lust to the B of fear and are unbelievable and bathetic when they try for a higher note, than like the Sherwood Anderson of "I Want to Know Why." Anderson himself derives from Twain, and sometimes Knight's narrative voice sounds like Huck Finn with additional dialogue—especially chapter titles—by Bertolt Brecht. He has a feel for phenomena: "It was warm, and we would dive under the water. When we did that we could see each other all outlined in a sort of cold fire that comes from the phosphorus in the water" (72).

Style as such and subjective record as narrative mode are foregrounded by repetition. Early in chapter 1, the narrator (his name is Dick Dempsey, but the reader remembers him as the "I" who tells this story) is on top of a boxcar: "I lay there, and it was cold, but I couldn't think about it. The way I felt I didn't care if school kept or not. That's the way I felt" (2). Four other chapters end with variations on the way he felt, and other formulaic repetitions recur throughout.

Chapter titles are terse—"TOUGH TO TAKE" and (my favorite) "THIS GIRL IS DIFFERENT." They are frequently used in the manner of Brecht's estranging placards, to ironically undercut, in advance, the characters' emotional responses. In chapter 26 the narrator's lover asks him to tell "things you love me like" and he improvises:

> "Well, I love you like mountains that are blue and gold, and like the smell of the sea up here, and like the bugle playing taps late at night."
> "And like whisky, too."
> "Sure, like whisky too. The first drink. And like getting up in the morning after it's been raining but now the sun is out, and like being in the forest where the big trees are, and like a Rolls Royce engine. I love you like all those things." (109)

The narrator is not lying; he really does love this girl. But the chapter title is calculated to flatten response: "LIKE WHISKY AND MOUNTAINS AND MUSIC."

The fatalism of the novel is evident in its title, *You Play the Black and the Red Comes Up*, which echoes James M. Cain's *The Postman Always Rings Twice*. But fate works differently in Knight. In Cain's novel the protagonist gets away with the murder of his girlfriend's husband but is to be executed for the murder of the girlfriend—which, in fact, was an accident. In *You Play the Black and the Red Comes Up* the narrator intends to murder his profane love, Mamie, because of his need for his sacred love, Sheila. But in a not unexpected symmetrical irony Sheila, not Mamie, is killed by his device and he is convicted for her murder. At this point, however, Knight gives an extra spin. Another character commits suicide, leaving behind a false confession to the murder. The narrator, who has accepted the plot logic of his impending execution, is horrified by this reversal and confesses to the attempted murder of Mamie and anything else he can think of, but no one is interested and he is forced to go free. This replicates his frustration early in the novel when he tries to relieve his guilt over some stolen money by gambling it away at the bar from which it was stolen. He bets dead against the odds . . . and can't lose: "By this time I didn't know what to do. I had kept playing the black, and the red wouldn't show up. I'd never seen a wheel come up one color ten times running. The old saying is that you play the black and the red comes up—but the saying wasn't true this time" (31).

It is as if the narrator finds himself in the wrong plot. Since Genter, the character who saves him, is a moviemaker, the narrator earlier releases his guilt over a crime he was involved in by confessing it under the transparent guise of a film scenario. Genter's "confession" plagiarizes from this scenario. The narrator was resigned to the James M. Cain plot line of his story: "I guess I got what was coming to me. If I didn't do what they said, I guess I tried to do as much to someone else. So I guess that when one door opens another closes, like. I planned things and it seems like justice works out and I get it anyhow, even if I didn't do it." But Genter objects that it is all too pat, "like a Hays-office ending to a movie plot" (119) and, in effect, cuts the execution scene.

Throughout, the narrator seems tranced, in a fashion Edmund Wilson saw as endemic to California: "I have heard a highly intelligent Los Angeles lawyer who had come to California from Colorado remark that he had periodically to pinch himself to remind himself of the fact that he was living in an abnormal, a sensational, world which he ought to get down on paper, but that he could never pull out of the trance sufficiently to react and to judge in what he still at the back of his mind considered the normal way" (Wilson, 240). Wilson then cites a passage from *You Play the Black and the Red Comes Up* as a veracious account of this sensation and compares the novel favorably to Aldous Huxley's *After Many a Summer Dies the Swan*. But Wilson complains about California novels generally: "It is probably a good deal too easy to be a nihilist on the coast at Carmel: your very negation is a negation of nothing" (Wilson, 241–243).

Early on, Genter tells the narrator: "It's the climate—something in the air. You can bring men from other parts of the world who are sane. And you know what happens? At the very moment they cross those mountains . . . they go mad" (44). Toward the end of the novel, the narrator muses, "And I thought about all the things they'd said about Genter after he was dead, but it didn't matter; because he knew more than they did. Anyhow, he was the only man in California with enough sense to know he was crazy" (132). In the passage cited by Wilson, the narrator, riding a boxcar crossing the mountains out of California, feels his experiences, sacred as well as profane, slipping away from him: "It was like all I had done in California was just a dream. And at first it felt good, and then it felt worse, because Sheila was only a dream with everything else. And that was bad" (130). Bertrand Russell cites the sentence "The golden mountain does not exist" as a paradigm of linguistic paradox.[20] How can you name something, with a definite article, that does not exist? Yet the sentence creates a nostalgia; we long to return to this golden mountain, especially because it does not exist. The narrator remembers going toward the California mountains with his sharecropper father, feeling "that if we ever got over those golden mountains everything would be different and the land would be different—like the promised land in the Bible" (75). In fact, the narrator finds Sheila: "THIS GIRL IS DIFFERENT." This may explain the novel's strange, compelling ending when the narrator sees the golden mountains again from his freight train headed east and flips out of the boxcar, hurting himself so badly he blacks out. But when he awakens he has lost the pain and knows he can walk all night: "it was pitch-dark but I wasn't afraid of losing my way. I knew where I had to go, and somehow it was like something would be sure to tell me how to get there" (133). And at last he is close to the golden mountains:

> And the minute I saw them I was me again and I could feel again, and I could feel Sheila was gone. I could feel my insides hurting me where they were empty because Sheila was dead and I knew as long as I lived that pain would always be there. It was the only thing left of her. The only thing I could have. And having it made me so happy that I began running down the slope.
> I ran down through the fields, through the great white paper poppies and the Indian-blankets, and I snatched them up in my arms as I went. And I ran on and on, down the hillside to the big desert that I had to cross to get to my golden mountains. (134)

It is clear enough that the jump from the freight car fatally injures the narrator and the rest of the chapter is a visionary experience as he is dying or even after death. California as unreality is paradigmatic. Both heaven and hell, its reality is found in loss and pain.

I want to briefly consider one last novel in this section, though it is not American and not strictly a crime novel. But it not only makes an original combination of the justice theme and the amnesia theme but also carries the idea of time and place in the crime novel to its logical conclusion, thus all the more evidencing the narrative logic I have been arguing for. This is *The Third Policeman* (1940, 1967) by the Irish man of letters, Flann O'Brien.[21] The novel opens memorably:

> Not everybody knows how I killed old Philip Mathers, smashing his jaw in with my spade; but first it is better to speak of my friendship with John Divney because it was he who first knocked old Mathers down by giving him a great blow in the neck with a special bicycle pump which he manufactured himself out of a hollow iron bar. Divney was a strong civil man but he was lazy and idle-minded. He was personally responsible for the whole idea in the first place. It was he who told me to bring my spade. He was the one who gave the orders on the occasion and also the explanations when they were called for. (7)

The narrator decides the only way to keep Divney from retrieving the money from where he hid it and running off is to keep him constantly under surveillance; they share the same bed for *three years*. Finally, Divney is apparently worn down and tells the narrator where Mathers's money is hidden—in Mathers's own house under a floorboard. The narrator sneaks into the house, pulls up the floorboard, and then "something happened": "I cannot hope to describe what it was but it had frightened me very much long before I had understood it even slightly. It was some change which came upon me or upon the room indescribably subtle, yet momentous, ineffable. It was as if daylight had changed with unnatural suddenness, as if the temperature of the evening had altered greatly in an instant, or as if the air had become twice as rare or twice as dense as it had been in the winking of an eye . . ." (23).

A number of odd things transpire: the narrator finds the box has disappeared; he hears a cough behind him and finds himself involved in a long conversation with the man he has murdered, decides to go to the police barracks to get help in finding the box, notices that he no longer remembers his name, and finally comes upon an architecturally original police barracks: "It looked as if it were painted like an advertisement on a board on the roadside and indeed very poorly painted. It looked completely false and unconvincing. It did not seem to have any depth or breadth and looked as if it would not deceive a child" (52–53). The narrator is then arrested for the murder of Mathers, not because of any evidence against him but simply because he is at the station and they need to arrest someone. The narrator responds with a fine legal point: that having no name, he has no legal existence, therefore cannot be tried or found guilty or hanged. The policeman, however, outflanks this objection with masterful logic, pointing out that a legally nonexistent person cannot be tried or found guilty but can easily be hanged: "The particular death you die is not even a death (which is an inferior phenomenon at the best) only an insanitary abstraction in the backyard, a piece of negative nullity neutralised and rendered void by asphyxiation and the fracture of the spinal string. If it is not a lie to say that you have been given the final hammer behind the barrack, equally is it true to say that nothing has happened to you" (102). The reader wondering how Woolrich's structural paranoia could be topped now knows. If you do not exist, you cannot be guilty, nor can anyone be guilty about you. But as we shall see in the English novels of chapter 5, murderers are compounded all of deceit and thus lack being to the point of disappearance. But then hanging would be superfluous in relation to the narrator since, as the reader has doubtless inferred, he is *already dead and in hell*, blown up by a bomb Divney planted under the floorboard. Hell, for O'Brien's character, is not other people; rather it is being himself in, as O'Brien describes it in a letter to William Saroyan, "a sort of hell which he earned for the killing" (200). This letter, quoted in a publisher's note at the end of *The Third Policeman*, also quotes from another O'Brien work: "Hell goes round and round. In shape it is circular and by nature it is interminable, repetitive and very nearly unbearable" (200).

There are other shapes and other temporal structures of imagined hells. In this chapter I have shown a variety of hells generically proper to the crime novel. The moral truth of these is questionable: looking into the void can become a morbid obsession, a self-serving indulgence, or, worse yet, an amusement. But, then, in the crime novel what is not problematic is not functional.

4

Devil or Angel

Fatal

Passion

in the

American

Crime Novel

L'amour est un enfant de Bohême
Il n'a jamais, jamais connu de loi,
Si tu ne m'aimes pas, je t'aime
Si je t'aime, prends garde a toi!

GEORGES BIZET, *CARMEN*

Devil or Angel
I can't make up my mind.
Which one you are
I'd like to awake and find.

BLANCHE CARTER, "DEVIL OR ANGEL"[1]

AT THE END OF *I, The Jury* Mike Hammer realizes that the lady he has had the hots for is also the criminal he has been trying to detect. She responds to his discovery by undressing before him, certain of her sexual power. But Hammer, after drooling a bit, shoots her in the crotch. Though a bit extreme, this sadistic fantasy is, within the rules of the tough detective genre, not immoral but exemplary. The hero's quest in the Hammett-Chandler-Spillane tradition is not, as in the English form, to rescue a social world because, as we have seen, his is always already irredeemably corrupt but to preserve his own isolated ego from losing itself in commitment to some other, usually female: "Spade set the edges of his teeth together and said through them: 'I won't play the sap for you'" (*The Maltese Falcon*, 195). John Cawelti describes the resultant ethos: "the price of survival would seem to be a terrible emptiness, a restriction of human possibilities, a cynical rejection of deeper emotion and commitment. . . . Only a rejection of all emotional and moral ties can help a man survive in a treacherous world."[2] The genre notably lacks guidelines for woman's survival.

As noted in chapter 3, the American tough detective form correlates with the American romance. Its misogyny is a specialized version of the central myth of the American romance: the hero's protection of his personal identity by flight from the entangling alliances of social definition.[3] Thus, the tough detective credo is hardly exaggerated by Steve Martin's parody in *Dead Men Don't Wear Plaid:* "Guns don't kill detectives, love does." Woman's paradoxical double function is to serve as negative sign of society or as negative sign of desire, as exemplary of stultifying conformity or fatal deviance. It is a perfect double bind. The genre *assumes* the romantic evaluation of passion examined and denounced in Denis de Rougemont's *Love in the Western World: "passion is linked with death, and involves the destruction of anyone yielding himself up to it with all his strength."*[4] Tough detectives know this, so they decline the gambit, as in Philip Marlowe's unregretful departure from Dolores Gonzales, whose entire characterization blatantly compounds misogyny with racism: "I looked back as I opened the door. Slim, dark and lovely and smiling. Reeking with sex. Utterly beyond the moral laws of this or any world I could imagine" (*The Little Sister*, 278).

In contrast, crime protagonists go straight to the end of the line. Not that fatal passion is merely the obverse of the tough detective pattern; the relation is more dialectical, exploratory. The crime novel centering on fatal passion is a kind of *reading* of the American detective genre, a reading guided by alertness to what could be *revised*, thus providing a whole new set of plot opportunities as well as suggesting at least a very different ethos. The crime protagonist may prove out the tough detective's greatest fear: passion gets him dead (though sometimes with curious slippages, excesses, and qualifications that undermine the purity of the misogyny). But the crime novel may outright subvert the misogyny of the tough detective form: the protagonist may risk commitment and *thereby* save himself or he may be destroyed *because of* his evasion, becoming the dupe of his own culturally constructed fears. He then is the victim of the *myth* of the femme fatale.

The Americanized model of the femme fatale owes much to James M. Cain, yet even here we find some equivocation; in addition, the influential film versions of his two best novels, *The Postman Always Rings Twice* and *Double Indemnity*, differ significantly from the novels. Still, these works are classic instances of "the longing for what sears us and annihilates us in its triumph," of the potential of death aggravating desire "to the point of turning this into a wish to kill either the beloved or oneself, or to founder in a twin downrush" (de Rougemont, 41, 44). Indeed, in Cain's novels compulsiveness is not so much an aspect of character as a substitute for it. Luchino Visconti's film version of *The Postman Always Rings*

Twice is *Ossessione*; Cain's characters try, unsuccessfully, not to overcome but to live up to their obsessions:

> "We're just two punks, Frank. God kissed us on the brow that night. He gave us all that two people can ever have. And we just weren't the kind that could have it. We had all that love, and we just cracked up under it. It's a big airplane engine, that takes you through the sky, right up to the top of the mountain. But when you put it in a Ford, it just shakes it to pieces. That's what we are, Frank, a couple of Fords. God is up there laughing at us." (88)

This is Cora in *The Postman Always Rings Twice*, and that her language seems exemplary of a vehicle inadequate to its tenor is Cain's theme. Both this novel and *Double Indemnity* center on characters who grope at a transcendence that is not in them and not in the situation; their desire is finally an embodiment of a cliché: it *is* bigger than both of them. This leads to the split in these two novels; in them a surface realism is insistently presented:

> It was nothing but a roadside sandwich joint, like a million others in California. (*The Postman Always Rings Twice*, 1)

> That was how I came to this house of Death, that you've been reading about in the papers. It didn't look like a House of Death when I saw it. It was just a Spanish house, like all the rest of them in California, with white walls, red tile roof, and a patio out to one side. (*Double Indemnity*, 217)

This establishes a level of identification for the mass audience by portraying ordinary places and people, but into this ordinariness Cain imports a tacky version of the archetypal:

> She looked like the great grandmother of every whore in the world. The devil got his money's worth that night. (*The Postman Always Rings Twice*, 89)

> She's in her stateroom getting ready. She's made her face chalk white, with black circles under her eyes and red on her lips and cheeks. She's got that red thing on. It's awful-looking. It's just one big square of red silk that she wraps around her, but its got no armholes, and her hands look like stumps underneath it when she moves them around. She looks like what came aboard the ship to shoot dice for souls in the Rime of the Ancient Mariner. (*Double Indemnity*, 37)

The operatic quality of such scenes, alternating with the drabness of setting, has not escaped Cain's critics.[5] In opera commonplace if violent characters generate sublime arias from their desire, jealousy, and revengefulness. But Cain's novels lack the social and political subtexts of such operas as *Cavalleria Rusticana* and *Carmen*, though Frank once fancies himself and Cora as "a couple of gypsies" (27). Cain's characters cannot sustain their arias or embody their archetypes. Cora is a bit of a whore but not the great-grandmother of every whore in the world; and, though a groundwork is established for it, Phyllis Nirdlinger is not appropriately cast as Life-Death or Hecate, goddess of the moon, earth, and underworld. The attributions are forced, giving the characters more symbolic weight than they can carry. But this is Cain's point: his novels work best when he emphasizes the gap rather than attempts to bridge it. What gives a certain pathos is the gap itself, characters attempting to negotiate a desire that they cannot understand, much less articulate. Desire cannot express the self because Cain's characters lack self and have nothing to express. Desire destroys them, but this seems hardly a loss. More really a gift than a curse to these characters, desire gives them a kind of galvanic energy; they glorify desire essentially by bringing nothing to it. They are that which passion passes through. Geoffrey O'Brien puts it perfectly: "If the Cain hero ultimately embraces his own catastrophe, it is because it is the most interesting thing that ever happened to him."[6] The function of fatal passion in Cain, then, parallels the privileging of schizophrenia and paranoia examined in chapter 2: it enlivens characters, sometimes even giving them a shadow of justification as over against a stultifyingly normative social order.

Desire is both generalized and particular. It is generalized in that the characters of *The Postman Always Rings Twice* and *Double Indemnity* desire the other not as a unique individual but as the pure embodiment of lust. Cain believes that bodies are more interesting than faces, noting that his stories "involve women whose figures are more vivid than their faces. . . . In women's appearance I take some interest, but I pay much more attention to their figures than I do to their faces. . . . Their faces are masks, more or less consciously controlled. But their bodies, the way they walk, sit, hold their heads, gesticulate, and eat, betray them."[7] His heroes fall in love at first sight not with persons but bodies. Walter Huff is initially unimpressed with Phyllis Nirdlinger: "A woman was standing there. I had never seen her before. She was maybe thirty-one or two, with a sweet face, light blue eyes, and dusty blonde hair. She was small, and had on a suit of blue house pajamas. She had a washed-out look" (219). But then "she was walking around the room, and I saw something I hadn't noticed before. Under those blue pajamas was a shape to set a man nuts . . ." (220). But Walter is a platonic lover compared with Frank Chambers: "Then I saw her. She had been out back, in the kitchen, but she came in to gather up my dishes. Except for the shape, she really wasn't any raving beauty, but she had a sulky look to her, and her lips stuck out in a way that made me want to mash them in for her" (2). But what most appeals is Cora's smell, referred to throughout and sensed by Frank even at Cora's trial: "it seemed funny to smell her, the same smell that had always set me wild, in the middle of all this stuff" (69). That is, biology is anomalous to legality. What Frank loves about Cora is her crotch, her heat. Seemingly this should lead to a promiscuous love ethos; any other hot woman should do as well as Cora. But, oddly, this is not so. It is only Cora's heat that Frank is hot for, only Phyllis that drives Walter nuts.

The paradox is structurally identical to that explored by de Rougemont: "Tristan and Issult do not love one another. They say they don't, and everything goes to prove it. *What they love is love and being in love.* They behave as if aware that whatever obstructs love must ensure and consolidate it in the heart of each and intensify it infinitely in the moment they reach the absolute obstacle, which is death. . . . Their need of one another is in order to be aflame, and they do not need one another as they are. What they need is not one another's presence but one another's absence. *Thus the partings of the lovers are dictated by their passion itself,* and by the love they bestow on their passion rather than on its satisfaction on its living object" (32). Precisely the gratuitousness of the desire affirms it. Both Frank and Walter have a try at loving nice women as alternatives to the enslaving passion. The role of the second woman is transparent in *The Postman Always Rings Twice.* After a period of strain caused by their complicity in murder and their mutual betrayal, Frank feels relieved to see Cora off on a trip: "She got some clothes in a hurry, and I put her on a train, and going back to the parking lot I felt funny, like I was made of gas and would float off somewhere. I felt free" (94). In the parking lot he meets a girl: "I looked at her, and I felt the same way I had walking away from the train, like I was made of gas, and would float out from behind the wheel" (95). Clearly, she exists as an antithetical function of Cora, as Frank finally recognizes: "She didn't mean anything to me, Cora. I told you why I did it. I was running away" (112). The second woman is not an alternative form *of* desire but a retreat *from* it.

In *Double Indemnity* the function of the second woman is less overt. Walter's reaction from the primary woman is more extreme: "I loved her like a rabbit loves a rattlesnake. That night I did something I hadn't done in years. I prayed" (284). A page later, Lola, Phyllis's stepdaughter (thus adding wicked stepmother to her archetypal attributes), appears in his office as an evident answer to his prayer. Walter convinces himself he is in love with her in language that clearly invalidates the sentiment expressed: "I had gone completely nuts about her. Having it hanging over me all the time, what I had done to her, and how awful it would be if she ever found out, that had something to do with it, but it wasn't all. There was something so sweet about her, and we got along so nice, I mean we felt so happy when we were together" (295). After Walter has been shot by Phyllis, the still unknowing Lola visits him in the hospital: "She sat looking at me, and all of a sudden she leaned over close. I turned my head away, quick. She looked hurt and sat there a long time. I didn't look at her. Some kind of peace came to me at last. I knew I couldn't have her and never could have had her. I couldn't kiss the girl whose father I killed" (323). That he can't kiss Lola is exactly right, but the reason is that she is merely Phyllis's antithetical function, the madonna to Phyllis's whore. These contrasting types are a Cain protagonist's good and bad dreams, externalizing the desire that he cannot bring to full consciousness and has no language for. The reader must infer from plot and convention the unconscious, existential motives in a Cain protagonist to fill in the blank spaces he actually presents. But women serve as surrogates (as well as scapegoats) of these subconscious depths. That is why, if Phyllis did not exist, Walter would have to invent her. She can be the goddess of death only in his projection, and if her masquerade is unconvincing it is because of the limits of his imagination.

What is interesting about the films made from these novels is how they fill in Cain's blanks. Geoffrey O'Brien claims that Hollywood films ignored Cain's description of Cora in the novel and made her into "the one thing that could 'explain' the mystery of her power—a raving beauty" (73). But Lana Turner's beauty is not raving nor yet expressive. Her very lack of emotional range, of hinted-at subtext, of projected intelligence or repressed intensity, gives her a certain rightness as the movie Cora. She is a beautiful blank surface on which desire can be projected, an invitation to fantasy. That she was "too poised and glamorous for Cora"[8] is not quite the case. It is true that one cannot imagine the plea "Rip me, Frank. Rip me like you did that night" (89) coming from Turner, as it does from the novel's and the movie remake's Cora (Jessica Lange), but Turner's lacquered artificiality combines with a certain underlying nervousness to convey a quality not unlike that which Cora attributes to herself in recounting her own Hollywood moment: "They gave me a test. It was all right in the face. But they talk, now. The pictures, I mean. And when I began to talk up there on the screen, they knew me for what I was, and so did I" (12). Part of Turner's appeal is our feeling that she did get away with it, that her characters have the aura of a hash-house waitress who made it in Hollywood, that she embodies Cora's impossible attempt at self-transcendence. So her playing a hash-house waitress who wishes, as it were, that she could be Lana Turner has a certain resonance. Turner expresses, that is, the gap between desire and expression, tenor and vehicle, big wish and little wisher.

The original works better than the remake, but neither quite catches the tabloid fantasy and California reality of the novel. But the film of *Double Indemnity* is arguably better than Cain's novel. It is a rare conjunction of talents—Cain's, of course, but as much or more those of Raymond Chandler, Billy Wilder, Edward G. Robinson, Fred MacMurray, and Barbara Stanwyck. These talents exceed Cain's prototext. Chandler simplified the novel, excising what was most melodramatic and sharpening the tough-guy dialogue into a more effectively mordant irony; Wilder's direction distilled this irony, as if a natural essence, from a pictorial background of mean ordinariness; and MacMurray, in what became his favorite role despite an initial reluctance to play so negative a character,[9] creates as cold and calculating a protagonist as can be found in Hollywood film. But the film centers on Barbara Stanwyck's hard-edged performance of a Phyllis both more commonplace and convincing, and more sexy and menacing than the novel's.

The Phyllis of Chandler/Wilder/Stanwyck is not Cain's implausible death goddess in a red robe but rather the ultimate in tacky, blatant, aggressive sexuality *heightened* to the level of the archetype Cain aimed at. We are prepared for Phyllis before our first sight of her by Walter's voice-over retrospective, especially a line taken from the middle of the novel but shifted to the beginning of the film as a framing device: "I killed him for money and a woman. I didn't get the money and I didn't get the woman." Our first view of Phyllis is at the top of a flight of stairs, draped provocatively in a towel. In a line altered from one in the novel and taking on several layers of subtext in Stanwyck's delivery, she says, "Is there anything I can do for you?" (The novel has "Is there something I could do?" [219].) Shortly thereafter, we see Phyllis undulate downstairs, the camera, following Walter's point of view, focusing on her legs. Walter cannot help but note her anklet, a detail of great significance that is an invention of the film, not the novel. Phyllis lounges in a chair and crosses her legs, flourishing her anklet and her sexuality at Walter, as if a banner with a strange device. Walter comments several times on the anklet, asking at one point what is engraved on it. He has obviously been trying to read it, and her. In fact, the engraving is appropriately her name, so the anklet is an emblem of identity. Turner's beauty is just there, a lucky accident of nature; Stanwyck's is an intention, an idea, fully conscious and aimed at Walter like a gun. A dialogue replete with double entendre, basically a sexual duel, is capped with lines that sound like a Safeway version of Henry James. Phyllis: "I wonder if I know what you mean." Walter: "I wonder if you wonder." Stanwyck's Phyllis, then, is not only sexier than Cain's but smarter, helped by Chandler's dialogue, Wilder's direction, and the actress's own considerable intelligence.

I am not trying to make the movie out as benevolent in its sexual politics. Chandler was a misogynist and Wilder a womanizer; neither could be mistaken for a male protofeminist. The Phyllis of the film is still a femme fatale, a collective construction of male imaginations. Yet the effect of the film's purely materialistic interpretation of Phyllis as opposed to the novel's partly metaphysical one tends to give the character a certain justification, significant if slight.

The novel's Phyllis identifies with death: "Maybe I'm crazy. But there's something in me that loves Death. I think of myself as Death, sometimes. In a scarlet shroud, floating through the night. I'm *so* beautiful, then. And sad. And hungry to make the world happy, by taking them out where I am, into the night, away from all trouble, all unhappiness . . ." (233). This is not only operatic but it would *only* work in an opera, as an aria sung by a Cain version of the Queen of the Night. Phyllis's plot is gratuitous: "I haven't any reason. He treats me as well as a man can treat a woman. I don't love him, but he's never done anything to me" (232). The film husband is not only an obnoxious, stingy lout that the audience cannot help but dislike, but clearly far less intelligent than his wife. Janey Place argues that forties *film noir* gives us "one of the periods of film in which women are active, not static symbols, are intelligent and powerful, if destructively so, and derive power, not weakness from their sexuality."[10] This is somewhat true of *Double Indemnity*. If the novel's Phyllis is unconvincing because she seems a fantasy of Walter's passed off as a character, his moral alibi really, the movie's Phyllis complicates Walter's attempt to limit her to his definition. It is true that in the novel as well as the film, Phyllis appeals to a preexistent corruption in Walter; in both, he has been waiting for the ideal insurance scam to turn up. Still, in the novel he has moments of mawkish sentimentality that seems designed to make him less irredeemable than Phyllis, that make her seem his corrupter. The film Phyllis's motives are more grounded. She is getting on in the world in a way open to talent.

The contrast is most striking in the ending of the film. Previous departures from Cain were mostly added dialogue and subtracted scenes, Cain's plot remaining relatively intact. But the beginning and ending of the film completely discard Cain and substitute Chandler. The novel ends with Walter and Phyllis on a ship to Mexico, their scheme exposed, mutual suicide their only alternative, Phyllis wearing her red gown. The last lines are:

> I didn't hear the stateroom door open, but she's beside me now while I'm writing. I can feel her.
>
> The moon. (327)

The goddess of death claims her sacrifice from a point of view altogether Walter's. But in the film, we see Walter call Phyllis at her house, intending, as his voice-over narrative tells us, to kill her. But the narrative adds, "What I didn't know is that she had plans of her own." To be sure this draws from an earlier scene in the novel where Walter arranges to meet Phyllis at a park, intending to kill her, and is instead shot and wounded by her. But again, the novel scene is entirely from Walter's point of view and reflects his version of entrapment. The film's Phyllis has a point of view all her own. After Walter's call, the camera switches to Phyllis, preparing for his visit like a good hostess, arranging the furniture, and, finally, with obvious symbolism, putting a gun under the seat of her chair. Walter enters and tells her that his boss has figured out her role in the murder while missing his and that this version is good enough for him. She responds, "Maybe it's not good enough for me, Walter; maybe I don't go for the idea." She follows through on *her* idea by shooting him. Wounded, he advances on her, daring her to shoot. She doesn't, and he asks, "Why didn't you shoot me again, baby? Don't tell me it's because you were in love with me all this time." She admits that she has been using him from the start, "until a minute ago, when I couldn't fire that second shot." It is as if Chandler and Wilder anticipated by over twenty years a memorable line from a notorious *film blanc:* love means . . . never shooting him twice. The rest of the scene goes as follows. Walter: "Sorry, baby, I'm not buying." Phyllis: "I'm not asking you to buy. Just hold me close." Walter: "Goodbye, baby." And he shoots her. Twice. Joseph Kruppa points out the wicked misogynist joke in this: Phyllis can't keep her gun up.[11] But with the surplus meaning so often found in crime films, Phyllis's failure is due to her momentary compromising of her materialism, which was, in a way, her integrity, the very source of her glittering, diamond-hard appeal. This Phyllis, who as a sex object is a culturally constructed commodity, is also a joke on her creators, answering the question "What do men want?" Some like them cold.

There are films that are all subtext, their overt narrative self-evidently absurd. In Vera Caspary's novel *Laura* and the film made from it, the authentic center of contention is over who controls the definition of the eponymous heroine. Laura seems merely the "innocent catalyst for men's idealisations," especially in the first part of the story when she is believed dead yet her "beautiful, dominating portrait . . . haunts the characters and determines the action."[12] She seems as trapped within the frame of male fantasy as the ladies in Poe's "The Oval Portrait" and Hawthorne's "The Birthmark." If the outcome is not so predictably fatal, it may be because the competition among the men in *Laura* opens a certain space for its heroine to define her own identity by playing off against the contradictory versions pushed on her. In so doing she escapes the portrait's frame, refusing to be idealized to death, and, though without conscious intention, even reverses the field, becoming the touchstone of male sexual identity in a game "characterised by a certain anxiety over the existence and definition of masculinity and normality."[13]

The plot of *Laura* is well known: Mark McPherson is the detective assigned to investigate the murder of Laura, a beautiful career woman who was the protégée of the wittily malicious radio performer, Waldo Lydecker, and the fiancée of Shelby Carpenter, a handsome and impecunious socialite. The story is at first told by Lydecker (as first-person narrator in the novel and voice-over narrator in the film), who offers it "not so much as a detective yarn as a love story" and somewhat wistfully wishes he were its hero (19). McPherson, who had never seen the live Laura, falls in love with her portrait, thus becoming part of a three-cornered rivalry for the rights, as it were, to her image. When Laura turns up alive and becomes one of several suspects for the murder of the woman whose facially disfigured body was mistaken for hers, her choice among these men becomes, literally, a survival issue for her. The distinctions are clear and the choice ultimately inevitable—which does not reduce a not innocent pleasure in seeing traditional moral and sexual conventions confirmed. Moreover, much of the interest of the story is in the shading and implicit qualification of these conventions. *Of course,* Laura will choose the tough, stoical detective McPherson, over Shelby, the self-indulgent overgrown boy whose main attraction is his resemblance to the men pictured in advertisements, and over the waspish Lydecker, whose voice rises into the feminine register when he is upset. Laura's maid emphasizes McPherson's difference: "'a man,' Bessie said. 'Most of them that comes here are little babies or old women'" (188). The film casting was perfect: Gene Tierney as Laura, Dana Andrews, Vincent Price, and Clifton Webb as the men (though that is the very term in question) in her life. Yet in both novel and film, McPherson is not merely an uncomplicated emblem of normative masculinity; he has a repressed sensitivity, a barely controllable intensity, and more than a shade of neuroticism. He shares with Lydecker an unequivocal contempt for the lightweight Shelby, but their feelings toward each other are equivocal. In McPherson's section of the novel he admits, "I despised the guy and he fascinated me" (131). Of McPherson, Lydecker says: "By all that is logical I should have despised Mark McPherson. I could not. For all his rough edges, he was the man I should have been, the hero of the story" (21). The suggestion of an underlying identity is not accidental: both love the same dead (as they suppose) lady; Lydecker has written a story about necrophilia and McPherson's fascination with Laura's portrait is a psychological version of it. It seems only logical that the one attempts to murder Laura and the other rescues her—but just in time, as if the plot acts out their mutual ambivalence about Laura. But it would never occur to McPherson to smash a beautiful object so a rival collector could not obtain it, as Lydecker had done and as he meant to do with Laura. McPherson falls as much in love with the real Laura as he had first with the ideal Laura, whereas Lydecker determines to destroy her once he sees she cannot remain his Galatea. Still it was Lydecker who first recognized Laura's innate quality. That Shelby Carpenter is not really in love with her is a left-handed compliment: she is too strong a person for him and he turns to lighter ladies for relief. So in both text and subtext of *Laura* the central conflict revolves around the fact that Laura turns out to be *alive*.

Point of view is not only a technique but a foregrounded problem in the novel and film of *Laura*. Caspary's novel has three narrators: Lydecker, McPherson, and Laura. The film emphasizes Laura as she-who-is-looked-at: "The power to incite murder which is visually inscribed to Laura's magnificent portrait is revealed to be a product of the neuroses of the men around her, not of the power she wields."[14] So in the film, Laura has no voice-over, it being, in an effective irony, Lydecker, her would-be murderer, who "struggles to retain control over his protégé's story against the investigations of the detective McPherson, who silences his controlling voice half-way through the film. . . ."[15] So, as with unreliable narration in fiction, in viewing the film again it is the voice-over narration that is looked at, not through. Our own conventional responses may well be part of what is put into question. The reader-viewer is implicated in his/her initial answer to the riddle posed by this woman who refuses to stay framed.

Frederic Brown structures *The Screaming Mimi* (1950) around and against the conventional expectations of the male reader of tough-guy paperback thrillers. But the novel carries its own warning label, an elaborate cautionary addressed to this reader. The novel begins with the proclamation that, as incredible as it seems, a drunken Irishman, Sweeney, made a resolution and kept to it. This puts us immediately into a world constructed out of stereotype and prefabricated expectation. Irishmen, always drunk, rarely make much less keep resolutions. But though these propositions may be certain, they don't *quite* fit the case:

> His name really was Sweeney, but he was only five-eighths Irish and he was only three-quarters drunk. But that's about as near as truth ever approximates a pattern, and if you won't settle for that, you'd better quit reading. If you don't maybe you'll be sorry, for it isn't a nice story. It's got murder in it, and women and liquor and gambling and even prevarication. There's murder before the story proper starts, and murder after it ends; the actual story begins with a naked woman and ends with one, which is a good opening and a good ending, but everything between isn't nice. Don't say I didn't warn you. (143)

Reader as much as character is tested on the validity of a certain wish, and presence of mind in the face of its fulfillment. Sweeney believes that "you can get anything you want if you want it badly enough" (145) and this is so. Sweeney, a Chicago reporter, happens upon a crowd looking through the glass doors of an apartment building at a woman who has been wounded by a knife slash. They cannot help her because her large and savage dog is trying to protect her. This in itself represents a perverse mass audience wish-fulfillment in its association of sex and violence. But as the woman struggles to her feet, the dog, trained, pulls the tab on the zipper of her gown: "Gently the dress fell off and became a white silken circle around her feet. She had worn nothing under the dress, nothing at all" (149). The woman is rescued and Sweeney makes his wish: to spend a night with *this* woman. Since he had never seen her before, his compulsion must have to do with the sado-masochistic eroticism of the scene he has witnessed. The lady is, in fact, a stripteaser, her dog trained not only to perform the zipper trick but then to walk between her legs and stand there, "his head raised to look out over the audience as though daring any man to approach that which he now guarded." Sweeney, in attendance, interprets: "Cerberus guarding the portals of Heaven" (226). This suggests that her vagina, which evidently attracted the psychopathic Ripper, needs the defense of her formidable dog, Devil. But it also suggests that her sexuality is not only threatened but is itself a threat. This literalization of *vagina dentata* is another instance of Freud serving as Bullfinch. Her act is called "Beauty and the Beast." The attack on the stripper, Yolanda Lang, sensationally reported by Sweeney's newspaper, makes her act the hottest one in town, playing to a packed house. Evidently what happened to her in conjunction with the kinkiness of her stripper act has tapped into communal fantasy and it works out so well for her that a publicity stunt might be suspected except that a Ripper *is* terrorizing the city, having murdered three women before the attack on Yolanda. Sweeney determines not only to spend a night with Yolanda but to track down the Ripper. Sweeney finds that one of the victims worked in a gift shop but was to have been fired for having stolen a statuette. At first, he sees no significance in this but changes his mind when told its suggestive title: "Screaming Mimi." In another questionable wish, he declares, "I would like to meet this Mimi" (183). The statue is of a slim nude figure, expressive of virginity but, as the shopowner puts it, "in a very peculiar way. . . . Virginity in this case, is expressed through fear, horror, loathing" (183). This is "not only in the face but in the twisted rigidity of the body. The mouth was wide open in a soundless scream. The arms were thrust out, palms forward, to hold off some approaching horror" (184). Sweeney reflects that "it would appeal only to a sadist, or to someone who had *some* abnormality in him. And yet he, Sweeney, had paid over twenty-four dollars of good money to take it home with him" (185). Its very name is a perverse joke—its catalogue number was SM-1, and someone in the wholesaler's office nicknamed it Screaming Mimi, with the obvious pun on screaming meamies (and Brown's own play on *S* and *M*). Clues accumulate to the point where Sweeney speculates that the statue may be of a previous and unknown victim of the Ripper; it is the Ripper Mimi shrinks from. Installed in Sweeney's apartment, Mimi's image of victimization becomes an unavoidable psychological presence to him:

> He put Mimi down, very gently. He wished she'd stop screaming, but she never would. A silent scream can never be silenced. (235)

> He locked the door on Mimi, leaving her alone and screaming in the dark. (240)

He traces the real-life model of Mimi and discovers she was one Bessie Wilson who apparently died in a sanatorium. The Ripper's attempt on her life—"Guy over six feet, two-twenty pounds, in a nuthouse uniform that started out being grey but that ended up being red, with blood in his hair and on his face, and coming at her with a ten-inch carving knife" (264)—though he was killed before he could reach her, caused permanent trauma. But then *this* Ripper is dead, suggesting, as does the name itself, that he is simply one example of a type, a potentiality. By now it should be evident that Sweeney himself has a discomfiting affinity that shows in his fascination with the statue and his attraction to Yolanda. Sweeney wrote, as eyewitness, the voyeuristic account of Yolanda's wounding and unintended striptease for his paper, *The Blade*. Brown rubs this in: "If you saw that pun yourself, forgive me for pointing it out. *You* got it, yes, but somebody else would have missed it. It takes all kind of people to read a book" (161). Of course, this clever reader has been reading something which the author warned him "isn't a nice story," perhaps because, like Sweeney, he wants to find out more about the naked woman promised him for the book's beginning and end. Like Sweeney, he gets his wish.

By this time you have probably guessed: Bessie Wilson is Yolanda Lang. So Bessie-Mimi-Yolanda has progressed from being the target of a single murderous gaze to being the target of the collective lustful gaze of a paying audience, Sweeney a member of it. In the conclusion of the novel, Sweeney gets all his wishes: he spends a night with the nude Yolanda and discovers the true identity of the Ripper, who has, in fact, been internalized in Bessie-Mimi-Yolanda. Her manager had stabbed her simply to divert suspicion when he realized that seeing Screaming Mimi had triggered a murderous psychosis. As she stands before Sweeney, "[a] nude high priestess holding the sacrificial knife" (299), he can freeze her into place only by a nonstop interpretive retelling of her story. Rescued finally by the police, he realizes that he had proven out his theory—he got exactly the two things he badly wanted and simultaneously at that.

This conclusion could be read as a particularly outrageous example of male chauvinist mythologizing: the victimization of woman transmuted weirdly into victimization by woman. But surely the book as much deconstructs as it evokes such fantasies. Popular fiction is attacked for offering uncomplicated, unearned wish-fulfillment. But in *The Screaming Mimi* the underlying assumptions of the wish are logically matched to its ironic fulfillment. Sweeney is attracted to sex laced with violence. He gets violence laced with sex. Victim and victimizer trade places in Bessie-Yolanda but, to a degree, in Sweeney as well, who as journalistic voyeur and purveyor of titillation exploits the violence of which he very nearly becomes the victim. And it should be remembered that the beast, Devil, stationed between Yolanda's legs, is, in fact, male. Is it too much to say that Bessie-Mimi-Yolanda is the victim of the perverse communal sexual fantasy exploited by the tough paperback genre to which Brown's novel self-reflectively belongs?

The ultimate deconstruction of the femme fatale American style is Jim Thompson's *A Hell of a Woman* (1954). This is another setup of the reader. Initially it appears that Thompson's protagonist-narrator, Frank "Dolly" Dillon, is a victim of female wickedness. Certainly this is how *he* sees it. In love with the sweet kid Mona, he is trapped in marriage with the "lazy selfish dirty slob" Joyce. But the Black Lizard paperback cover seems to indict Mona: we see a tough, worried-looking man in the background while a tougher lacquered-looking blonde leers at us in the foreground above the caption "Love now, pay later—she lured him into the world's oldest trap." So early on we are set up for the alternative possibilities that Frank is either trapped between a madonna and a whore or trapped between two whores. But the cover does not quite fit: the woman on it is Joyce's age and projects her brassiness and assurance, but the caption could only fit Mona since Joyce, far from doing any luring, wants out of the deal. So the cover and caption make sense only as Frank's conflated projection of both women; it is his constructed image of "Woman" which the novel proceeds to deconstruct. What we have is a pathological misogynist compelled to convert any madonna he encounters into a whore.

Frank's house is in fact filthy, but this is because Joyce, as she tells him, has given up on the series of sordid habitations consequent upon Frank's inability to keep a job. When Frank retorts that his mother kept a pristine cold-water flat for her seven children, Joyce, having clearly heard this before, responds in outrage: "But I'm not your mother! I'm not some other woman! I'm me, get me? Me, me!" He says, "And you're bragging about it?" (25). Frank finally wins the argument by knocking Joyce into a tub full of dirty bath water with "the sweetest left hook you ever did see" (26) and exits laughing.

No sympathy with the protagonist could survive this, even when he returns to his flat to find it all torn up, his clothes carefully cut into ribbons, his socks and underwear stuffed into the toilet, Joyce's revenge for his indifference to her impending departure:

> "Good luck and my best regards to the boys on the vice squad."
> "D-Dolly . . . is that all you can say at a time like this?"
> "What do you want me to say? Peter, Peter, Pumpkin Eater?" (28)

Frank doesn't understand the implication of his own allusion, nor does he learn better, as did Mother Goose's protagonist:

> Peter, Peter, pumpkin eater,
> Had another, and didn't love her;
> Peter learned to read and spell,
> And then he loved her very well.[16]

Frank cannot read his women or even distinguish them. Remembering Joyce at the beginning of their relationship (in her pre-Frank period she had "one of the nicest little efficiency apartments you ever saw . . ."), he gets muddled: "No, now wait a minute! I think I'm getting this thing all fouled up. I believe it was Doris who acted that way, the gal I was married to before Joyce. Yeah, it must have been Doris—or was it Ellen? Well, it doesn't make much difference; they were all alike. They all turned out the same way. So, as I was saying: I said, What kind of a guy do you think I am? And she said . . . they said . . . I think you're nice" (29). Frank is a classic version of the schizo-psychopath of chapter 2 for whom all women are serial versions of his own stereotyped construction: "To hell with that damned bitchy Joyce, and Doris, and Ellen and . . . and all those other tramps" (61). The ellipsis signifies the infinity of the series.

How self-deluded Frank is becomes clearer as a new and thereafter counterpointed narrative begins about halfway through the novel, "THROUGH THICK AND THIN: THE TRUE STORY OF A MAN'S FIGHT AGAINST HIGH ODDS AND LOW WOMEN . . . by Knarf Nollid" (93). Knarf tells us of repeated predicaments he gets into, naturally "through no fault of my own" (95), such as his wife's unreasonable behavior when she somehow slipped and fell into the bathtub. He concludes by assuring us that "though I seldom complain you have doubtless read between the lines and you know that I am one hard luck bastard" (102). Reading between the lines yields the one truthful word in the second half of the sentence.

In creating this monster of misperception Thompson obviously draws on Jung and Sartre as well as Freud. A send-up of the misogynist tough guy, Frank must reject his anima, the "Dolly" in him, precisely because, a fortiori, he so desperately needs mothering; in a bizarre scene the returned Joyce comforts him after a nightmare:

> "There," she said. "No, baby, around this way. Tha-ats my boy! Now, down a little, just a little more . . . and then closer, darling. Very close to mother . . ."
> And she drew me close.
> And slid the gown off her shoulders. (110)

His inevitable murder of Joyce is another doubled narrative, justified
for Frank, an unfortunate accident for Knarf. What infuriates Frank
is that she doesn't believe the lies he lives by. Earlier he proclaims, "I
will leave you to be the judge, dear reader" (154). He *has* inadver-
tently supplied the terms of judgment.

Jeffrey Burton Russell argues in *Mephistopheles: The Devil in the
Modern World* that Kant developed a still-persuasive account of
radical evil: "Kant's view is a demythologized version of original sin.
The essence of sin is the lie, which consists of the refusal to recognize moral law and set it above our own egoistic desires. This is not
a chronological event involving Adam and Eve and the distant past
but a principle of human nature."[17] Constructing the world in consistent bad faith, the liar deals with an impulse to evil by projecting it. In Simone Weil's definition, "A hurtful act is the transference
to others of the degradation which we bear in ourselves. That is why
we are inclined to commit such acts as a way of deliverance."[18]
Though Frank is clearly mad, nowhere in the book is it suggested
that he is not then responsible. He is exemplary of what the philoso-
pher Mary Midgley calls the "paradox of responsible negligence,"
defining this as "a deliberate blindness to ideals and principles, a
stalling of our moral and intellectual faculties." Frank becomes increasingly obsessive but, as Midgley says, obsessiveness is a choice:
"To let obsession take one over is . . . always to consent, in some
degree, both to one's own death and that of others. Or—to look at it
another way—a destructive attitude to others and to one's own nature, can be satisfied by cultivating an obsession."[19] Frank's alibi is
in fact the tough guy's wised-up recognition that all women are
bitches, all streets are mean, all promises empty, and all realities
ugly. He cannot afford to recognize the self-abnegating love of Joyce
and Mona, for this would require divesting his character armor and
there may no longer be anyone inside.

Frank puts anyone who tries to emotionally reach him into a
double bind, not only Joyce but Mona, doubly a victim as childhood
kidnap victim who supposes her brutal abductors to be her family
and as a waif whom Frank will inevitably and eventually construe
into his series: "Well she finally started in on me. I didn't have it
tough enough, I guess, so she had to make it tougher. Watching me
all the time like I was a goddamned freak or something. Not saying
anything unless I spoke to her. You know: a lot of little things. Wearing me down little by little" (173). The reader does know; having ter-
rorized her into abjectness, Frank now holds *that* against her. She is
submissively walking behind him when she is run over by (or throws
herself in front of) a truck in Dallas.

The novel ends with another double narrative, but the two narrative streams now run in parallel sentences rather than chapters. Frank now calls himself Fred Jones, so Derf Senoj resumes the struggle against high odds and low women. Except this time it is the mirror self that has the greater purchase on reality. "Fred" has crossed over to the other side, so we need *Derf*'s account, in italics, to reveal the truth of Fred's narrative. Fred is staying with the beautiful and sophisticated Helene in a fine apartment house whereas *Derf* is holed up in a fleabag with a hooker, *Helen*. Helene fixes Fred a cocktail while *Helen* and *Derf* drink cheap wine, smoke grass, sniff coke, and shoot heroin. Then Helene, snipping her split ends with a large pair of shears, informs Fred that he has been as disappointing as all her other men and must pay. (This obvious inversion of Frank's series suggests fear of inadequacy as a source of it.) She approaches Fred with the shears extended at the exact moment *Derf*, completely zonked, puts his foot through the window. Then *Derf* straddles the window sill above the shards of glass as Helene prepares to liberate Fred from his misogynistic guilt. As the self-diminished *Derf* defenestrates, Fred gets the last word:

> You're no different from the rest, Fred. And you'll
> *my leg through the window. I straddled it, rocking back*
> have to pay like the rest. Don't you want me to,
> *and forth, and it didn't take hardly any time at all. Helen*
> darling. I nodded and she began unfastening and
> *came to the door of the bathroom, and she began*
> fumbling and then, then she lowered the shears and
> *laughing, screaming. I threw myself out the window.*
> then she was smiling again and letting me see. There,
> she said, that's much better, isn't it? And, then, nice as
> I'd been, she started laughing. Screaming at me. (182)

The joke is on him.[20]

5

Pale Criminals and Murderees
The Problem of Justice in the English Crime Novel

If once a man indulges himself in murder, very soon he comes to think little of robbing; and from robbing he comes next to drinking and Sabbath breaking, and from that to incivility and procrastination.

THOMAS DE QUINCEY, *"MURDER CONSIDERED AS ONE OF THE FINE ARTS"*

IN THE DIALECTIC OF fatal passion, lovers are simultaneously realized and undone by their passion. Violence becomes the metaphor of a freedom from society's rules wherein the lovers' doom, seen as punishment for transgression, reaffirms the reader's moral norms (and in film the Hays code). But in another turn of the dialectic, it becomes the *liebestod* for which the lovers, however unconsciously, yearn.

This code operates, however, only in the American rather than the English crime novel. Passion in the English form appears in a mode diametrically opposite: far from seeing mediocrities become oddly awesome as carriers of the passionate sublime, we see passion demystified as a delusion of the mediocre. Fatal passion is a main American theme because it expresses the romance theme of the conflict between boundless desire and the inevitable, but to Americans *never fully acceptable*, social restraints upon it. Desire, in England, is not so entitled. Finally, the English crime novel has no stake in deflecting misogyny since misogyny is not a convention in the English detective novel. False consciousness in the English form is centered on egoism, the valuation of the self over social rules and obligations, rather than misogyny. Whereas the American protagonist may be blind to a woman's love, the English protagonist is more likely to presume upon it. Thus the English tension is not between desire and restraint or misogyny and love but between selfishness and obligation, deeds and their deserts, the problem basically of justice.

Justice is not merely a different problem from that of fatal passion but a different kind of problem. Fatal passion is oppositional to rationality, especially rationality as encoded in the social system, whereas justice is arguably the greatest invention of the rational intellect. Moreover, while fatal passion is inherently paradoxical in its linking of desire with death, eventuating in a desire for death, the problems of justice arise primarily in practical application, an attack on a given system of justice being based on a more embracing concept of justice as it applies to a specific social order. English crime novels, like English mainstream novels, privilege social-historical problems over the psychological-metaphysical ones found in the American romance. Indeed, many English crime novels are semidocumentary, drawing on actual cases, sometimes even on trial transcripts. But in the classic English *detective* novel the problem of justice is minimalized to a temporary uncertainty as to the identity of the criminal resolved by the detective's grand flourish of deduction at the conclusion. Story and world are justified by this expected conclusion. Whereas the English *crime* novel deflects into the problematic. Hence the term some English writers use for what I call the crime novel: the inverted detective story. The crime novel inverts the detective story precisely by its problematizing of justice. Instead of whodunit the riddle is whether he/she will be brought to justice or to what degree he/she is truly guilty. Even when the English crime novel is closest to the values of the detective novel, a disturbing shift of focus will put us in a discomfiting relation to characters and action. These deflections fall into a clear pattern of permutations:

1. A guilty protagonist's crimes are eventually detected, and he/she is properly punished. This comes close to detective-story norms, but the murderer-as-protagonist shifts focus from the rationality of detection to the irrationality of murder. Moreover, even if our response to the protagonist is punitive rather than sympathetic, a disturbing emotional imbalance permeates the novel in contrast to the usual avoidance of strong feeling in classic English detective fiction.

2. A guilty protagonist is punished, not for the crime committed but another of which he/she is innocent. Or he/she may be destroyed in some nonlegal fashion relatively or completely unrelated to the crime. So justice of a sort may work out but with an ironic perversity that undermines its associations with reason.

3. A morally and legally guilty protagonist for whom we have some sympathy murders an unsympathetic person. We hope the protagonist brings it off but wonder if we ought to.

4. A morally and legally guilty protagonist for whom we feel considerable sympathy murders a relatively unsympathetic but not fiendish person and is executed for it. The execution, perfectly legal and of the "right" person, seems to us a worse crime than the crime.

5. An innocent character is punished for a crime he/she did not commit. The opposition to detective fiction is self-evident.

6. The category of guilt/innocence may be confused by (a) an intended victim who turns the tables by murdering his/her would-be murderer; (b) a murderee who all but incites his/her own murder; or (c) a guilty bystander who is in complicity with murder by, probably unknowingly, inciting it or, quite consciously, concealing knowledge of it.

7. Finally, and perhaps most subversive of the underlying ethos of the detective story, a guilty character successfully frames an innocent one. This is what villains in detective stories try to do, only to be foiled by the superior acumen of the detective. But here wickedness succeeds and innocence is undone.

The above list is arranged in ascending order of deviancy from the detective-story ethos and shows a range of possibilities, though some are rarely taken up. Moreover, some fall between categories and some overlap, bringing into play two or more categories. But most categories show at least one superb criminal performance. Finally, there are two character types that cut across many of these plot types: the pale criminal and the murderee. Indeed, we shall see that most murderers in this chapter are pale criminals, though not all victims are murderees.

The pale criminal of Nietzsche's typification in *Thus Spoke Zarathustra* is a person who commits an act of violence that he or she is not up to and allows himself or herself to be defined by that one act: "An image made this pale man pale. He was equal to his deed when he did it; but he could not bear its image after it was done. Now he always saw himself as the doer of one deed. Madness I call this: the exception now became the essence for him."[1] These pale criminals lack the courage of their impulses; they betray impulse by freezing their essence in a single past act rather than delivering themselves to processual flow. By rationalizing their act and defining themselves in terms of it, they deny its irrational spontaneity. In contrast, the conception of the pale criminal in the English crime novel approximates Nietzsche's only in its emphasis on the criminal's falling short of the significance of the act through false consciousness and bad faith. But the source of false consciousness is opposite, proceeding from the criminal's rationalized refusal *to* define the self in terms of the act. The English crime novel holds that the self is least authentic when self-centered, selfish. The English criminal commits a murder that inflates ego but diminishes self, has prudential rather than impulsive motivation, and is emotionally enabled by false consciousness and bad faith.

Some of these criminals are so inept that they seem dependent on the helpfulness of "the murderee," a term F. Tennyson Jesse coined in *Murder and Its Motives* (1924): "there appears to be a race of human beings who lay themselves out to be murdered—they are murderees." Jesse cites victims who walk into deadly situations despite well-founded suspicions as well as those who blindly trust obviously dangerous characters. Perhaps Jesse's hairdresser went too far in claiming that " 'you'll never find a nice girl in a trunk,' " but the stupidity of some victims of both real and fictive violence does seem almost culpable. The existence of murderees is itself one of the puzzles of crime: "Perhaps at some future date, when the laws of attraction and repulsion are more fully understood than they are at present, it will be discovered that murderees send out waves that correspond as do the waves of wireless between certain stations. Meanwhile this curious question must remain something of a mystery."[2] Though the murderee is a less common type than the pale criminal, the two are not infrequently found in the same novel, symbiotically related. This is the case in the novel by Shelley Smith (Nancy Bodington) to be discussed in the first category of plot types.

1. A guilty protagonist's crimes are eventually detected and he/she is properly punished.

Smith's *The Crooked Man* (1952) plays inventively on the themes of punishment for the wrong crime (category 2) and the perverseness of the murderee (category 6b), but what is most interesting is the fury of her punitive pursuit of her protagonist. The original English title of her novel is *Man Alone*, possibly a sideblow at the version of existentialism that emphasized a heroic posture in the face of alienation and nihilism, then expounded in postwar England and America. Her protagonist, Thomas Bates, is alienated and nihilistic but neither heroic nor intelligent. He is sly, egoistic, cowardly, stupid, and evil.

His wickedness is enabled by the remarkable gullibility of the chief murderee, Grace Pickering, whom Bates somewhat reluctantly rescues from drowning. He capitalizes on her immediate casting of him as romantic hero to decamp with her purse, which, disappointingly, contains only a few shillings. Accidentally meeting her again, he easily convinces her that someone else stole the purse. He marries her under a false name (Frederick Noble!), manipulates her into withdrawing her life's savings, and runs off with them. He then marries Annie Guin, but while walking with her sees Grace yet again, ditches Annie (after stealing her jewels), and persuades Grace, newly affluent from a bequest, that their separation was somehow her father's fault. (The father had, in fact, correctly assessed "Noble's" character and tried to block the marriage.) Bates then arranges for Grace and himself to make wills leaving their fortunes to each other and contrives her apparently accidental electrocution.

Smith characterizes Grace's romantically muddled consciousness convincingly enough to make her a credible murderee. But then she is tracking the reality of the George Joseph Smith murder case. Smith, as "Henry Williams," married Beatrice Constance Annie Mundy, staying with her long enough to steal 138 pounds. Accidentally encountering her in Weston-super-Mare, he persuaded her to come back to him. They wrote mutual wills and he murdered her in a bathtub. Under his real name he married Alice Burnham against the strong opposition of her father. Smith insured her for 500 pounds, following which she was found dead in her bath, as was a year later Margaret Elizabeth Lofty. Alice Burnham's brother read an account of the inquest of this latest victim and sent word to the police of the suspicious parallels, at which point Smith's crimes began to catch up with him.

Shelley Smith conflates the murderee traits of the Mundy murder with the suspicious father of the Burnham murder. George Joseph Smith's final crime was the murder of Margaret Elizabeth Lofty. For this, Shelley Smith substitutes Bates's abduction of the insane heiress Ruth Dunville, whom he marries *without* planning to murder her: "It did occur to him that she would be just the right sort of wife for him; a woman who asked no questions, never spoke, and blindly did as she was told. She would need to be his idea of a perfect wife since he must put up with her forever. The fact that, as an insane person, she could not devise a legal will, was to save her life. Since she could not will her fortune to him, he must share it with her. He had already decided that she should have a nurse and keep to her own room" (140–141). Naturally, it is this woman's suicide which is taken to be murder; Bates is hanged for the one death he did not bring about. That is, Shelley Smith shows clearly, justice of a sort. Her Bates is a submediocre human being with only two strong emotions: hatred of the world and love of self. These come together in his vision of paradise:

> he had been pierced by the sharpness of his sudden desire for the Paradise of a world unpeopled, all to himself. It had never occurred to him to imagine for himself a heaven other than in the terms taught him in the institution [an orphan asylum]: a Heaven of harps cascading eternal psalms against a boredom of infinite blue, with seas of jasper and chalcedony below, hard and slippery as glass; and everywhere, as far as eye could see, people, an endless multitude of people, clothed in white, praising everlastingly, with himself—if he was there at all—nothing but a meaningless dot against so many. But the whole world to oneself! That was ecstasy! The mere conception caused the soul to expand with delight. The pressure of deceit and envy that distorted so cruelly one's personality would no longer exist, and instead one would know the pure bliss of being oneself, master of the solitudes. (5–6)

Bates is hating and hateful, and the force of Shelley Smith's novel comes from her clear hatred of his ultimately nihilistic egoism. To simply describe such a mediocrity's self-love produces automatic irony, but Smith's contempt intensifies this effect: "He cherished a mad dream of some miraculously steady and respectable life with unlimited money in the bank to be spent exclusively on his adored self, to be lavished on his unthwarted and richly, enviously, esteemed self" (13). When he has a bit of money, he is torn: "On the one hand, his congenital avarice could hardly bear to let go of a single note and on the other, he could not resist showering presents on himself—votive offerings at the shrine of his idol. For once his darling self should have everything money could buy" (51). This authorial contempt is the necessary, compensatory counterweight to Bates's overweening egoism. It is part of Shelley Smith's symbolic punishment of Bates that his legal punishment is technically unjust. There is a certain hard comedy in his assurance of his technical innocence: "There were three weeks left for Thomas Bates in which to make his soul. Instead he soothed himself with a lullaby, rocking over and over in his mind, I shall appeal! I shall appeal! He still refused to believe they could hang him, because he had not killed Ruth Dunville, and it would be an intolerable injustice. He clung to that, as though Justice had always been his watchword" (184). As he has lived by false appearances, by the letter of the law, so does he die by them.

His solipsistic egoism is what justifies the extraordinary literary terrorism of the novel's ending when Bates, being led to the gallows, is greeted:

> an appalling howl was carried on the clear air from the ramshackle tenements distantly overlooking the prison yard; it could even be seen that every window was crammed with red-and-purple-faced figures, banging metal, calling, waving, shrieking hysterically, with hatred and with *laughter.* . . . That there should be laughter was shocking. The scene itself appeared to quiver with the gruesome inhuman racket. The astonishing spectacle of so much hatred all directed at him seemed completely to unnerve Bates; terror of this hydra-headed monster suddenly loosened his knee joints and turned his bowels, with its intimations of punishment he had never foreseen; so that he had to be dragged across the yard, lifted to the scaffold, and held upright there while his last glimpse of the world was extinguished in the stuffy folds of cloth that smelt like death itself. (185)

He encounters, briefly, the reflected image of his own hatred and a nullification of his identity equal to his nullification of others.

Smith's matching of crime and punishment in the spirit of Dante's *Inferno* is internally logical but likely to prove disturbing to modern readers queasy about the concept of retribution.[3] If the crowd's emphasized laughter seems gratuitously cruel, this may be Shelley Smith's deliberate affront to less rigorous notions of crime and punishment. At any rate, it is far from the avoidance of punishment and emotional disturbance common to the detective novel. Moreover, the implicit equation of execution audience to novel audience may not overjoy the reader. In fact, here is where the novel departs most dramatically from the George Joseph Smith case. Bates's viciousness does not exaggerate Smith's; in a letter to Beatrice Mundy, Smith justified his decamping by accusing her of having given him a social disease. Eric R. Watson, editor of *Trial of George Joseph Smith* in Notable British Trials, speculates on Smith's last thoughts: "If, stupefied and terrified as he was, he was capable of coherent reflection, we may be sure his last thought was one of self-pity." And the judge proclaimed to Smith, "An exhortation to repentance would be wasted on you." In all this, Shelley Smith's novel tracks quite closely the George Joseph Smith affair. But as Smith was carried to his execution, the waiting crowd fell silent.[4]

2. A guilty protagonist is punished but not for the crime he/she committed but another of which he/she is innocent.

Or he/she may be destroyed in some nonlegal fashion relatively or completely unrelated to the crime.

An ironic providence operates of the sort rather well described in John Reynolds's *The Triumph of God's Revenge against the Crying and Execrable Sin of Wilful and Premeditated Murder* (1704):

> But God's providence and justice . . . is as different as it is mirac-
> ulous; for sometimes he protects and defers it of purpose, either to
> nullify or to harden our hearts, as seems best to his inscrutable will
> and divine pleasure; or as may chiefly serve and tend to his glory, yea
> sometimes he makes the murderer himself as well an instrument to
> discover, as he hath been an actor to commit murder; yea and many
> times he punisheth one sin by and in another, and when the mur-
> derer is most secure, and thinks least of it, then he heaps coals of fire
> on his head, and suddenly cuts him off with the revenging sword of
> fierce wrath and indignation.[5]

In other words, murder will out but sometimes with an odd indi-
rectness of divine aim. The classic is the Francis Iles (Anthony
Berkeley Cox) novel *Malice Aforethought* (1931), which besides the
convention of the justly unjust punishment depicts with fine irony
the psychology of egotism and self-delusion.

In this novel, Dr. Bickleigh murders his wife, Julia, who lords it
over him on grounds of superior birth, puts him in the wrong where
she is actually at fault, and is unforgivably inconsiderate: "He
looked sadly at the joint in front of him. There was no knuckle left
on it, and the knuckle was the only part he liked. Unfortunately,
Julia liked it too" (7–8). So the stuff of murder is comically petty
domestic tyranny; in this sort of crime novel murder and cold lamb
knuckle go together. Dr. Bickleigh at five feet six and at thirty-seven
is two inches shorter and eight years younger than his wife: "Not
that she had ever been grateful to Edmund. That she was thirty-five
years old, had years ago parted with any hopes that she might have
entertained of marriage, and possessed a face not unlike that of her
own favorite horse (as her sister Hilda, a candid woman, immediately pointed out on learning of the engagement), weighed nothing
against the fact that she was a Crewstandon" (13). Bickleigh's height
and class combine along with his wife's continual reminders of his
"wormhood" (30) to produce a massive inferiority complex, especially toward women. This results in a compulsion to womanize,
driven partly by "primitive masculinity" (32) but primarily by out-
raged ego.

Madeleine Cranmere supplies the last link in Bickleigh's motive by buttering his battered ego with flattery so blatantly false that only someone in so much need of reassurance could swallow it and by casting their relationship in a platonically pure light that fits exactly into his daydreams. Julia moves him to a frenzy of rage and denial by merely describing Madeleine's true character:

> She is a *poseuse* of the very worst description. She is acting the whole time. . . . She is obviously hysterical, and yet at the same time I could detect in her a callous calculation which quite disgusted me. Her selfishness is inconceivable; nothing interests her but herself and her own silly emotions. In short, I should call her utterly untrustworthy, egotistical to the point of mania, and the most dangerous kind of liar there is—the liar who can deceive not only other people, but herself as well. (90–91)

This is all so true it swings the reader's sympathy somewhat toward Mrs. Bickleigh, who in an odd, unloving way really does have her husband's best interests at heart. She would even have been willing to give him up to a less awful woman. But it is just this genuinely disinterested concern that seals her fate. Convinced of his (and Madeleine's) version of Madeleine, Bickleigh takes this gem of psychological analysis as a final insult added to some of Julia's real enough injuries of him and contrives her murder.

His apparently perfect murder of her precipitates in him a major change, though one logically related to his inferiority complex. He becomes a megalomaniac. In a way peculiar to English crime novel protagonists he compares himself, favorably, to real-life models, those in de Quincey's "Murder Considered as One of the Fine Arts." He agrees that "Murder could be a fine art: but it was not for everyone. Murder was a fine art for the superman. It was a pity that Nietzsche could not have developed de Quincey's propositions" (154). Bickleigh misses de Quincey's irony even as he illustrates de Quincey's ironic prediction—that murder leads to prevarication. The lie is a basic violation of the social contract and thus the most important moral category of the English crime form, as opposed to the American form's tendency to see *society* as the lie. His misunderstanding of Nietzsche is equally clear: "There was a quite perceptible difference between what he had done, and proposed to do, and murder: though he could not altogether define it" (155). Clearly he is the English sort of pale criminal. Murder gives him the self-confidence to actually seduce a former flirtee, the now-married Ivy, but his grandiose plans to murder practically everyone who annoys him go with the delusion that poor Julia's life was so unhappy that

"She was most probably most grateful to him by now, wherever she was" (139). This of a woman whose worst flaw was her patent self-satisfaction. Later as difficulties mount, he regrets that Julia is not around to advise him! Bickleigh escapes conviction when the vindictive Madeleine, star witness of the prosecution, is exposed as exactly the hysterical poseuse Julia had perceived. But Bickleigh's satisfaction is qualified by his financial ruin. He reflects, "a nice system that allows that sort of thing to happen to an innocent man" (235). This outrageous self-vindication leads directly to the ironic finale of the novel. Having taken his stand on technical, jury-verdict innocence as opposed to actual moral innocence, he is arrested for a murder which he did not commit and which was not a murder. Bickleigh's murder of his wife was taken by a jury as an accidental death from disease rather than the intentional killing "with malice aforethought" (211) that it actually was. He then attempts to murder Madeleine by infecting her with botulism but ineptly infects her instead with a typhoid disease that she survives. On the basis of this blunder, he is finally charged and convicted for the typhoid murder of Madeleine's husband, an actual result of the bad plumbing of Madeleine's manor house, *about which Bickleigh had earnestly warned her.* The novel concludes: "On the 2nd June, Dr. Bickleigh was executed for the murder of Dennis Hubert Blaize Bourne. He protested his innocence to the last" (237).

Iles's sardonic tour-de-force was nicely brought to television, with Hywel Bennett poisonously convincing as Bickleigh, both sinister and ridiculous. As much as in the novel, we see how the embarrassment of ridiculousness may motivate murder, thus implicating the sometimes ridiculous reader who has the odd fantasy of revenge and no less the completely self-assured reader whose ridiculous relations and friends may be covertly brooding on who knows what.

The protagonist of Julian Symons's *The Man Who Killed Himself* (1967) is Arthur Brownjohn, short, bald, and, like Bickleigh, married to a domineering woman of a higher social class. He too is a connoisseur of murder, his favorite reading the Notable British Trials series. The structure of this novel is economically conveyed in its first two sentences: "In the end Arthur Brownjohn killed himself, but in the beginning he made up his mind to murder his wife. He did so on the day that Major Easonby Mellon met Patricia Parker" (11). Brownjohn's dilemma is that with the addition of a wig, false beard, and loud clothes he *is* "Major Easonby Mellon," with an alternate job, a matrimonial agency which is really a low-level confidence game, and an alternative wife in London. But he is himself duped by Patricia Parker, who pulls the badger game on him. Her blackmail demands make the Mellon identity economically counterproductive. Moreover, Brownjohn has been conned out of some money he secretly withdrew from his wife's bank account by Mr. Clennery Tubbs. So Brownjohn's problem is his wife, and Mellon's problem is his livelihood. Their joint solution is to manufacture evidence of an apparent love affair between Mrs. Brownjohn and the mythical Mellon, drawing for inspiration on the letters quoted in the Notable British Trials account of the Thompson-Bywaters case. Then "Mellon" murders Mrs. Brownjohn and disappears, leaving Brownjohn a distraught but affluent widower. All this works perfectly except that in his new home, a cottage in Sussex, Brownjohn drinks a bit too much and cannot resist donning wig, beard, and loud clothes to take a turn around his garden as "Mellon," where he is seen by some startled neighbors. Later, Tubbs, remet, discovers the Mellon wig and is accidentally killed in a struggle over it. Brownjohn disposes of the body but is eventually charged with the murder of Easonby Mellon (the identity conferred on Tubbs's recovered body). The police case is that Brownjohn hired Mellon to murder Mrs. Brownjohn and then killed him—after all, Mellon had been seen at Brownjohn's cottage! Brownjohn finally *confesses to the murder of Easonby Mellon* but does not stand trial because by this point he has lost his hold on *any* identity. The psychological theme of the novel, underlying its irony, is that when Brownjohn murders his wife and eliminates his alternate identity of Mellon he has destroyed the relational sources of identity: "The things in which he had taken pleasure . . . seemed to have no existence independent of the people with whom they were associated" (134). The ultimate victim is himself.

Symons's second novel in this trilogy, *The Man Whose Dreams Came True* (1968), employs the same plot device but with the twist of a wish come dreadfully true. Anthony Jones's dream is to live in luxury in a foreign land. In pursuit of this dream he welshes on gambling debts to a dangerous clubowner and become accessory to and fall guy for a murder, but eventually, by an almost providential series of circumstances, he not only escapes conviction at his trial but wins enough money gambling to prepare to set off for Caracas with the clubowner's mistress. But this *cannot* work out for a character who is such a loser that when he tries to forge a check on his employer he misspells the name. In an ironic turn his two biggest scores, the sexual conquest and gambling luck, combine to do him in. Here again, the reader has a creepy relation to the protagonist, despising him and worrying for him at the same time. The reader may be *embarrassed* by his or her relation to a protagonist so sly and abject and enter into a certain complicity with the author's ironic destruction of him.

3. A morally and legally guilty protagonist for whom we have relative sympathy murders an unsympathetic person. We hope the protagonist brings it off but wonder if we ought to.

The most interesting play on this formula is Oliver Onions's *In Accordance with the Evidence* (1912). The first-person killer directly challenges the reader; as he moves in for the kill, he asks, "If you can see what else I could have done, tell me. I am willing to learn" (274). He clearly expects an endorsement of his homicidal intent, and this is not easy to withhold. The narrator, James Herbert Jeffries, is a giant of a man, both tall and heavy. He is highly intelligent, desperately poor, a savage, solitary brooding man who in his early days "hated pretty well everything and everybody" (19). If a misanthrope, he is not a cynic, and the covert love he begins to feel for Evie Soames is painfully idealistic. His unknowing rival is his physical, mental, and social opposite, a butterfly to his bear, Archie Merridew. Jeffries's already precarious position is worsened when, in an emotional turmoil at seeing the developing intimacy between Archie and Evie, he fails half of his business school examination on method. Archie, of course, passes, solely due to Jeffries's tutoring help. Jeffries now begins an elaborate plot against Archie, meantime staying close to the now engaged Archie and Evie by courting Evie's friend, Kitty, a deception about which he feels more guilt than his eventual murder of Archie.

This narrator is clearly out to affront our generic and moral expectations. His immediate motivation *is* moral: he discovers that Archie plans to marry Evie despite being under secret treatment for a social disease. Jeffries even gives Archie a last chance to cancel his engagement before carrying out the murder. Archie's own lack of moral responsibility dooms him. Earlier Jeffries induces him to write a suicide note under the guise of an exercise in dictation, supposedly drawing on a newspaper story of the death of a seamstress.

> "Dearest mother, I cannot face the disgrace. I hope you will forgive for the trouble I am bringing on you. I have put it off as long as possible, hoping things would get better, but there is only one end to it."

("Kid, eh?" murmured Archie, writing.)

"I trust God will forgive me. I am not afraid to die, I am afraid to live and face it. I cannot do E. this wrong. Please, dear mother, think of me as I used to be. I have tried and tried, but it is all no good, and I am better out of the world. Give my love to everybody, and try, dear mother, to forgive me."

"Time!"

Archie leaned back in his chair.

"Phew! Was that five minutes? Seemed short," he said. "Just a breather before we transcribe." He lighted a cigarette. (269)

The genius of Jeffries's scheme is that the apparent suicide note expresses just those sentiments that Archie's mother and Evie fondly suppose him—as a gentleman—to hold. The blindness of these women to Archie's actual cynicism and callousness guarantees the success of his murder. The Archie they know is an ideological fantasy.

In the first part of the novel, where Jeffries does everything right and is treated like a dirty dog while Archie does everything wrong and is taken as a charming boy, the reader can empathize with Jeffries's hatred of Archie. But the murder, by hanging, may induce a certain queasiness. Were Jeffries caught, we could have it both ways. Like most of our killers, Jeffries "intends to suffer no consequences" (259). The question of accountability is thus doubly raised, the protagonist daring *hubris* as well as murder, challenging providence. In the conclusion we discover that Jeffries has become wealthy and influential; he has refused a knighthood. But does he not, at least, suffer deep inner remorse? He tells us: "I do not start at sudden sounds, nor fear to be left alone in my library when it grows late. I play with my clean-born children. Evie is happy with me" (276). Dismissed here is an entire literary apparatus of retribution to be found in Poe, Dickens, and innumerable melodramas.

4. A morally and legally guilty protagonist for whom we feel considerable sympathy murders a relatively unsympathetic but not fiendish person and is executed for it. The execution, perfectly legal and of the "right" person, seems to us a worse crime than the crime.

Ernest Raymond's *We, the Accused* (1935) could only be told in the third person, for it is the author's role to supply the perspective the characters lack, to comment on their strivings and failings with a compassionate rather than punitive irony, to judge, in effect, the world's judgments. Near the end of the novel, the prison governor, faced with the ugly duty of executing a man he has come to like as well as pity, reflects, "How on earth could that decent little fellow, considerate for all, have done so shocking a deed? It defeated the imagination" (505). But such a reflection reveals his sympathetic imagination, his ability to transcend the limits of self in which most are self-imprisoned: "But so the people come to the still places and go, and each is the centre of his own world which no one else has ever visited or seen" (54). Raymond's mission is to encompass these isolated worlds, seeing them in a cosmic perspective compounded of Christian charity and naturalistic pathos. In this vision the characters are diminished in contrast to the cosmic backdrop but enlarged by the author's objective sympathy. The nearest this authorial voice comes to condemnation is of those characters who most completely lack imagination or compassion, especially those who dress up their blood lust in the guise of duty and justice. This author means to do justice to his characters.

One of these small centers of self, the palest of pale criminals, is Paul Presset, fifty years old, "a small, thin man with a weak chin and meagre limbs" (19), insecure about his lower-class origins, timid and shifty in manner, married to an older woman who cannot resist continually using as weapons against him her higher-class standing and engrained knowledge of the "U" ways of middle-class speech and action as well as the superiority she feels innately endowed with by the possession of a small income. At the end of the first chapter the author foreshadows the gap between inconsequentiality of person and consequence of act by presenting Paul on his way to work: "a small figure in a well-brushed black suit, bowler hat, and square-toed shoes, with a bag in his right hand and an umbrella hooked over the left arm; walking briskly towards the rumbling traffic of the Caledonian Road, and destined to a fame as wide as half the world" (21).

Paul is led toward destiny by the pull of desire and fantasy. Paul is "in love with" Myra Bawne, thirty-one, girlishly pretty but fading. That his desire is quite consciously adjusted to what he could reasonably hope for does not entirely undercut its reality, but theirs is the most apologetic of affairs: "At first Myra was terrified of the hotel vestibules, the long lobbies, and the hostile rooms. Her real tendency was to fly from life, not to run and grasp it like this; and the same tendency was in Paul, not to be overcome without strain and heat: he might over-persuade her, and reassure her, and try to provide strength for both, but his heart palpitated, and the moisture stood on his brow as he went with his tale to the reception bureau or guided Myra along the carpeted corridor, at the heels of a bell-boy in buttons. He was not a facile sinner" (94–95).

Paul is given to fantasy about his wife's death, prompted by her own continual complaints about her health, though these result from a hypochondria which is actually a considerable source of comfort to her. A hard, dull, self-centered person, she has no idea of how great is the gap between them: "She was not a woman to look towards any far horizons, and so was tolerably content with her life, and imagined her husband to be the same. She did not know that she was the negation of all his hopes. She did not know that when he came to bid her goodbye each morning, the sight of her, blowsy, dishevelled, and hard-eyed, on her disordered bed was a lash across the face of a very hungry man" (17–18). Paul cannot divorce his wife without losing his job and without his job he could not marry Myra. There seems only one way out.

The murder scene becomes excruciating, again because of the extension of imaginative sympathy. Paul's egotism is not of the monstrous magnitude of Bates's and Bickleigh's; indeed it may be no greater than that of the reader of the novel. And Elinor loses her hatefulness when in a pensive mood induced by a near-fatal attack of influenza she reflects on how little love she has ever inspired. Paul "is saddened by this glimpse of a hidden Elinor, disappointed and wistful and utterly solitary as he" (120). This rare moment of understanding contributes to Paul's doom because Elinor's illness provides him a cover for her poisoning, and her pathetic request for burial in the same churchyard as her mother emotionally bars him from cremating her incriminating body. Later she accepts what *we* know is a poisoned drink because, touched by his apparent consideration, she wants to acknowledge it. She feels most kindly toward Paul at the moment he is murdering her. As the poison takes effect, Paul feels exultant at Elinor's death but genuinely solicitous about her unanticipated suffering: "[he] sat at her side, holding her hand to comfort her, and occasionally resting his palm on her brow. Doing this, he was conscious of no hypocrisy because he was incapable of clear thought. He was just an elemental human being, stabbed by the sight of pain" (172–173). The moral calibrations of this passage are rather fine as it pulls at and readjusts our sympathy. Paul is an inept criminal and soon suspected. He flees with the innocent and trusting Myra, and the police pursuit, complete with tracking dogs, is imagined by Raymond as a kind of atavism. The police "with their panting jaws and eager, following eyes, looked kin to the animals. Exulting, the lust to punish went across the vast loneliness of the downs" (311).

This chase is on the Sussex downs but the fugitive lovers finally lead the police to the other end of England, the mountains of the Lake District where the extension and framing of their flight against a grandly barren natural world becomes part of the argument of the novel: "To go up and over Irton Fell is to go over a curve like the summit of a world. At its highest point Myra and Paul saw the vast view of the mountains that ring round Wastdale Head. . . . Massive, overwhelming, the dark mountains suggested forces too great for the strength of two puny creatures: to fly or to fight were alike useless . . ." (340–341).

In the mountains, at an overlook known as the Judge's Seat, Myra comes to a realization. She knows now that Paul has consistently lied to her, that he is, in one aspect, a shifty, deceitful, selfish man. Treasured moments together now seem drained of authenticity: "memory itself was poisoned and slain. Surely there could be no experience so awful as this destruction of the past" (332). Her realization is that she can recover the past and endure the present only by a love that encompasses the world as well as Paul: "If she continued to hate the world, she could not love Paul. But if she began to understand and forgive and pity all, she could struggle back to him" (333). She forgives Paul without rationalizing his "inconceivable self-centeredness" (333) precisely because she has moved to a larger traditional religious center, the center from which speaks the narrative voice of the novel. Paul's act is not excused but neither is the act of the state, which merely increases the sum total of evil. On the eve of Paul's execution the prison governor, looking at his watch, mumbles "with a bitterness that surprised him, 'Well . . . now for murder number two, what?'" (506).

5. An innocent character is punished for a crime he/she did not commit.

Raymond's novel shows a society neither natural nor Christian. Its normative feelings are snobbery, egotism, and a kind of primitive as well as punitive violence directed toward its least resourceful and most defenseless members. This too is the world of F. Tennyson Jesse's *A Pin to See the Peepshow* (1934), based on the Thompson-Bywaters case. Mrs. Thompson, executed along with her lover, Frederick Bywaters, for the murder of her husband, was the perfect judicial murderee. A victim of fantasy, her fantasy of herself as romantic heroine and the public's fantasy of her as a figure of dangerous female sexual appetite, she may have been executed really more as a

demonstration against sex than crime.[6] Filson B. Young in his introduction to *Trial of Frederick Bywaters and Edith Thompson* in the
Notable British Trials series is unusually forthright about his belief
in her innocence. Noting her bad luck of having an appeal come up
just when the Home Office was making one of its periodic public
shows of toughness, he declares her sentence to be "technically justifiable on legal grounds [but] essentially unjust."[7]

What happened was that on midnight October 3, 1922, Percy
Thompson was stabbed to death by Frederick Bywaters as
Thompson and his wife were walking down Belgrave Road from Il-
ford Station to Kensington Gardens Street. Mrs. Thompson was convicted as an accessory, though the only real evidence against her
were letters she had written to Bywaters, the meanings of which
were open to interpretation—as in the phrase "daring all," which
could be taken as a reference to murder or merely intercourse.[8] The
prosecution never produced evidence of a specific plan centered on
October 3, but an imperfect defense strategy, the implausibility of
some of Mrs. Thompson's testimony (Young notes her attorneys
should not have allowed her to testify), and the obvious hostility of
the judge toward her resulted in the guilty verdict and sentence of
execution. Young persuasively portrays Edith Thompson as charming, vital, and foolish. Hardly the "corrupt, malignant sorceress por-
trayed by the prosecution," she was a dreamer: "Her chief consciousness was hardly ever in what she was doing at the time, but
inhabited a world of desire and make-believe."[9] Even her tendency
toward lying proceeded not from self-interested calculation but
from imaginative self-absorption, "a desire to escape from the unin-
teresting actualities of life." She was, as Young says, "the chief victim of her own tragic personality."[10]

Despite the usual disclaimer, F. Tennyson Jesse's novel draws ex-
tensively on the Thompson-Bywaters case, not so much transform-
ing Young's Notable British Trials account (a series to which Jesse
herself had contributed) as expanding it, developing its implications.
Clearly, Jesse's Julia Starling is closely based on Edith Thompson.
The book begins with "Day Piece to Julia," showing her at sixteen as
a girl with "a sort of dashing assurance," a "zest for life" (11, 16).
It ends with "Night Piece to Julia," which concludes with her execution. As Jesse told her Paris publisher, she wrote the Day and
Night sections first: "And in that frame I placed the life of an over-
emotional, under-educated, suburban London girl, who had no more
idea of murder than the unfortunate Mrs. Thompson had."[11] The
theme of the novel is the fate of a woman intensely alive and imaginative but trapped by the conventions of class and the deficiencies of

sentimental education in prewar England, and, finally, legally murdered by the grand institutions of "justice."

The novel's evocative title comes from the Day Piece scene in which Julia, at school, pays "a pin to see the peepshow." The pin has no intrinsic value, the collecting of them "a purely arbitrary rite decreed by fashion." The peepshow is a white cardboard box with a round hole cut at each end, one covered with red transparent paper, one empty. But what one sees in it is another world:

> It was a mad world, compact of insane proportions, but lit by a strange glamour. The walls and lid of the box gave to it the sense of distance that a frame gives to a picture, sending it backwards into another space. Julia stared into the peepshow, and it was as though she gazed into the depths of a complete and self-contained world, where she would go clad in snow-shoes and furs, and be able to tame savage huskies and shoot bears; a world of chill pallor, of an illimitable white sky, both only saved from a cruel rigour by the rosy all-pervading light.
>
> It might have been possible for someone less eager and much older than Julia to apply an eye to that box and see nothing but cardboard advertisements and cotton-wool, but it was not possible for her. For the moment that she gazed into that space of some ten inches by five, she was lost in a fourth dimension of which she had never heard. (15–16)

Julia seeks this fourth dimension generally in random emotions, then specifically in sexual ones. She does not know where else to look, her upbringing having produced neither a true Christian nor an honest pagan. Her concept of religion gives her "No measure by which to live . . . nothing that would make her give up any tempting experience that lay just beyond her nose" (49). But neither does her upbringing allow for honest acceptance of pleasure: "the English mingling of the romantic and respectable in her, which she owed to her upbringing and not to her own nature, made her unable to accept that nature's true conclusion—the logical acceptance of passing pleasure . . ." (259–260). She cannot let herself go in her brief relation with a young soldier because, though moved, she is not In Love. She supposes that "such stirrings as were hers ought to be accompanied by sentiment" (132). As the epigraph to this section from Sterne's *A Sentimental Journey* suggests, "They order, said I, this matter better in France" (217).

The symbol for the English disorder is a broken statue of Apollo, green with damp, in St. Clements Square: "the strings of his lyre were made of whitewashed wire and had snapped, and were now curled up aimlessly, his hand poised over them. There were bird droppings on his shoulder" (74). The problem is partly that Julia is in the wrong class to receive a proper sentimental education. The sympathetic prison doctor reflects:

> Two things were hanging Julia Starling—her birth certificate, and her place in the social scale. If only she had not been seven years older than Carr [the lover], and if only she had been higher or lower in the world! In the class above hers the idea of divorce would not have shocked, and a private income would even have allowed her and Carr to live together without divorce, and no one would have been unduly outraged. Had their walk in life been the lowest, had they been tramps or part of the floating population of the docks down London River, they could have set up in one room together, and no one thought twice about it, as long as the husband wasn't a big strong man who made a row and tried to do them in. (499)

So Julia Starling hangs not for murder—which she didn't commit— nor yet adultery but for being in the wrong fantasy in the wrong class at the wrong time.[12] For that matter, she goes in for make-believe no more than the institutions that do her in. The novel's epigraph, from *Measure for Measure*, asserts the universality of the human masquerade:

> But man, proud man!
> Dressed in a little brief authority;
> Most ignorant of that he's most assured,
> His glassy essence—like an angry ape,
> Plays such fantastic tricks before High Heaven
> As make the angels weep . . .

This describes the Crown's attorney and judge who doom Julia. At one point in the trial Julia drifts into a reverie about the elaborate costuming of judges and priests, fantasizing that "if all the clothes in that court were suddenly whipped away by the hand of a fiery angel, and everyone found himself or herself naked, the trial would come to an end. People with hair on their chests, and all the funny little incidents of the human body displayed all over them, couldn't have conducted a trial; and yet that was what they all were—just tiny little people with hair in odd places, and toe-nails that needed cutting, and tiny, bewildered hurt souls inside all of them. They only got on with their business at all, or with any business, by dressing it all up" (437–438).

6a. The category of guilt/innocence may be confused by an intended victim who turns the tables on his/her would-be murderer.

Burke N. Hare (a suspicious name for an editor involved in crime—does he know where the bodies are?) in his introduction to Richard Hull's (Richard Henry Sampson) *The Murder of My Aunt* (1934), points out that inverted detective stories, wherein the riddle is not of whodunit but whether they will catch him, are often written from the murderer's point of view, posing the dilemma "that the reader may wind up empathizing with a distasteful character, an experience which can easily be rather distressing. In *Malice Aforethought* Iles, by writing condescendingly of his characters, keeps them at arm's length. If Hull had not made Edward into such a buffoon, he would be unbearable" ([v]). Hull acknowledges a debt to Iles, explaining, in the third person, why he turned to crime: "It can't be said that he was ever a very successful accountant, and in 1935 he began to think he would be more interested in writing. The decision to do so and to concentrate mainly on a particular type of detective fiction was made after reading Francis Iles' *Malice Aforethought*" ([vi]). Hull goes on to say that he "specialized in unpleasant characters because he [Hull] says there is more to say about them and that he finds them more amusing" ([x]).

Edward, the would-be first-person killer, is the only but by no means favorite nephew of Mildred Powell, who lives in the Welsh countryside a few hilly and curvy miles from the village of Llwll, a name Edward has much fun reviling in the first two pages of the novel, most of which consists of his journal. A bit over halfway through his narrative he informs us, "I have really a very kind, unselfish, and forgiving nature" (60). This is from a man who is carefully (within the limits of his intelligence) plotting his aunt's murder, who throws a rock at "an irritating bird," and whose only sport is croquet since "what are games for, except to release one's complexes by a little flavoring of spite" (40). From the beginning Edward's narrative reveals him as fat, vain, lazy, petty, vindictive, and, above all, extraordinarily obtuse. After his first murder attempt fails, he is the only one in the area not to know he is suspect. His second attempt is a device timed to begin a fire at a time he will have a secure alibi. He drives off in a car stuffed with his best possessions. On his return he sees his supposedly deceased aunt in the road and, taking her for a ghost, drives straight at her. What follows is a fine comedy of cross-purposes:

> With a startled scream the figure leapt to the side of the road and catching one foot on the warning white stone by the side of the road, toppled over onto the ground. It was not until I was almost at the gate of the back yard that it occurred to me that this was very curious conduct for a ghost. After all, whatever you may say about spi-

rits from the other world, they do not trip over stones. . . . I put La Joyeuse into reverse and glided quietly and quickly back to the spot, just as the apparition collected itself and got on the road again. Once more the figure hopped off the road; I only just missed it.

"Really Edward," came my aunt's voice, quite unmistakably natural and lifelike, "you're becoming crude in your methods. And as for coming back again—well!" (100)

At this point, Edward *speculates* that his aunt may be suspicious of him, taking this as evidence that she "has a very unpleasant mind" (110). His original attempt backfired when his beloved Pekingese rather than his aunt perished in a crash caused by his sabotaging of her car, and he is still bitter about her less than enthusiastic response to his plan to erect a tombstone with the touching epitaph: "To darling So-so, his master's only joy. A victim of speed" (77). Clearly what he needs in an aunt is a good murderee and his aunt Mildred is massively unqualified. In the aunt's postscript to Edward's diary she shows special outrage "when finally Edward, with a reference to his Pekingese, threw in my teeth his own attempt to kill me . . ." (171). She has, of course, been assiduously reading his diary since the car "accident" and as she observes of the novel's title after Edward meets a fatal "accident": "Well, (of) can be possessive can't it? Can mean 'of or belonging to'" (174).

The Murder of My Aunt is a classic comic crime novel, though its protagonist is too ridiculous and its would-*not*-be murderee too formidable to allow for what F. Tennyson Jesse saw as the factor differentiating the crime novel from the detective novel: "the function of the crime story is above all to give the nerves a frisson."[13] For a crime novel with both comedy and a frisson I recommend Shelley Smith's *The Cellar at No. 5* (1954), which matches two totally incompatible old ladies, Mrs. Rampage and her "companion," the aptly named Mrs. Roach, and proves at length that even killing a roach is not without its complications.

6b. The category of guilt may be confused by a murderee who all but incites his/her own murder.

I find Francis Iles's *Before the Fact* (1932) a richer, stranger novel than its more celebrated predecessor, *Malice Aforethought*. Fairly well along in this novel Lina Aysgarth, its protagonist, reads a book:

It was a penetrating piece of work, about murder and murderers. Analyzing her subject, the authoress had suggested that just as there

are born murderers so there are born victims: murderees, whose nature is to get murdered; persons who, even when they see murder
bearing down on them, are incapable of moving out of its way. Lina
laid the book on her lap, and stared into vacancy. Was she a murderee? (242)

The book is, of course, F. Tennyson Jesse's *Murder and Its Motives*
and Lina is the most convincing and abject of murderees. Time and
time again the reader longs to scream "Watch out" to her, to shake
her out of her passivity, to get her to stand up and go. But not only
does she stay with her husband after she learns that he is a liar, a
thief, and an embezzler, not only does she continue on after her realization that he, with malice aforethought, caused the death of her
father and then of his own best friend, but she continues to nurture
and protect him until he, inevitably, gets around to her.

If Lina is the epitome of the murderee, her husband, Johnnie, anticipates the model Cleckley psychopath as described in Hervey
Cleckley's *The Mask of Sanity*. Formally designated "the Cleckley
psychopath" in the *Encyclopedia of Psychology*, the type is summa-
rized as follows: "'while not deeply vicious, [the Cleckley psycho-
path] carries disaster lightly in each hand.' These persons may be intelligent and often display great charm, enhanced undoubtedly by a
lack of nervousness or other neurotic manifestations. Yet they are
fundamentally unreliable with a remarkable disregard for truth and
seem incapable of real love or emotional attachment. . . . They lack
genuine remorse or shame, often rationalizing their behavior or lay-
ing the blame on others. They have a 'specific loss of insight,' that is,
an inability to appreciate how others feel about them or to antici-
pate how others will react to their outrageous conduct."[14] Lina, despite her best efforts, finally cannot help but recognize just such
qualities in Johnnie; when she can no longer maintain delusion she
grants forgiveness:

> Johnnie with his infantile moral blindness, could never see those
> things as any ordinarily decent person sees them: as Lina herself saw
> them. Lina saw Johnnie as a murderer. Johnnie saw himself either as
> one driven by circumstances to a certain unconventionality of ac-
> tion, or else as a rather clever person. Probably he had managed to
> persuade himself, too, that he was doing his father-in-law quite a
> kind turn.
> Euthanasia. (178)

Her feeling is partly maternal. One of the first things she notices
about Johnnie is how his expression reminds her "of a small boy participating in some joyful, small-boyish crime, smiling at his accom-

plices" (9). In fact, what makes the Cleckley psychopath so dangerous to others is that "the absence of fear, the happy-go-lucky insouciance that emerges when shyness, self consciousness, guilt, and apprehension are dispelled, is a cardinal attribute of 'charm.'"[15] Lina comes to believe that Johnnie *needs* her. Even after Johnnie's murder of his friend, "If anything Lina felt more protectively responsible for Johnnie than ever. Johnnie could not be held to account for what he did: Johnnie simply did not know. Lina's protectiveness did not extend to the world in which Johnnie was loose" (208). Late in the novel Lina feels herself being looked at by Johnnie "in an odd, most un-Johnnie-like way; and since then she had intercepted much the same sort of look several times. It was a peculiar look as if Johnnie could not make up his mind whether he liked what she was wearing, but liked *her*, so much that it did not matter what she wore" (228). The slowest reader could interpret this better than Lina: "Now at last she was convinced that Johnnie would never again do anything that would upset or hurt her, not merely because he respected and was even a little frightened of her, but because he adored her. It was a very comfortable feeling" (229).

Finally Lina realizes that "Johnnie, her child—Johnnie, her whole life, was going to kill *her*" (235). There is some comfort: "It really was an odd comfort to Lina all this time that Johnnie loved her. Johnnie intended to kill her, yes; but he did not want to kill her. Johnnie was looking just as miserable in these days as Lina herself was feeling. The idea of killing her plainly depressed him very much indeed. He would do it with tears in his eyes" (244). Still, worries never cease: "She was worried lest Johnnie might do something silly. A person in full health cannot just drop dead without a lot of fuss and bother afterwards. There would have to be an inquest and (she could not help shuddering) a post-mortem. Johnnie was always so confident that he might not choose his moment carefully enough. Lina did wish she could advise him about it openly" (251). She does her best to help: "Lina wondered whether anyone else had ever been an accessory before the fact to her own murder" (253).

The authorial irony engendered by holding principally to Lina's point of view throughout the novel has an effect more disturbing than in even the most complicitous instances of first-person-killer point of view. One is suspended between horror, pity, and contempt for this lamb leading herself to the slaughter and the black humor of the novel is of the most discomforting sort. It is no mystery why Alfred Hitchcock in his film version, *Suspicion* (1941), was forced by his studio to reveal at the conclusion that it is all a great mistake, a series of misunderstandings, that no one has been murdered, that

Cary Grant really loves Joan Fontaine as much as Lina persuades herself that her "child," Johnnie, loves her. After all, how could such a charmer be a killer? The wish-fulfillment around which *Rebecca* (book and movie) is built was inverted, before the fact, by Iles.

6c. The category of guilt/innocence may be confused by a guilty bystander who is in complicity with murder by, probably unknowingly, inciting it, or, quite consciously, concealing knowledge of it.

The classic novel of guilty bystanders is Marie Belloc Lowndes's *The Lodger* (1913). Currently in critical disrepute, it is, in fact, a psychologically convincing portrayal of how two quite decent people come into collusion with the serial murders of a psychopath. Lowndes's protagonists are the Buntings, a couple long in service who have invested their savings in a house, the two upper stories of which they plan to rent. But no renters appear and as the novel opens we find them on the edge of losing their house, their money, and their status: "they were now very near the soundless depths which divide those who dwell on the safe tableland of security— those, that is, who are sure of making a respectable, if not happy living—and the submerged multitude who, through some lack in themselves, or owing to the conditions under which our strange civilization has become organized, struggle rudderless till they die in workhouse, hospital, or prison" (9). Then, providentially as it were, the lodger appears, saving the Buntings from financial, social, and psychological nullification by taking both their lodgings. True, the lodger seems rather odd with his tall, cadaverous frame, Inverness cape, and old-fashioned top hat, with the black bag he guards so carefully, with his nervous, jumpy ways, his aversion to "flesh meat" (28), and his quavery, high-pitched voice in which he reads aloud biblical passages, all with the same theme: "a strange woman is a narrow gate. She also lieth in wait as a prey, and increaseth the transgressions among men" (36). Meanwhile the newsboys in the street are crying out the latest crime of "The Avenger." The Avenger is clearly based on Jack the Ripper, and the novel does not make much of a mystery about the identity of the lodger and the Avenger. The suspense lies in when the Buntings will suspect and what they will do about it.

Mrs. Bunting is the first to begin to wonder but works hard at fending off the thought because the lodger's respectability and sobriety meet her highest expectations; even his misogyny doesn't much trouble her: "Mrs. Bunting had no very great opinion of her sister women, so that didn't put her out. Besides, where one's lodger is concerned a dislike of women is better than—well, than the other thing" (46). It is not *quite* that she prefers a lodger who butchers women in the street to one who has intercourse with women in his room. She comes, for that matter, to like him: "And then—and then, in a sort of way, Mrs. Bunting had become attached to Mr. Sleuth. A wan smile would sometimes light up his sad face when he saw her come in with one of his meals, and when this happened Mrs. Bunting felt pleased—pleased and vaguely touched. In between those—those dreadful events outside, which filled her with such suspicion, such anguish and such suspense, she never felt any fear, only pity, for Mr. Sleuth" (124–125).

Belloc convinces the reader of the naturalness of Mrs. Bunting's becoming a sinner by omission. The novel also effectively withholds overt judgment of the Buntings, leaving it to the reader whether to see their weakness as a form of wickedness. There is considerable irony but it inheres primarily in the plot, the invention: two decent, respectable people knowingly harboring a psychopathic killer. Just to tell this story so coolly and objectively precipitates irony.

7. A guilty character successfully frames an innocent one.

There are several interesting performances in this category, such as Bardin's American thriller, *The Last of Philip Banter* (1947) and Julian Symons's *The Color of Murder*, but in both the moral horror potential to this variation is diminished by the worminess of the victims. Both seem to ask for it, though not to the degree that they get it. Probably this was calculated by the authors as a means of relief from the implications of the theme, which shockingly inverts the expectation of justice. Indeed, the finest book in this category, Edward Grierson's *Reputation for a Song* (1952), is so excruciating that I cannot bring myself to discuss it at any length. Suffice it to say that the murder victim is framed after the fact, leading to the acquittal of a particularly loathsome killer.

6

Civilization and Its Discontents

Simenon, Millar, Highsmith, and Thompson

Much Madness is divinest Sense—
To a discerning Eye—
Much Sense—the starkest Madness—
'Tis the Majority
In this, as All, prevail—
Assent—and you are sane—
Demur—you're straightway dangerous—
And handled with a Chain—

EMILY DICKINSON

If I owned Hell and Texas, I'd rent out Texas and live in Hell.

PHIL SHERIDAN, SPEECH,
FORT CLARK, TEXAS, 1855

MOST OF THE CRIME novels I have so far discussed I consider classics of the genre. But the four writers of this chapter stand out for their careers in crime. Georges Simenon, Margaret Millar, Patricia Highsmith, and Jim Thompson play, in their quite different fashion, with and against the conventions and formulae while creating a special quiddity. Each is central to the genre and *sui generis*. Each equivocates in one way or another about who in a given story is *really* the "beast in view." The original target of obloquy may be revealed as victim rather than perpetrator of violence or as both victim and perpetrator. Stigmatic terms tend to bleed outside the category of the idiosyncratic to become at best endemic social possibility and, at worst, pandemic social stain.

These writers, except Simenon at times, do not deny personal moral responsibility; they are not immoralists or yet nihilists (although Thompson has been taken for one). Rather they revitalize conventional morality, highlighting the incidence of a covert pathological relationship between righteous judgment and psychological projection. Their writings depict not only the rules of conventional morality as provisional and precarious but, even more disturbingly, the array of socially agreed-on assumptions that are taken to substantiate civilized life. Relevant to these writers is Joseph Conrad's definition of society as basically a criminal conspiracy: "L'homme est un animal méchant. Sa méchanceté doit être organisée. Le crime est une condition nécéssaire de l'existence organisée. La société est essentielment criminelle—ou elle n'existerait pas."[1] And their characters frequently have some negative epiphany in which self and world dissolve into script, stage set, and lighting.

Georges Simenon

A Simenon character should never blink for the known world may vanish in the interval—in his crime novels, that is, since Maigret's bourgeois rectitude stabilizes Simenon's detective series. Indeed, Maigret could be seen as a kind of reaction-formation to the world of the crime novels. He can understand, partly through empathy, motives inarticulable by the criminal himself. Maigret solves crimes, mends destinies, and generally tidies up the universe with this resource of empathy while himself secured from too complete an identification with criminal motives by his "ineradicable lower-middle-classness."[2] But in Simenon's crime novels (what he called *romans dur*), there is no such safety net; Simenon has said, "As soon as I name my main character I become him. It is not my intelligence which writes the novel, but my impulses."[3]

This statement comes from an English television interview conducted by a psychiatrist, J. Stuart Whitely, and a forensic pathologist, Francis Camps, an instance of the attraction Simenon's crime novels hold for medical professionals. *Le Cas Simenon* (the title of a book on him by Thomas Narcejac) compels such interest because the novels carefully and minutely report the feelings and thoughts of their deviant protagonists without clues to how to judge and interpret these. Whitely found Simenon as "obsessional" as many of his protagonists, and Simenon recounts his agreement with Charlie Chaplin on their fortunate position as artists: "the difference between us and other psychopaths is that they pay to be cured and we are paid to cure ourselves."[4] Earlier in the interview Professor Camps likens Simenon's relation with his protagonist to a psychiatrist's with a psychopath: "Inbau . . . wrote a book on interrogation and described interviewing a young sex killer. Just at the moment of the completion of the interview the father came in and said to the boy, 'You didn't do it.' And the boy answered, 'Yes, I did, Dad. And Doctor Inbau almost did it too.'"[5] This could serve as a parable of writer-character-reader relations in the crime novel. Simenon's characters are phenomenologically acute at tracking their sensations, feelings, and moods but capable of only the crudest version of intellection. As Lucille Frackman Becker in her useful book on Simenon observes, these characters "are creatures of instinct rather than of intelligence."[6] In what sense then are they "guilty" of the crimes they sometimes rather vaguely commit? Becker quotes Simenon on Dostoevsky: "What he contributed above all, in my opinion, is a new notion of the idea of guilt. Guilt is no longer the simple, clearly defined matter one finds in the penal code, but becomes a personal drama that takes place in the individual's soul."[7] Even Maigret, Simenon's model of bourgeois civility, sees his courtroom testimony as deflected from reality by legal form: "Everything he had just said was true, but he had not made the weight of things felt, their density, their movement, their odor. . . . Everything was falsified here, not through the fault of the judges, the jurors, the witnesses, the penal code or the procedure, but because complicated, living human beings were summed up in a few sentences."[8] Judges, in a Simenon crime novel, are seen as more ideologically complicitous: "it is their business to support the world's ideas."[9] Morality, then, is relative: "Morality seems to change everywhere every thirty or forty years; so why believe in it."[10] Consequently, crime is relativized into nonexistence: "I have tried to make it understood . . . that there are no criminals."[11] Or, within the logic of the position, there are no criminals *except* judges. Criminal judgment implies the existence of the person judged—as an integral, self-consistent being with the power of choice. The Simenon hero is a polar opposite to the golden age private detective who solves crimes by recognizing the exact equation of manners with morals in a world where physical and social signs are never finally indecipherable, as well as to the tough-guy detective whose integrity is what his criminal milieu can threaten but never finally subvert. Simenon characters are instantly subverted because what they suppose to be their center is mere quotidian habitude beneath the illusory world of which there is no foundation, metaphysical or theological, at least none for which they have a name. The recurrent motif in his novels, as Simenon says, is "a sudden sensation of unreality of the environment, of people, of the outside world, which one of my characters experiences."[12] And with one step outside the magic circle of collective illusion the world dissolves into a series of signs that, latent with meanings that never quite cohere into a sign system, refuse to declare themselves. The world may always be a mirror for the individual, but that of Simenon's crime novels reflects "l'homme désintégré."[13]

Noting that Simenon "suggests more than he expresses," Claude Mauriac cites Gilbert Sigaux's observation that "the choice of a certain quality of silence is not a choice that leads to the elimination of problems but to stating them without recourse to speech."[14] The consistent flatness of scale in Simenon's language is precisely expressive of his world. (After reading Simenon, Sartre and Camus appear positively effervescent.) It is a weird literary distinctiveness: so many signs that point nowhere in particular, being neither autonomously self-reflexive nor philosophically enunciative. In a Simenon crime novel all is straightforward and clear; no reader can fail to follow the plot and Simenon's presentation of the responses of his characters is, for modern fiction, extraordinarily lucid. Yet somehow the final effect of character, book, and author is enigmatic, as of a puzzle unsolved. Whitely felt this in his interview: "Simenon is like the anti-hero of the non-Maigret books, a person about whom we know a great deal of intimate information and yet who remains an enigmatic figure."[15]

Any selection out of Simenon's astonishingly prolific output must necessarily be arbitrary, and I chose two novels that especially interested me, *The Man Who Watched the Trains Go By* (*L'homme qui regardait passer les trains,* 1932) and *L'homme de Londres* (1933).

The Man Who Watched the Trains Go By

Kees Popinga, the man who watched the trains go by, appears nearly a caricature of the bourgeois life, a man "who had settled ideas about people and the world at large" (7), who "has been doing the selfsame things night after night for the last fifteen years, till every movement, every attitude, had become almost automatic" (9), who believes he has the best house in "quite the healthiest and most attractive part of Groningen" (10). The signs of potential deviance are so indirect as to escape even his own notice. "And if, in an introspective mood, he had set himself to discover if there were a streak of wildness latent in his mental make-up, nothing is less likely than that he would have thought of a certain queer, half-guilty feeling that crept over him whenever he saw a train go by—especially a night-train, with all its blinds down, rife with mystery" (7). From this passage on, of course, the criminal reader anticipates Kees's journey to the night side. It begins when by happenstance he encounters his employer, the respectable Julius de Coster, drinking heavily in a disreputable bar. De Coster explains that after milking his firm for years, he is about to fake his suicide and disappear. He urges Kees to "see the world with different eyes," suggesting "perhaps it'll be the making of you" (20). Kees does just this, soon deciding that he had been tackling the world's problems "from the wrong angle" (130–131). The reader will recognize Kees's realization as a perspective shift but of a sort opposite to that of the detective novel. In Simenon the quotidian world is put askew; as Gavin Lambert observes, "the effect is like watching a movie in which the camera remains slightly tilted throughout."[16]

As Kees first hears de Coster's revelations, "it seems to him that the conversation was taking place in a dream-world, and that once he stepped out into the street he would be back in the world of real life" (21), but when he does so *this* world seems no longer real. His very appearance of stable bourgeois identity had concealed its opposite: "In fact, Kees Popinga had often dreamt of being someone quite different from the Kees Popinga everybody knew. That was why he always tended to overplay his part, out-Popinga'd Popinga, so to speak—for he knew that, were he to give way on the smallest point, there were no lengths to which he mightn't go" (28). And so it happens. Kees decides his major priority is to choose between de Coster's wife, Eleanore, or his mistress, Pamela, both newly available. He picks the mistress and so takes the night train to Amsterdam.

There is a significant typographical and narrative gap between Kees's cool announcement to Pamela that "it comes to this: I've decided to spend an hour or so with you" and the next sentence: "When he left the hotel he was, if that were possible, still calmer" (46). He embarks on a yet later night train to Paris at about the time Pamela's body is discovered and takes advantage of the border customs inspection to catch up with the journal he has begun to keep: "*Took the 23.26 at Amsterdam, second class.*" A few minutes later he is moved to add: "Cannot make out why Pamela started laughing at me when I told her what I wanted. So much the worse for her. I couldn't let it go at that. By now, presumably, she understands" (47–48). Sometime after he arrives in Paris he discovers from a newspaper that he can be described as having "brutally murdered" Pamela and that since his crime was "motiveless" he must be "a homicidal maniac" (58). He does not particularly feel like one and, in fact, feels less and less like anyone in particular. Kees, then, is another version of the schizophrenic protagonist but in the current *clinical* sense of a person lacking affect.

Kees is as unable as any other crime novel protagonist to pass up a mirror. After seeing himself described as a criminal maniac and sexual degenerate, he "went down to the lavatory for the sole purpose of examining himself in the looking glass" (135). Throughout the novel what he sees there is questionable: "a blurred, rather enigmatic visage," but this he observes "with complacence" (117), whereas he is both fascinated and irritated with the categorical definitions of him in the newspapers. Certainly Kees Popinga is not what he used to be, a standard-issue, socially defined self. He sees a newspaper photograph that literally cuts him out from social and family identity; it has been cropped out from a family picture. Is such loss of social self a disfigurement or, as Kees assures himself, an opening to potentiality?—"There were no limits to his possibilities now that he had ceased playing the part of Kees Popinga, the model citizen. . . . For the first time in his life he had an absolutely free hand. Incredible that, through all those years, he had sweated his soul out keeping up appearances . . ." (70). But what, in particular, are the possibilities to which there are now no limits and what cards will Kees play with his free hand? Is there anything in Kees to keep up or bring out except appearances? The police describe him as having "no special peculiarities" (57).

Kees objects to various descriptions and analyses of himself. He is irritated at the presumption of a porter at Groningen station that he had been in "a state of great excitement" (65). (Some years ago in France Valéry Giscard d' Estaing devastatingly insulted Jacques Chirac by describing him as "un peu agité.") He considers writing to the psychologists who have been analyzing him in newspapers to "ask them to defer forming opinions at this stage" (151). But the lack of another person, a *significant* other, to give limits (and perhaps possibilities?) to the self reduces Kees to making faces at the mirror. But fixed traits, old or new, are dangerous to Kees: "if he didn't wish to become known as 'the man with the cigar' he must take to smoking cigarettes, or a pipe. It went against the grain, as a cigar was, so to speak, a facet of his personality; but, now that his mind was made up, he promptly crushed out what remained of the cigar and filled the ugly little pipe he'd bought at Juvisy" (118). But if every trait is a sign of self and each such sign a clue to the police, wouldn't cigarettes, pipe, or even nonsmoking be potentially dangerous? As Jacques Dubois notes, the ideal for a deviant would be to become a man without qualities.[17] Is in-sign-ificance, a kind of white writing of the self, the only recourse? Is it possible?

No wonder that Kees has moments of wanting to embrace his newspaper identity. He has to suppress the impulse to announce to his reading public, "Let me introduce myself, ladies. I'm Kees Popinga, the thug from Amsterdam!" (95). Thinking of habits that could betray him if on a police description or published in a newspaper, "he felt an almost uncontrollable impulse to do them—to behave in character with the personage thus depicted" (120). The alternative to the social self limited by custom may be no more than the graphic self inscribed in journalistic cliché: "I'm Kees Popinga, the Grey Ghoul!" (68). As Kees liberates himself from social constraint, he becomes, in ratio, subject to the compulsions of the imp of the perverse. He is out of touch with not only his feelings but his actions and perceptions. He does not let himself know that Pamela is dead until he reads it in the newspapers—increasingly the market in which he exchanges identity. When a French underworld figure, Jeanne, draws the line at having sex with a lady-killer (even though she has previously helped him while knowing his identity), she becomes for him a Pamela-imago, as it were, and his attack on her is inevitable: "When, after washing his hands, which had some traces of blood on them, he started putting on his shoes, he was as calm as after the Pamela affair" (104). In the event, Jeanne lives through the attack, but the curious abstraction in the phrase "the Pamela affair" is matched by his journal entry on Jeanne: "*Saw Jeanne at her flat; she didn't laugh. As a precaution stunned her slightly*" (117).

Is then Kees's perspective shift an instance not of ontological insight but personal pathology? In fact, he is not some Gallic parallel to Arthur Brownjohn, the difference having to do with French as opposed to English general ideas about the relation of the individual to the social world, the French taking for granted a degree of intrinsic alienation, intrinsic antagonism, in this relation. Natalie Sarraute sees the modern period of literature as *The Age of Suspicion*.

The French have their reasons which the English do not know. French and American writers have a certain affinity to nihilism quite foreign to the English point of view. Julian Symons satirizes and relativizes social and moral conventions with sophisticated intelligence, but one never doubts that his world is bounded by an ultimate normativeness, that its creator will never invite you on *un voyage au bout de le nuit*. There is a different specific gravity to the idea of the social contract in Simenon: as more problematic, it is as well more poignant. A powerful image of what it can mean to be cut off from the social contract is in yet another mirror reflection in *The Man Who Watched the Trains Go By*. Kees, in a bar, looks up and sees his face in the glass:

A face expressing nothing, neither anguish nor despair, hope nor fear. Its blankness reminded him of a face he had seen ten years before at Groningen, that of a man who had just been run over by a tram and had both legs cut off. But the injured man didn't know that yet; the pain had not had time to make itself felt. And sprawling in the road he gazed up, completely puzzled by the women who fainted as they caught sight of him, and wondered what on earth was wrong with them and with himself, and why he was lying there surrounded by an excited crowd. (173)

Certainly one motif in the novel is that as Kees explores what it means for the first time in his life to have "an absolutely free hand," he is more and more not only being cut off but cut down, mutilation rather than potency being the outcome of rebellion. Yet it would be mistaken to take the novel as implicitly a justification of the claims of normative society as against those of a pathological deviant. If to deviate is crippling, cutting down the self and throwing perception askew, to belong is deadening, inauthenticity and bad faith being the requisites for social tranquillity. For that matter, the clearly pathological numbness of affect evident in Kees's afterthoughts on the attacks on Pamela and Jeanne seems more an importation from his quotidian world than a disease specific to deviancy. The relation between the normative and deviant might be conceived as less a Manichean battlefield than as a figure that looks like a rabbit from one perspective and a duck from another. Thus, while Simenon's image of alienation from the social world is that of mutilation, it is not clear that Kees as a person normal to the point of nullity had anything to lose. Kees starts out small, diminished by such ironic chapter titles as that announcing his decision to take on a de Coster woman: "*How Kees Popinga, though he had slept on the wrong side, woke in good form; and how he was hard put to choose between Eleanore and Pamela.*" His perspective is absurd in so taking for granted their availability. Yet when he ends up naked on a railroad track in a failed suicide attempt, the image ambiguously suggests not only the logical final image of social divestiture, but also a curious philosophical realization. In *The Novel of Man*, Simenon asks, "Will our age give us the portrait of man naked?"[18] Without accepting Kees as representative man, we may still feel a certain nervousness about how to take the final passage, wherein Kees, now socially categorized by his presence in an insane asylum, shows his psychiatrist the exercise book in which he is supposedly writing his memoirs:

There was nothing but the title:

THE TRUTH ABOUT THE KEES POPINGA CASE

The doctor looked up in surprise evidently wondering why his patient had written no more. And Kees felt called on to explain, with rather a forced smile: "Really, there isn't any truth about it, is there, doctor?" (199)

Who gets the best of this exchange, doctor/critic or patient/ character? Earlier, in a letter to a newspaper, Kees "nearly added 'paranoiac' after his name, as a last fling" (179). Simenon once told Maurice Richardson that some French medical schools recommended *The Man Who Watched the Trains Go By* "to students of psychiatry as a better study of paranoia than any text book."[19] But within the text Simenon launches a preemptive strike against psychological closure. Even the irony that undercuts Kees seems, retroactively, an attempt, finally unsuccessful, by the narrative voice to contain the implicatory empty space opened up by the character.

L'homme de Londres

In the confrontation of Simenon's everyday characters with the destiny that comes upon them, Gilbert Sigaux sees "une sobre grandeur, un tragique gris."[20] If Kees is too light for this description, it is exact for Maloin, the protagonist of *L'homme de Londres*.[21] Simenon says his aim in characterization is to make his protagonist "heavy, like a statue. . . ."[22] Never did he succeed better than in Maloin.

L'homme de Londres is a novel densely specified and allegorically suggestive, the allegory usually intimated by the physical detail. Maloin is the night-shift switchman at the ship-train terminal in Dieppe. He is married, with a son in school and an older daughter who works in a butcher's shop. He seems unalterably encased in everydayness: "Il faisait la même chose, à la même heure, au même endroit, depuis bientôt trente ans" (8). He walks to work within a time made up of "des heures comme les autres," which are only later constituted as "des heures exceptionnelles . . ." (5). Ensconced at work in the glass-enclosed booth overlooking the harbor from which he operates his switches, he happens to become sole witness to a smuggling transaction followed by a murder. He wonders later why he did not call for help. In fact, *it just did not occur to him.* In the course of the death struggle he witnesses, the smuggled valise falls into the bay with the victim. When the killer flees, Maloin, almost as an afterthought, recovers it, finding it stuffed with English bank notes. Its secret presence in his work locker acts as a kind of reagent that transforms Maloin's life, crystallizing the latent content of longstanding relationships, introducing him to a mysterious new one, and ultimately detaching him from his niche in his world and reflecting him to himself as no longer the sum of his habits but as a problem for which there are no sure answers.

An initial change is his reversal from detached observer to exposed target of observation. Initially, watching the smugglers from his tower, Maloin feels as amused as when he has spied on lovers' trysts. Even after the murder he cannot help smiling as he looks first at his locker, where the suitcase is hidden, then out the window at the killer, the man from London, now frantically searching for it in the harbor. But the superiority of this perspective is undercut when walking home from his work as he unexpectedly encounters the man and is unable to disguise an increasingly obsessive fascination. In a surrealistic moment, the two look at one another, anxious, astonished, neither capable of detaching his gaze. Maloin has been seen seeing. He realizes immediately that he should not look at his tower; naturally, he does so and the man follows his glance at the now vulnerably conspicuous tower. People in glass cages shouldn't cast glances.

The suitcase entangles and incriminates Maloin without his getting any use from it. The amount of money goes beyond his imaginative resources, and it is only when he takes his daughter on an intoxicating shopping trip, spending his savings while using the suitcase money (which he cannot use directly until converted to francs) as a kind of imaginary credit source, that "il découvrait de nouvelles perspectives" (114). Significantly it is in relation to his daughter that the money makes sense to him; a latent content in his feeling for the daughter, Henriette, is catalyzed. This emerges, before the shopping spree, when he glances through the window of the butcher shop where she works and sees her on hands and knees scrubbing the floor. Especially troubling is that he can see a glimpse of the bare flesh above her stockings. Without a clear idea of what is upsetting him—he is the only one actually looking—or of what he wants, he precipitates a grandly farcical scene, in the French style, with the butcher's wife and manages to get his daughter fired. The money in the suitcase is his rationalization of this behavior, which surprises him as much as anyone else: "Je n'ai pas le droit de laisser ma fille une minute de plus dans cette maison, se disait-il sans conviction. Quand on a cinq cent mille francs et plus . . ." (73). We see clues to this odd behavior when, in shepherding his daughter home, he happens to see the local prostitute, Camélia; when, in trying to justify himself to his wife, he claims that as Henriette scrubbed the floor the passersby saw most of her behind; and when he later bluntly asks Henriette whether the butcher has ever tried to make love to her. Sexual jealousy and repressed incestuous desire combine with class resentment to produce the scene later of the shopping spree, in which one of his purchases is a fur coat for Henriette like that of Camélia. These partial releases of repression make the trip a "jour de fête" for Maloin (117). For the moment he floats in the happy universe of those privileged by money; the wonderfully friendly salespeople call Henriette "madame."

But Simenon has created a zero-sum world, and as Maloin spends money he really does not have, his thoughts compulsively return to the man from London, the penultimate possessor of this money. He guesses correctly that the man cannot leave Dieppe because the only money he had was in the suitcase. When they chance upon each other at the seawall, Maloin feels embarrassed, as if caught in a lie. This man, about whom he knows practically nothing, has become a presence for him, his face already easier to recall than that of the brother-in-law Maloin has known for fifteen years. Of course, the man, having worked out what happened to the suitcase, is a threat, but this has less to do with Maloin's preoccupation than a growing sense of sympathy based initially on a kind of structural identity—their common, equally dubious, claim to the money. When the murder victim's body surfaces and the man from London, identified as a man named Brown from Newhaven, becomes the subject of an intense manhunt, Maloin puts himself in his place, worrying that he may lack food or shelter.

The relation is heightened when Maloin discovers that his daughter has surprised a man in their utility shed and, on impulse, locked him in. Certain it is Brown, Maloin orders his wife and child to keep their mouths shut. But he thinks uncomfortably of how the rain must be leaking into the shed, that Brown must be hungry, cold, and frightened there, that he could even die of exposure. The shopping trip comes soon after and as Maloin buys his daughter shoes and a fur wrap, he thinks of Brown, crouched in the shed. Brown is being hunted by that social world so respectful to Maloin and his daughter as they make their purchases.

When Maloin returns to his tower, his "cabine vitrée," his thoughts compulsively circle back to his shed, his "cabane." He feels almost as trapped in the one as he knows Brown to be in the other. Earlier he had resolved to return the suitcase to Brown if Brown spoke to him; now he resolves to offer to split the money. This decision precipitates Maloin into an ultimate relation to Brown.

Maloin is a dour, inexpressive man. He and his wife are virtually strangers to each other and even his relation with his daughter is clouded by unacknowledged desire. His solitary job has got him in the habit of talking more to himself than others: "Maloin fronça les sourcils, plissa les ailes du nez, se gratta la tempe et poussa un soupir. Ce sont des habitudes qu'on prend quand on vit seul des heures entières: on fait des grimaces, des gestes, on grogne, on dit de temps en temps quelques mots" (16). When he looks at himself in the mirror after retrieving the suitcase from the harbor, he sees what looks like the same Maloin. And when his day-shift colleague casually asks him, "Tu te crois beau garçon?" he responds, "Sait-on jamais?" (21). Connected as he is to his social world by little more than habit pattern, Maloin cannot assimilate the suitcase to it. As he gets deeper into complications, his world becomes both more heavily oppressive and less substantially real. On the way to see Brown he finds himself, without having planned it, stopping at a *charcuterie* and buying, absurdly, peace offerings of a can of sardines, a sausage, and a bit of pâté while contemplating himself morosely in the mirror behind the counter. Increasingly, "Il ne se sentait pas dans un univers solide" (142). Before entering the shed he sits on a stone and wonders what will become of himself and his family, envisioning his house posed on the cliff like a child's toy. Things are slipping, the pâté has gone mushy, he looks bemusedly at the sausage as if he had forgotten who bought it. As the rain and fog dissipate, the sky and sea taking on a limpid beauty, he can no longer see the point of what he has done and is doing. He could go back to his house as if nothing had happened and life would go on as before. But he has spent money for necessities on luxuries, he has caused his daughter to lose a job that helped keep the family marginally solvent, and he is open to the smug reproaches of his brother-in-law.

The brother-in-law, whose face is now less distinct to him than Brown's, decides the issue. Maloin goes into the shed in a complete funk; yet, Simenon declares, "à ces moment-là, on est lucide. On voit tout, on entend tout, on se dédouble. Il se voyait lui-même, en quelque sorte, comme dans un miroir, tendant la grosse clef vers la serrure" (146). He can neither see nor hear but believes he can smell Brown, who appeared to his daughter like a "bête traquée." When Brown, addressed politely as "Monsieur Brown," makes no sign of response to repeated overtures, Maloin becomes flustered and delivers an extraordinary speech, like a classroom declamation, accusing Brown of lacking "chic" and childishly warning him to say something before he counts to three. Brown has been locked up for quite some time without food or water in a stifling shed, so it is understandable that what leaps out from a hidden corner to attack Maloin is "quelqu'un qui avait été Brown . . ." (150–151). Maloin manages to wrest from Brown his weapon, the crab hook Maloin uses to winkle out crabs from their niches. In his panic he is struggling no longer with Brown but with "cette chose vivant." The killing moves from active ("il frappa") to passive case: "Le crochet s'enfonça dans du mou et fit naître un râle." It is like the time he had to kill a rat by stomping it: "Il avait fallu dix coups! Le rat s'obstinait à vivre!" But finally "cela bougeait moins. Cela traînait par terre. Des doigts s'écartaîent lentement" (152). But the moment after his death, as his body takes on an hallucinating immobility, he becomes Brown again, even *Mr.* Brown, and Maloin, on his knees, implores Brown's pardon, declaring, truthfully, that he did not do it on purpose. He tries to restore Brown with brandy, but it spills down his face and runs over his Adam's apple. This extraordinary tableau in which Maloin tries to establish polite relations with a corpse is surely from the best movie Alfred Hitchcock never made. Finally, his voice sounding like someone's who has just wakened from sleep, Maloin formally acknowledges, "Vous êtes mort . . ." (153).

As Maloin recognizes that he has, in his own view of things, stepped irremediably over the line, he feels an odd calm, a calm that is a kind of emptiness. Something ultimate has happened: "Il faisait des gestes comme un homme ordinaire, mais il sentait bien qu'il n'était plus un homme comme les autres. Il avait franchi une frontière inconnue, sans pouvoir dire à quel moment cela s'était passé" (154). This frontier is not that which traditional morality posits between good and evil but, for Simenon, the more interesting line between those on the inside and those on the outside of the world of social routine.[23] Maloin is like a crab winkled out of its niche, the process completed by his own crab hook. But in a way this grants lucidity:

> L'air était si vif qu'il donnait de petits coups d'aiguille dans la peau. Il y avait vent d'est et la mer, le ciel, la falaise ressemblaient à l'intérieur d'un coquillage tant leurs tons étaient clairs et irisés. De loin, on voyait les pêcheurs à la voile bleue relever leur drague et lancer les coquilles Saint Jacques dans un panier. (155)

The world seems like a great shell, beautiful in its emptiness, as within it fishermen haul in coquilles Saint-Jacques to be winkled from their shells. This world and those processes most nearly connected with it, fishing an instance, is self-justifying: it is as it is. The social world, compounded out of egotism and deceit, mistaking convention for reason, is the problem.

Maloin's name can be construed as a compound of "bad"(*mal*) and "elected" (*oint*), and, though not a holy sinner, he has found his own back-door entrance to a qualified redemption. The fog that has covered Dieppe from the beginning of the novel has lifted; for the first time since he witnessed the suitcase transaction Maloin knows exactly what he must do. He goes home and has lunch, his manner lacking its usual surliness: "Il ne lui arrivait pas souvent de parler si doucement" (158). When his daughter, sensing an oddness, questions him, his response shows his new recognition of where he is:

"Qu'est-ce que tu as?"
"Rien."
Il n'avait rien. Un grimace involontaire. (159)

He retrieves the suitcase from his locker, proceeds to a hotel where an English detective hunting Brown is staying, waits in the lobby until the detective arises, and hands him the suitcase, explaining "Voilà!" (167). He then leads him to Brown's body.

But police proceedings lack the dignity of Maloin's simplicity. They insist on reducing the event to their official clichés, assuming Maloin killed Brown to protect the money. The commissioner is astonished when Maloin gives him a look "grave, profond, qui semblait venir de très haut et prendre la mesure du petit homme aux souliers vernis" (179–180). Maloin has realized the futility of explanation:

Maloin sourit, d'une sourire qui était comme un cadénas posé sur la vie intérieure.
    Il avait compris. Il n'essaierait plus de s'expliquer. Il donnerait docilement les renseignements qu'on lui demanderait, sans un mot de plus. (180)

Later, when going through the extraordinary French legal ritual of public reenactment of the crime, he silently apologizes to Brown: "Je te demande pardon, mon pauvre Brown, se disait-il, en lui-même. Ils veulent absolument me voir manier le crochet" (181). But when asked how he struck Brown, he replies, "J'ai tapé dans le tas," and is almost pleased at the stupidity of the crowd that construes his directness as callous flippancy. His real offense here is to deny the crowd its moral melodrama: wanting Hugo, they get Simenon. After this he welcomes the isolation of the jail with its "murs blancs" and is merely irritated by the lawyer the court forces on him: "Maloin regarda l'avocat comme il eût regardé un objet curieux mais inutile. . . . Quand on le condamna à cinq ans, sa femme et sa fille se jetèrent dans ses bras en sanglotant et après les avoir embrassés, il regarda autour de lui avec l'air de chercher quelqu'un" (185). Who but Brown, his accidental destiny? As he earlier reflects, "C'était idiot, mais c'était comme ça! Le plus revoltant, c'est que cela aurait pu être autrement. Cela n'avait tenu qu'à des hasards" (184).

The Simenon protagonist at some point discovers that his massively lawful world is a false construction. The apparent stability of self proves merely epiphenomenal to this construction, an aspect of mass inertia. He attains a privileged perception of the arbitrariness of the everyday. The exclamation points that stud Simenon's style register not surprising departures from the everyday but its amazing persistence when seen from the far side—as when the maid in the hotel needs to mop under Maloin's feet as he sits patiently waiting for the English detective: "Exactement chez lui, quand on lavait la cuisine et qu'il tenait les pieds en l'air pendant qu'on passait le torchon en dessous!" (166). The protagonist's deviance from social expectation may be in the direction of a clearer, more natural sense of the norm, as when Maloin, after killing Brown, sees what he must do: "Il mettait de l'ordre! Il n'aurait pas pu dire ça à quelqu'un, car on serait moqué de lui. Et pourtant c'était ainsi" (154). It is all simpler than the authorities can comprehend.

Margaret Millar

Far from being ossified, civilized society in Margaret Millar's Southern California has not yet been achieved. The problem in her novels is to attain a rational adult identity in a society of overage children. This society has rules so patently absurd that conformity to them is more destabilizing than rebellion. To attain what used to be the traditional expectation of rational, mature identity is in Millar's world a heroic quest against difficult odds. Superego and id predominate in this world in a curious covert alliance. The superego types encase themselves in the character armor of the authoritarian personality in an ultimately vain attempt to deny desire, which then all the more tyrannizes over them. The impulsive types spend their energy fictionalizing the world to accord with desire. Avid and solipsistic, they apprehend others only as constructions of desire or inimical blocking figures to it. Or the type may be so fey as to be outside the boundaries of social and moral definition, dangerously innocent. The two novels in this section exemplify respectively the struggle of a woman to free herself from a conspiracy of crazily authoritarian relatives who want to keep her a child and the absurd tragicomedy of a superego-bound character trying to socially enclose the feyest of mermaids and, of course, in her destructive element immersing himself.

A Stranger in My Grave

Millar terms her writings detective fiction, though acknowledging she does not go in for "the actual detection part."[24] She uses detective conventions but deviates always into crime. In the detective novel, the puzzle is primarily one of event, solved by reconstructing time and space through the perspective shift that revisions the world of the novel as a set of signs which are clues to what happened and "whodunit." Millar's reader, however, is faced primarily with signs of character and must calibrate the degree of reliability of various narrative points of view to solve a puzzle really of persons (or of personae, as in *Beast in View*).

Hermeneutic glimpses, teases, and red herrings proliferate in the paradoxical title and dual points of view of *A Stranger in My Grave* (1960), but as in classical tragedy, resolution is precipitated by recognition, specifically of family identity in this peculiarly American variation on *Oedipus*.

The alternation in point of view frames the novel, each chapter beginning with one or two sentences in first person set off by italic type and isolated by a typographical gap from a standard type face, with third person discourse carrying the narration. The first person sentences seem to be from a letter, enigmatic signs from a past not specifically located in time, whereas the narrative is set in the present, Southern California, 1959. The protagonist, Daisy Fielding Harker, an attractive, rather girlish housewife in her thirties, is in both narratives, split between them really, unable to put herself together until she can discover the substance of the first discourse and integrate it and herself into the second, the present time in which she feels lost, an essential part of herself having been misplaced somewhere in the past. Daisy knows nothing of the letter, yet her "times of terror" (9), with which the novel begins, are explicable only in the story told obliquely in the letter.

Daisy's terror begins with a dream in which she mounts a hill to a local cemetery and is drawn to a grave, one that bears her own headstone with the correct birth date of November 13, 1930, but a death date of December 2, 1955, four years earlier. In some way, on that date she died. Her mother unintentionally moves Daisy forward by a verbal slip as she argues that Daisy ought not "to sit here brooding because you dreamed somebody killed you" (26). This is not what Daisy said, but it feels right to her: "*I died* had become *someone killed me*" (27). She was "psychically murdered" (31) on December 2, 1955, what she now thinks of as "The Day" (25). Though another, literal murder occurred on that day, the real mystery of this book is "who killed Daisy Harker." This murder Daisy is determined to solve.

Daisy's husband, Jim, is indulgent about the pattern of half-starts and dropped subjects Daisy fell into after her psychic murder: "ce-

ramics, astrology, tuberous begonias, Spanish conversation, uphol-
stering, Vedanta, mental hygiene, mosaics, Russian literature, all
the toys Daisy had played with and discarded" (12). It suits husband
and mother to keep Daisy incomplete, a frivolous child-woman who
may, however, need acting classes—her mother's recommenda-
tion—to keep up her role. What disturbs her husband about Daisy's
new project is that "she had stepped out of her usual role, had
changed lines and costumes, and now the director was agitated because he no longer knew what play he was directing" (57). The last
thing her benign tyrants want in Daisy is self-reflection, concomitant with autonomy: "Jim loved her insofar as she fitted his conception of the ideal wife. Her mother loved her as a projection of herself,
but the projected part must be without the flaws of the original"
(172). She should reflect *them.* Both in a sense love her, or at least
their image of her, but she is being *killed* with such kindness. Her
mother assures Daisy that she is loved, leading Daisy to the recognition, contrary to fifties gender ideology, that "Being loved was not
the problem" (172). She wants to change her grammatical category
from passive to active; the project she must carry through is that of
herself.

Since Daisy can find present identity only through reconstruction
of the past, she needs help, a trained investigator, to recover "The
Day," but in 1959 this will be a man and men do not take Daisy seriously. She offends their logic, asking her lawyer's help because
"something has sort of happened" (29), compounding this felony
with the admission that the something is a dream, thus putting her
two removes from male legal reality. Later, unhappily realizing how
much he has failed Daisy, the lawyer realizes how "he had been willing to accept her in her role of the happy innocent, the gay little girl,
long after he'd discovered that she was not happy or innocent or gay"
(33). Even Stevens Pinata, the bail bondsman and part-time investigator, who ultimately helps her find "The Day" and herself, initially types her as "the kind of woman whose darkest secret could be
bleached out with a little chlorine" (45). Sensing his assessment, she
tells him that she is "quite sane . . . *And* rational, if the two can possibly go together." To Pinata, this is tautological, and he is put off
balance when Daisy makes the Dickinsonian distinction that "sanity" may be mere conformity to an irrational society; it is "as if a pet
parrot . . . taught to speak a few simple phrases, had suddenly
started explaining the techniques of nuclear fission" (48).

Daisy, sleeping beauty and child-woman, is waking up and growing up: "*I felt quite happy, in a sleepy kind of way. And then suddenly something woke me, and it began, the terror, the panic*" (14).

Wakeful, she has perceptions that are oddly valid: "Jim's face, staring down at her, was out of focus so that he looked not like Jim but like some kind stranger who'd dropped in to help her" (13). Jim's attempt to reassure her—that, whatever her problems, she still "look[s] pretty as a picture, to coin a phrase"—is undercut with a sardonic ur-feminist decoding: "I went to the best embalmer" (17). Her mother tells her how lucky she is to have a husband so wrapped up in her, and Daisy imagines "a double mummy, two people long dead, wrapped together in a winding sheet" (21). So much for togetherness. By now we know what made Daisy feel dead.

The italicization of Daisy's awakening associates it with the italicized letter, moving toward completion as the chapters progress; in both consciousness is informed with pain. The letter is font and origin of the hermeneutic traps of the novel: *the reader alert to the physical clues prevalent in the detective novel is likely to miss the psychological clues prevalent in the crime novel.* The former, in fact, are red herrings distracting attention from the latter so as to delay the reader's recognition. The perspective shift in the novel is from the conventional decoding of physical evidence to reconstruct an event to the intuitive apprehension of tacit signs so as to reveal a self. The self then recovers the event that shaped it.

We can infer that the letter is from Daisy's father. But who is this? In chapter 4 Stan Fielding, alcoholic ex-husband of Daisy's mother, blows into town just long enough to get into trouble and is out again even before Daisy appears with the money to repay his bail bondsman, Stevens Pinata. This is how Daisy happens on Pinata and launches her investigation. Fielding's voice is immediately recognizable to Daisy when she receives his call for help:

> "Hello, Daisy baby."
> Even if she hadn't recognized the voice she would have known
> who it was. No one ever called her Daisy baby except her father. (34)

When she shows concern for his health, not usually a strong point with alcoholics, he responds, conventionally, "Fine. Oh, I've got a touch of this and a touch of that, but in the main, fine" and asks her for money to get him out of "a bit of a pickle." He knows she will give it to him because, as he assures her, "You're a good girl, Daisy, a good daddy-loving girl" (35). He and Pinata talk as they await Daisy's money, even exchanging confidences. Pinata is a foundling, so named because abandoned at a church on Christmas Eve. He is not certain of his parents' ethnic identity. But when Fielding commiserates—"Fancy that, not knowing who you are"—he responds, "I know who *I* am . . . I just don't know who *they* were." But by virtue of his name he has communally shared in discrimination against Mexican-Americans. Fielding sees himself as opposite: "I know all about my grandparents and great-grandparents and uncles and cousins, the whole damn bunch of them. And it seems to me I got kind of lost in the shuffle. My ex-wife was always telling me I had no ego, in a reproachful way, as if an ego was something like a hat or pair of gloves which I'd carelessly lost or misplaced" (39). So we have two characters, Fielding and Daisy, who have family but misplaced egos, and one, Pinata, who has a stable ego and a misplaced family. He seems to have the best of it.

Chapter 5 centers on Daisy's commission to Pinata to reconstruct "The Day." By this point we have five fragments of the letter, a starting point for reconstructing the ego, firm or shaky, implicit in *its* signs. But do these *need* interpretation? Foregrounded as enigma by initial placement in each chapter, italicization, and, indeed, eloquence, the letter presents itself as riddle. Yet its provenience seems self-evident: it was written by Daisy's father, Fielding is Daisy's father, and by the end of chapter 4 he is telling Pinata that he would much rather write to than see Daisy: "That's what I'll do, I'll write her a letter" (42). Could the following lines, the first five fragments of the letter, each ending in an ellipsis, be *this* letter or an earlier one from Stan Fielding?

My beloved Daisy: It has been so many years since I have seen you . . . (9)

Perhaps, at this hour that is very late for me, I should not step back into your life . . . (19)

But I cannot help it. My blood runs in your veins . . . (27)

When I die, part of me will still be alive, in you, in your children, in your children's children . . . (33)

Anyone who has been reading character as closely as plot in this novel will realize that Fielding *could not* have written this. Besides the difference between "My beloved Daisy" and the revolting "Daisy baby," the letter is more eloquent and less glib than Fielding's characteristically smooth evasions. Fielding, who is sophisticated enough to speculate on the state of his ego, would not write a phrase as grammatically awkward or as emotionally expressive as "at this hour that is very late for me." And Fielding's exploitative relation to Daisy centers not on blood but money. In its tone and rhythm, in its awkwardness of grammar and dignity of spirit, the letter is quite expressive, but not of Fielding.

When Daisy and Pinata visit the cemetery, the cross she dreamed about is there but her name is not on it; it reads:

CARLOS THEODORE CAMILLA
1907–1955

Inquiry reveals that Camilla, "the stranger in Daisy's grave" (85), died on "The Day" in 1955. He is the ghost who haunts this narrative. The reader will have realized before Pinata and Daisy that Camilla has to be Daisy's biological father, author of the letter. Repudiated by Mrs. Fielding out of sexual guilt and racial hysteria, killed, in ambiguous circumstances, by Fielding on, of course, "The Day," Camilla is the absent presence of this novel. Throughout the novel we have seen photos of Camilla, have heard about him under his nickname of Curly, and, of course, have been reading cumulatively the letter, sent to Daisy, intercepted and hidden by her mother, and finally on the last two pages of the novel read for the first time by Daisy and for the first time as a continuous, completed discourse by the reader.

But Daisy does not, until the conclusion, know any of this. What she discovered and subsequently repressed on "The Day" was that her husband had had an affair culminating in illegitimate paternity. But the trick of it is that there was no affair and no illegitimate child. Daisy was taken in by an elaborate sham designed by her mother and husband to prove his potency and her infertility, so as to divert her from the truth, which is that they want her to be a child and not have one. As her mother sees it, a child would be "marked by a stigma that must not be passed on" (240). Paternity in Sophocles' *Oedipus* is primarily a question of dynasty. In Millar's novel it is, in American fashion, a question of race. Daisy has been infantilized by husband, mother, and pseudofather to protect her from the realization of her blood relation to the racial other. Growing up, Daisy opts for the risks of realization against Pinata's advice that she not listen too hard or see too much. She is getting an idea of what she wants and Pinata is it. Pinata scrupulously reminds her of his lack of family or racial identity, but after her mother's overinvestment in these, she can feel the attraction in traveling light: family in this very American book (by an author of Canadian origin) can only impede identity; it is false consciousness institutionalized. The recognition scene to which she has been led by Camilla's ghost delivers her from the claustrophobic love and paranoiac pride of family. She cannot know what her children will look like or their precise racial mix, but to her they will be gifts and their name will of course be Pinata.

Mermaid

One of the most arresting (and not infrequently arrested) character types in modern fiction and film is the naïf, a character above or below or sideways to the governing conventions of propriety, who has a catalytic effect on the social order, precipitating chaos and sometimes violence by his or her affront to the social code.

If the character comes crosswise of the law, it will be primarily insofar as the law differs from justice and encodes a kind of social stupidity. The character's innocence may seem almost in itself an offence, as with Eudora Welty's Uncle Daniel Ponder: she may generate chaotic desire by simply standing still, radiating aura, as with Eula Varner; or, combining spontaneity and innocence with a certain malice aforethought, characters may work their way up from simple perception of the falsity of social conventions, like Alice Walker's Celie, to subversive forays against whatever is smugly assumed, like Catherine in Truffaut's film *Jules et Jim* or Ann Elizabeth McGlone in Frances Molloy's *No Mate for the Magpie*. These characters differ in their knowingness: they may be fools, wise fools, or even tricksters. However, all are, in varying degrees, socially unassimilable but justified by their desire and spontaneity. Boudu *should* be saved from drowning.

There is a certain anomaly in a character *type* that embodies *originality*, a *convention* of *nonconformity*. Cleo Jasper, the eponymous protagonist of *Mermaid* (1982), is clearly a type of naïf, innocent of social convention. The only question she would seem to pose is how wise a fool she will turn out to be. We are introduced to her as she comes into a law office and announces she likes the little cage— that is, the senior partner's private outside elevator. Denied a ride on this, she excuses herself to the receptionist with charming naiveté: "I'm bothering you, aren't I? My brother Hilton is always telling me I mustn't bother people, but how can I help it if I don't know what bothers them?" (13–14). She watches the lawyers return from lunch and picks the one with the nicest face, Tomas Aragon.

What Cleo came for, apart from seeing the little cage, is to find out her "rights." A student at Holbrook Hall, advertised in the more expensive magazines as a "facility designed to meet the special needs of exceptional teenagers and young adults," she is aware that another word for her exceptionality is "retarded" (19). Twenty-two years old, she is fourteen or fifteen in dress and appearance, and less than that in social awareness. A friend has told her about her "rights," including the right to vote, though she doesn't especially want to, lacking interest in "presidents and things." She just wants

to know if she *could* since "Hilton says voting is just for responsible people who don't have foggy times." Hilton is her brother, but
one who was already grown up and married at the time she was born
to a mother "too old to have a baby but she had one anyway and I'm
it." She went to live with Hilton when she was eight, after having
lived with her grandmother, who was "very nice, only she died," leaving Cleo with money she never gets to use because, as her brother
tells her, she is "exceptional." Cleo learns her rights, within the limits of her comprehension, pays Aragon a dollar fee, and decides to set
out for the museum, reassuring Aragon she knows the way: "He
watched her from the window as she left the building. The museum
was due north. She walked rapidly and confidently south" (22).

We are next introduced to Hilton Jasper, Cleo's brother and
quasi father. From the previous section, we could hardly have
avoided certain preconceptions about this character: that he is cul-
pably insensitive, a blamer, too aware of his own rights and not
enough of Cleo's. It is no surprise to find that he sits at the head of
his dinner table "as though he were a captain instructing his crew
on how to maneuver through stormy seas, which to Hilton meant
taxes, Democrats, inflation, undercooked lamb and bad manners"
(22). Unfortunately, the crew consists of his resentful wife, Frieda; of
Cleo; and later of his arrogant son, Ted, arriving home on college va-
cation. Ted is one year younger than his aunt Cleo. No wonder, then,
that Hilton has a twitch at the corner of his right eye. He is a rigid,
authoritarian personality who needs to have everybody and everything stay in order in a world where nobody and nothing will: "Bad
manners and taxes and crime and Democrats and unsuitable subjects for dinner conversation were sweeping the country. He was
only forty-five and he wanted to stop the world and get off" (25).

The reader may feel that the author is even stacking the deck a
bit, as one might expect from a notable conservationist writing of a
banker and oil executive. This remains to be seen.

Things come apart when Ted, peacefully smoking a joint, is visited in his bedroom by Cleo, who takes off her nightgown to ask his
opinion of whether she should wear tight blue jeans like other
women of her (biological) age. Ted tries hard to not look, but this is
difficult when she sits next to him. Hilton, on discovering his
twenty-two-year-old sister in the act of learning about something as
disreputable as bad manners, Democrats, and unsuitable subjects for
dinner, orders Ted out of the house and begs Cleo to promise never
to let another man touch her. Clearly, incest, at least of the emotional kind, is compounded. In the morning Cleo hears Frieda blame
her entirely for the events of the night, ranting that she "didn't

know right from wrong and had no intention of learning," that she might have a baby, that morons like her should be sterilized, and that she is a spoiled brat, a bad apple. Cleo doesn't see it this way:

> She wasn't an apple, a brat, a moron. She was Cleo. "I am Cleo," she said aloud. "I got rights." (33)

This comes as the last line in the first section of the book, "Child," and is the last we see of Cleo (though we hear a fair amount) until section three, "Mermaid," begins 133 pages later. At the start of section two, "Woman," two characters who know Cleo meet for the first time, as Hilton commissions Aragon to find the now missing Cleo. "Hilton Jasper wasn't quite what Aragon expected" (37), which ought to make the reader wonder as well. It is true that Aragon, at this moment surely a surrogate for the reader, "felt uncomfortable with the man, more uncomfortable than he had with Cleo" (40). For the reader these ratios of sympathy are cued by character type and moral conventions. We *already* know what to think of rigid Republicans as opposed to fay Naiads. But there may be a problem with being fay, one of which is that it is uncomfortably close to being fey. It is not that as our sympathies with Cleo are qualified, our judgment of Hilton is completely reversed. In the relationship of Hilton and his wife, Aragon finds no love but an abundance of "duty, guilt, sacrifice, anger" (61), clearly not Millar's idea of a justified life. But at some point we might need to reconsider Frieda's claim that Cleo "didn't know right from wrong" and recall Cleo's response to Hilton's not untortured question of whether she cares as much for him as for Zia, ice cream cones, TV, flowers, and strawberries:

> "I have to love Zia best," she said slowly, "because he never gets mad and when I talk to him he always listens like I was a real person."
> He turned and grabbed the back of the wicker chair to keep it quiet. "You *are* a real person, Cleo."
> "Not like the others. You said I didn't care about things. Real people care about things." (32)

Zia, it should be remembered, is the gardener's dog. When Cleo runs off she takes Zia with her but then rather casually abandons him. We should not decide that Cleo is evil instead of innocent; the problem is that she is innocent of evil, that she does not in fact know right from wrong, and that, because of these lacks, she is not quite a real person.

She does, however, have real effects. Aragon discovers that she has run off to marry Roger Lennard, a teacher at Holbrook Hall.

Roger meant to help her become a real person, learn her rights, vote! And he meant to help himself go straight; Mrs. Holbrook, to avoid complications, employs gay men to teach girl students. Roger's attempt is a disaster in both respects; Cleo leaves and he, unable to opt into heterosexuality, takes poison. Cleo then finds the banished Ted, they gravitate to the harbor, to Donny Whitfield's father's yacht, on which her Holbrook class had made a memorable excursion, and Cleo calls Donny at Holbrook to suggest a party. This makes sense to Donny, although his stay at Holbrook is a condition of criminal probation. It happens that Aragon, at the school to ask some questions, has been careless with his keys, and when he leaves so does Donny, in the trunk of his car. After a party that seems modeled on those in *The Great Gatsby*, Cleo, a fast learner about *some* things, informs Donny, "You got rights" (175), one of which is to commandeer the boat and, as captain, marry Ted and Cleo. She knows he can do this because she's seen it on television, where she has also picked up the information that after seventy seconds of intercourse she *must* be pregnant. Donny, asserting his rights, commandeers the boat at gunpoint, giving Cleo a .22 for auxiliary purposes. At some point during all this confusion Aragon has found his way onto the boat, which sets off vaguely in the direction of Ensenada. When Ted, coming out of a hangover, does not take to the notion of marrying his aunt, the offended captain starts shooting. Meantime, "Cleo began screaming with excitement and jumping up and down until she tripped on the hem of the white nightgown that was her bridal costume. The .22 fell out of her hand and slid across the deck in Aragon's direction" (195). But Donny has Aragon covered, so the lawyer decides his best chance is to join Ted, who, hit by a shot, has abandoned ship. Fortunately, Aragon has managed to bring two life-jackets with him and keeps himself and Ted afloat until rescued by a coast guard cutter. With Ted's subsequent death from the bullet wound, the closing of the Holbrook school, Donny's facing manifold felony charges, the total collapse of Hilton's marriage, and Roger's suicide, a pretty good score has been rung up. Frieda's opinion of her sister-in-law begins to make sense to Aragon: "It was the first time he'd thought of Cleo as a ruiner, a destructive force, more of a victimizer than a victim" (87).

In fact, Cleo is in no way responsible. Millar's novel is an exploration of what it might mean to be in no way responsible. Certainly, spontaneity: "The party ended early, with everyone going to bed wherever they lost consciousness" (175). For another, liberation from arbitrary social and legal categories: when Aragon suggests to Donny that he is violating the terms of his probation, Donny, inspired by Cleo and the liberating ocean air, responds with an instant deconstruction: "'Screw probation,' Donny said. 'Probation is for landlubbers. At sea it's only a word'" (191). This seems the irrefutable refutation of Cleo's earlier moment of doubt: "Maybe this isn't such a good idea . . . Maybe we don't have all those rights Roger said people had" (184). She even has doubts about whether Ted would be the perfect husband and father: "Ted had passed out on a couch and was lying on his back with his mouth open, snoring. Cleo listened to him for a few minutes, frowning. She wasn't sure she wanted a husband who snored; it might keep her and the baby awake" (178). Just before the shootout Aragon tries to persuade Cleo that she cannot marry Ted without a blood test, a license, and some person slightly better qualified than Donny to perform the ceremony, besides which the law frowns on marriage between an aunt and her nephew. But, the innocence of unmediated desire regained, Cleo responds, "I won't listen to you . . . I think you're a nasty man" (194).

There is a difference between Daisy's defense of intuition in *A Stranger in My Grave* and the refusal of Cleo to let reality interfere with desire. The two books act out distinctions between the intelligence of the journeying heart and the blindness of self-enclosed desire. Daisy's aim is to confront reality; Cleo's to evade it. Aragon's scruples may be, under the circumstances, extreme: "*I made the mistake. I left the keys in the ignition. My fault*—" (202). This may be overscrupulous, but if a small mistake, careless rather than venal, leads to a larger disaster, who would *not* feel guilty? Cleo, however, does not; there is no hypocrisy in her claim to Hilton: "I didn't really do anything much." Hilton, whom we dislike less and less as the book goes on, cannot see it that way: "His hands gripped the steering wheel as if they were trying to squeeze the life out of it. Nothing much. Roger Lennard was dead and Ted on the point of death. Rachel Holbrook's lifework in ruins and Donny Whitfield would almost certainly be sent to the penitentiary. Nothing much" (210–211). This extension of responsibility would be too complicated for Cleo, but when Hilton tells her that Frieda won't be coming back because she doesn't feel like it, "This simple explanation satisfied her because she understood it. If you wanted to do something, you did it. If you didn't, you didn't" (211).

Cleo's is a mermaid's point of view. She has no guilt to wash away; if the shower she takes toward the end of the novel is more than literal, it is because it relates this liminal creature—Ted's aunt, one-minute stand, and would-be wife; Hilton's sister in blood, daughter in effect, and lover in the fantasies he cannot even allow himself to have, child-woman-mermaid—to her natural element: "She went up to her room and showered and shampooed her hair. Then she stood in front of the full-length mirror in the bedroom, letting the water drip down her body, tickling her skin. She liked the way she looked, a mermaid escaped from the sea" (213). When she goes downstairs, Hilton is lying on a couch, his face to the wall: "She wondered if he was dead, so she touched him on the shoulder. It was like switching on one of the mixing machines cook kept in the kitchen. Hilton began to shake all over as if he were being ground up inside, his liver and heart and stomach and appendix, all ground up into hamburger. It took away her appetite" (213). Hilton's anguish comes from having been informed that Ted has just died of a wound from what Cleo calls "the teeny little gun" (214) she was holding. Millar doesn't tell us exactly how this happened; we might infer the gun went off when Cleo was jumping up and down with excitement, or perhaps in some foggy corner of her inaccessible mind, she aimed it. Now, however, she simply does not believe in the death, much less her responsibility for it, though able to discern that she is somehow out of place: "She brushed her hair, still wet, and put on the freshly laundered jeans and T-shirt, and wondered where mermaids went when they came up from the sea. There didn't seem to be a place for them" (214). Being fay is a problem for one who is but also, as we have seen, for those who aren't. It's like another character's explanation of why she had trouble with a former husband who was a teetotaler: "It's like being married to an aardvark. It's okay if you're another aardvark" (80).

The novel ends with Cleo's search for other aardvarks, her return to her element:

> Then she ran down the rest of the driveway to the street. She felt very light and airy, moving with the wind like a silk sail. And suddenly, magically, she knew what mermaids did when they came up from the sea. They went down to it again.
> She could see the harbor in the distance and she kept running toward it. Everyone on the *Spindrift* would be very surprised to see her and they would all have a party to celebrate . . . Donny and Ted and the young man who told her about voting and some of her other rights.
> None of that seemed important anymore. She was going to a party. (215)

There are two final comments necessary on *Mermaid*. First, the reader may object that she/he is not the naïf I posited who would feel an initial sympathy for mermaidism. Fair enough; this naive reader is based on myself. My second time through the novel I realized that what I had seen as confused characterization was my conventionally mediated confusion about the characterization. But since this misconstruction was cued by the author, the reader having been set up for a perspective shift, I was clearly Millar's ideal reader. Second, among various contemporary parables about emotional excess, self-centered hedonism, and the irresponsibilities of desire and the failures of public norms, parables such as those by Bellow, Updike, Percy, and Paul and Alexander Theroux, *Mermaid* stands up rather well.

Patricia Highsmith

Patricia Highsmith, one of the true masters of crime, comments, "I suppose the reason I write about crime is simply that it is very good for illustrating moral points of life. I am really interested in the behavior of people surrounding someone who has done something wrong, and also whether the person who has done it feels guilty about it, or just, 'so what.'"[25]

Graham Greene observes that a Highsmith novel does not guarantee the reader moral closure: "It makes the tension worse that we are never sure whether even the worst of them, like the talented Mr. Ripley, won't get away with it or that the relatively innocent won't suffer . . . or the relatively guilty escape altogether . . ."[26] One Highsmith novel, *The Tremor of Forgery*, concludes with the question still unanswered whether the protagonist's attack on a man resulted in his death. The man has disappeared: has he been covertly buried? Is he in hiding? Not only the moral definition of the event—manslaughter, justifiable homicide, accident—but the event itself is left in doubt.

Guilt, though central to Highsmith's fiction, tends to be rather free-floating. Highsmith characters may shrug off one person's murder while agonizing whether they have been *inconsiderate* to another. A character scrupulous to the point of absurdity is offset by another who feels abundantly self-righteous in the commission of premeditated viciousness. Greene praises Highsmith for having "created a world of her own—a world claustrophobic and irrational which we enter each time with a sense of personal danger, with the head half turned over the shoulder . . . Actions are sudden and impromptu and the motives sometimes so inexplicable that we simply have to take them on trust . . . Her characters are irrational and they leap to life in their very lack of reason; suddenly we realize how unbelievably rational most fictional characters are as they lead their lives from A to Z, like commuters always taking the same train" (9–10). The one rule that holds for Highsmith's world is that characters certain of who they are, how things are, what is good and evil, true and false, real and unreal, are *always* in the wrong. Highsmith rings the changes on her themes of the indeterminacy of guilt, the instability of identity, and above all the heavily compromised, even reversible binary opposition of deviance and the norm in all her novels. I have arbitrarily chosen one of these, *A Dog's Ransom* (1972), while my other choice and Highsmith's finest performance, *The Talented Mr. Ripley* (1956), was inevitable.

A Dog's Ransom

For Highsmith as for Simenon in his crime novels, police investigations epitomize social stupidity and malevolence. The police, in Highsmith, hardly ever know what they are doing except when it is something wrong. Her one sympathetic policeman becomes a murderer while also having some traits of a murderee. This is Clarence Duhamell, a young, painfully well-meaning patrolman in a New York City world that is, as much as Saul Bellow's Chicago, a type of the "moronic inferno." Late in the novel Duhamell is shot in the leg in a street incident. When asked who did it, he responds absurdly and exactly, "Oh—people on a Hundred and Fifth" (206). The criminals that shot him in a random incident do not concern him; his real worry by now is not about criminals but police.

The novel begins when Ed Reynolds, a middle-aged senior editor of a publishing firm, begins receiving gratuitously vicious anonymous letters, followed by the kidnapping of his dog and a ransom demand. Clarence, who is assigned the case as a routine affair, feels an instant respect and affection for Reynolds and Greta, his Jewish wife, an escapee from the Holocaust. He feels, unilaterally, a relation to them, and puts in extra work to track down the perpetrator. This is Kenneth Rowajinski, in his fifties and unemployed except at his avocation of paranoid megalomaniac. Clarence's zeal in finding Kenneth is exceptional for a policeman but so is his blunder of leaving him in order to check with Mr. Reynolds about how best to recover the dog. (Kenneth had, as a shrewder policeman would have known, killed the dog right off.) This gives Kenneth time to burn some of the ransom money so he can claim he bribed Clarence with it. He then takes up the delightful sport of harassing Clarence's girlfriend, Marylyn. *He* has been following *Clarence*. Marylyn, dubious anyway about going with a policeman, blames Clarence for the harassment and begins to break off from him. Meanwhile, the police are giving Clarence more trouble about the bribery charge than Kenneth about the dognapping. So it is no wonder that when Clarence sees Kenneth lurking in wait of Marylyn, he decides to give him a good scare, maybe even break his nose, but gets carried away and smashes him into oblivion with his gun butt.

How are we to take this? Legally, it is a far worse crime than Kenneth's but is it morally? Do we *feel* it to be? Kenneth is an exceptionally repulsive character, especially when we see him through his own point of view. This repulsiveness can be a weapon as in his accosting of Marylyn: "Kenneth had never seen such fear so quickly. He smiled, excited and pleased. '*I'm* the one who gave your friend five hundred dollars! You're his girl-friend?' Kenneth added a phrase and licked his lips, stammering from his own sudden laughter" (128). Is it poetic justice that his goggle-eyed repulsiveness is what carries Clarence away into squashing him? Has Clarence murdered a man or exterminated a cockroach masquerading as one? Reynolds, a more than ordinarily civilized man, is led by his reflections on the moronic inferno into fantasizing the very thing Clarence later does: "He was thinking what a disgusting city New York really was. You had to rub elbows, you did rub elbows with creeps like this one every day of the week, every time you rode a bus or subway. They looked like ordinary people but they were creeps. His heart was beating rapidly, and he was imagining tearing Rowajinski limb from limb, catching him by the throat and smashing his head against a wall. He could do it, he thought" (99). It would be a heroic effort for a reader who has had any experience with "creeps" to avoid participation in this sentiment. Yet if we have read any previous Highsmith novel, we know how she equivocates on the absoluteness of the distinction between ordinary people and creeps.

Despite the fact that we never lose sympathy for Clarence and never feel it for Kenneth, moral equivocation is central to *A Dog's Ransom*. Reynolds's anticipation of Clarence's act is one of a pattern of equivalences in the novel, some of them quite odd. Manzoni, a police officer, hates Clarence in much the fashion Kenneth hates Reynolds: for being nice, civilized, college-educated. He seizes on the bribery charge as an excuse to harass Clarence and, like Kenneth, tries to get at him through Marylyn. So when Manzoni's nastiness "reminds Clarence of Rowajinski" (123), the equation seems justified. But why should Clarence have a dream in which *he* is "a cripple, more crippled than Rowajinski, scorned and avoided by other people" (180)? In another dream, "he was not quite himself and not quite a different person either. He had killed two people, and he disposed of the second corpse, like the first, by stuffing it into a large rubbish bin on a deserted street corner. The second victim was Manzoni (the first was unidentified in his dream)" (204–205). But clearly the first is Kenneth, disposed of as Kenneth had the dog. Still in the dream "he became aware that he was an eccentric character, someone to be avoided, and Clarence realized what he had done, killed two people and disposed of their bodies in such a way that they were bound to be discovered fairly soon . . . Then he suffered guilt, shame, a sense of being cut off from other people, because he had done something that no one else had done or could do" (205). But couldn't they? Reynolds *wanted* to kill Kenneth, and Manzoni, in the end, does kill Clarence.[27]

Clarence feels guilty more of murder in general than specifically that of Kenneth. He is shaken by Marylyn's rejection of him: "Her firmness was devastating to Clarence. It came to him forcefully that what he had done was repellent, shocking to other people" (179). He confesses to Reynolds:

> "I felt that I had to tell you this, Mr. Reynolds." *Absently, Ed said,*
> *"You can call me Ed."* He felt dazed by what he'd just heard, as if it
> somehow weren't real. (181, my italics)

Whether or not the murder is evil, it is anomalous, as the wonderfully inconsequential phrase italicized above indicates. Reynolds's response to Clarence's deed is ambivalent, a visceral dislike of a man who, for whatever reasons, committed a murder counteracted by an idea of him as "a young man who had lost his temper against an evil that no one else was doing anything about" (183–184). Neither Reynolds, his wife, nor Marylyn have the slightest intention of betraying Clarence to the police. Marylyn speaks for their common outlook when she turns on a police interrogator: "This whole bloody town . . . is rolling in dope and the pigs are rolling in dough from it, and you waste your time trying to find out who killed a creep. What side are you on, anyway? I'll tell you. The cops are on the *creeps'* side" (234).[28]

Clarence's increasing misery has less to do with guilt about murder than with Marylyn's rejection and Reynolds's increasing coolness, an attitude Reynolds cannot himself account for: "Ed's thoughts were not clear to himself, because what had come to him was a feeling: Clarence was odd. Or *maybe* he was odd. He just didn't *look* odd" (183). What is very odd is Clarence's emotional investment in the Reynoldses; he desperately wants their approval, really their love. This is both credible and mysterious; Marylyn is puzzled and exasperated when Clarence insists that she meet the couple. Near the end of the story, as Clarence undergoes police interrogation and torture, the only thing about which he now feels guilty is being forced to telephone Reynolds. When he is allowed to return home, this is what is on his mind: "He was thinking of calling Ed, explaining, despite the hour. Then he decided against it: wouldn't it be more annoying to ring at this hour, when perhaps they were asleep? Clarence wanted to take a shower. Then he thought, no, ring the Reynolds now, before the shower, because after the shower it will even be later. Yes, he had to apologize, and tonight, otherwise he wouldn't be able to sleep for thinking about it" (242). This issue of being considerate calls forth more uncertainty, anxiety, and guilt than Kenneth's murder.

Clarence's realization that he has lost the Reynoldses as well as Marylyn sustains him in the final police interrogations. He begins to feel separate from the process, untouchable, even exhilarated; Manzoni and the rest have no purchase on him because he no longer has anything to lose. When Manzoni comes to his apartment and tries to force a confession, his indifference provokes Manzoni into shooting him, a murder that Manzoni, a regular guy, decently on the take, will have no difficulty getting away with. But Manzoni does not long occupy his last thoughts: "Any way you looked at it, Manzoni was safe. And he thought of Marylyn, a glimpse of the impossible, the unattainable. What a pity she had never understood, really, what it was all about. And Ed and Greta—they never understood that he would practically have died for them" (256).

Is *any* conventional response to all this possible for a reader?

The Talented Mr. Ripley

This is one of the best crime novels ever. Written early in Highsmith's career (1957), this book presents a "solution" to the Highsmith problem of guilt that is both utterly unacceptable and quite difficult to avoid complicity with. Even its protagonist's meretriciousness is disturbingly appealing; within the world of the novel it makes an odd kind of sense.

Certainly, Tom Ripley, Highsmith's extraordinary protagonist, is something of a problem from the conventional point of view—that, for instance, of Simone Trevanny, a character in Highsmith's *Ripley's Game*, for whom his appeal makes no sense: "'I cannot understand. I cannot,' she said. 'Jon, why do you *see* this monster.'" Her husband, Jon, surrogate to Highsmith's bemused reader, reflects, "Tom was not really such a monster. But how to explain?" (218).

How indeed? Tom may not be a monster or at least *such* a monster, but Simone's view of him has some warranty. She has, after all, found him hosting two bodies, the death of whom she rightly suspects him of having facilitated. Luckily, Simone is unaware of four earlier murders Tom has accomplished, but Tom's attempt to reassure her becomes rather counterproductive when circumstances force him to dispatch two mafiosi with a hammer before her very eyes: "Of all times, Tom thought, when he'd meant to create a peaceable impression on Simone" (242).

What to make of a character like Ripley is at least as much a problem for the writer as for the reader. In *Plotting and Writing Suspense Fiction*, Highsmith's peculiar how-to book, she proclaims, "I think many suspense writers . . . must have some kind of sympathy and identification with criminals, or they would not become emotionally engrossed in books about them. The suspense book is vastly different from the mystery story in this respect. The suspense writer often deals much more closely with the criminal mind, because the criminal is usually known throughout the book, and the writer has to describe what is going on in his head."[29] Though Highsmith denies identifying with her protagonists, Ripley is special. On the "South Bank Show" of British television Highsmith described *The Talented Mr. Ripley* as her easiest book, completed in only six months. Perhaps this was because "I felt that Ripley was writing it."[30] In *Plotting and Writing Suspense Fiction* Highsmith declares, "There is nothing spectacular about the plot of *Ripley*, I think, but it became a popular book because of its frenetic prose, and the insolence and audacity of Ripley himself. By thinking myself inside the skin of such a character, my own prose became more self-assured than it logically should have been." Further on she distinguishes *caring about* a protagonist from *liking* him: the former "is not the same as liking the hero. It is caring whether he goes free, or caring that he is caught rightly at the end, and it is being interested in him pro or con."[31] But Highsmith does like Ripley and involves the reader in this guilty pleasure. In *The Talented Mr. Ripley* we see Ripley, initially as nebulous to himself as unimpressive to others, invent himself, confirming fraud as his vocation and murder as his expedient.

The Talented Mr. Ripley brings up certain problems: who is Ripley, why do we care about him, and, not least, why does Highsmith protect him from being "caught rightly at the end?" An obvious and wrong answer would be that he embodies our own suppressed violence, as in those Clint Eastwood and Charles Bronson

films where we feel a nice rush as the protagonist blows away anyone who annoys him (these always happening to be the children of
darkness). But Ripley's murders are never elegantly choreographed
and aesthetically appealing, as in these films and, say, Francis Ford
Coppola's *The Godfather*. Rather they are spontaneous, spasmodic,
and clumsy, leaving an acid aftertaste as in, say, Francis Ford Coppola's *The Godfather: Part Two*. Though Ripley murders so many
people over the course of four books that Highsmith herself loses
count,[32] the point is never the murders per se but the fact that he
gets away with them. What one responds to in Ripley is not the triumph of the id but the evasion of the superego. Not his spasmodic
violence but his "singular lack of guilt"[33] makes him specially appealing to the hyperconscientious. The fantasy evoked is not of violence but impunity. Highsmith carefully builds anxiety in the
Ripley novels to be dispelled at last as if by the wave of a magic
wand. The surprising ease and stylistic verve of *The Talented Mr.
Ripley* results from a release of the repressed. The novel, written, in
a sense, by Ripley himself, shares his qualities: "free in spirit and
audaciousness. And he is amusing too."[34] No wonder that Highsmith emphatically responds to a German interviewer's question
whether Ripley will ever lose out: "Nein, nein! Nicht bevor ich
sterbe. Ich mogle immer mit seinem Alter. Leider kann ich das mit
mir selber nicht machen."[35] He won't go till she does!

The Talented Mr. Ripley begins with Tom being followed by a
man whom he fears is about to arrest him. (Tom has constructed a
minor scam with IRS forms. Though criminal, Tom's scam is more
a form of play since he has not had the nerve to get money from it.
Tom's nerve improves during the course of the novel and the series,
but it is important to recognize that he is always *playing* at crime.)
The man turns out to be Herbert Greenleaf, father of Dickie Greenleaf, whom Herbert mistakenly supposes to be a close friend of
Tom's whereas they are merely slight acquaintances. Even after
being apprised of his error, Greenleaf proposes that Tom take a leave
of absence from his job in order to retrieve Dickie from the Italian
seacoast town where Dickie is living a pleasant expatriate life and
return him to his responsibilities as scion of a large shipbuilding
concern. This presents no problem for Tom since the job he must
leave is fictitious, but when he arrives in Italy he finds it more appealing to insinuate himself into Dickie's enjoyable lifestyle than to
persuade him to renounce it. The spanner gets into the works when
Dickie falls out with Tom due to Tom's jealousy of Dickie's
girlfriend, Marge. Ultimately, Tom solves the problem by replacing

Dickie; he murders him, impersonates him, and forges a will leaving his money to Tom Ripley. He is also forced to murder Dickie's friend, Freddie Miles, who discovers the impersonation.

This plot outline necessarily focuses on Tom's actions, especially his murders, but Highsmith's interest is less in Tom as murderer than in Tom as actor, performer, role player, in Tom's ability not merely to escape the limitations of his identity, but the identity itself. Tom is pleased with himself in direct ratio to his ability to stand outside this self, objectify it, play it as a role. Thus, early in the novel we get the first of many mirror images: "Slowly he took off his jacket and untied his tie, watching every move he made as if it were somebody else's movements he were watching. Astonishing how much straighter he was standing now, what a different look there was in his face. It was one of the few times in his life that he felt pleased with himself" (12–13). On the ship to Europe he signals his "starting a new life" (31) with the purchase of a cap reminiscent of the mythical helmet of invisibility:

> A cap was the most versatile of headgears, he thought, and wondered why he had never thought of wearing one before? He could look like a country gentleman, a thug, an Englishman, a Frenchman, or a plain American eccentric, depending on how he wore it. Tom amused himself with it in his room in front of the mirror. He had always thought he had the world's dullest face, a thoroughly forgettable face with a look of docility that he could not understand and a look also of vague fright that he had never been able to erase. A real conformist's face, he thought. The cap changed all that. (31)

Appearance takes priority over reality or, to be precise, for Tom it *becomes* an effective reality, creating class, moral, and national identity.

Tom's very defects turn out to be functional in his eventual transformation—his other-directed oversensitivity to others, his diffidence, his self-dislike all make it easy for him to shuck off his rather minimal self and become the other he has so well observed. His initial blunder with Dickie is to approach him at the beach in a bathing suit, a self-exposure which goes against Tom's genius and has the reverse effect to that of the versatile cap: "Tom stood there, feeling pale and naked as the day he was born. He hated bathing suits. This one was very revealing" (41). But Tom's other-directed responsiveness soon has him unconsciously copying Dickie's walk as he becomes more and more Dickie's double:

> They sat slumped in the carozza, each with a sandaled foot propped on a knee, and it seemed to Tom that he was looking in a

mirror when he looked at Dickie's leg and his propped foot beside him. They were the same height, and very much the same weight, Dickie perhaps a bit heavier, and they wore the same size bathrobe, socks, and probably shirts.

Dickie even said, "Thank you, Mr. Greenleaf," when Tom paid the carozza driver. Tom felt a little weird. (58–59)

At this point in the novel, Tom has no thought of murdering Dickie. What he aspires to is a kind of cross between a blood brother and mirror image of Dickie, living Dickie's life concurrently with him. He fantasizes murdering not Dickie but Dickie's friend, Marge, who is the reality principle interfering with Tom's dream of sharing Dickie's life. In the most bizarre scene of the novel, Tom, alone in Dickie's room and dressed in Dickie's clothes, fantasizes himself as Dickie murdering Marge:

> "Marge, you must understand that I don't *love* you," Tom said in the mirror in Dickie's voice, with Dickie's higher pitch on the empha-sized words, with the little growl in his throat at the end of the phrase that could be pleasant or unpleasant, intimate or cool, accord-ing to Dickie's mood. "Marge, stop it!" Tom turned suddenly and made a grab in the air as if he were seizing Marge's throat. He shook her, twisted her, while she sank lower and lower, until at last he left her, limp on the floor . . . "You know why I had to do that," he said, still breathlessly, addressing Marge, though he watched himself in the mirror. "You were interfering between Tom and me—No, not that! But there is a bond between us!" (68–69)

What Tom has not yet realized is that he cannot be Dickie or even effectively play Dickie so long as Dickie is alive to be and do so. There cannot be two Napoleons in the same asylum. The conclusion of the scene above is that Dickie explodes Tom's act by catching him in the performance of it. Shortly thereafter Tom has an epiphany of Dickie's (and everyone's) irremediable otherness:

> He stared at Dickie's blue eyes that were still frowning, the sun-bleached eyebrows white and the eyes themselves shining and empty, nothing but little pieces of blue jelly with a black dot in them, meaningless, without relation to him. You were supposed to see the soul through the eyes, to see love through the eyes, the one place you could look at another human being and see what really went on inside, and in Dickie's eyes Tom saw nothing more now than he would have seen if he had looked at the hard bloodless sur-face of a mirror. Tom felt a painful wrench in his breast, and he cov-ered his face with his hands. It was as if Dickie has been suddenly snatched away from him. They were not friends. They didn't know each other. It struck Tom like a horrible truth, true for all time, true for the people he had known in the past and for those he would know in the future . . . (78)

To sum up, Tom now envisions relations with others as external and illusory, a matter of surface appearances. His initial response to this vision is to wish to die.

In a way he does this. He dies to himself as Tom and becomes Dickie, after murdering the original claimant to that identity. Tom so throws himself into being Dickie that his Tom-identity becomes more distant to him; he imagines telling Marge something "in Tom's voice" (105). In becoming Dickie, he appropriates not only the latter's clothes but his smile, he packs like Dickie, paints like Dickie, even tries "to think about what Dickie would be thinking about" (144). In sum, "Now, from the moment when he got out of bed and went to brush his teeth, he was Dickie, brushing his teeth with his elbow jutted out, Dickie invariably putting back the first tie he pulled off the rack and selecting a second" (119). Being Dickie is a vast improvement over being Tom: "It was impossible ever to be lonely or bored, he thought, so long as he was Dickie Greenleaf" (106). Finally, in one of Highsmith's nicest moments, Tom-as-Dickie is asked about Tom and responds, not untruthfully, that he doesn't know him very well.

But there are problems. As Tom splits Dickie's money between his own and Dickie's bank account, he reflects that "after all, he had two people to take care of" (117). He can only be Dickie to people who have never seen Dickie, and he is forced to murder Freddie Miles for stumbling across his impersonation. Worst of all, he must go back to being Tom when Dickie becomes the main suspect in Freddie Miles's murder. This prospect of becoming a real Tom as opposed to a fake Dickie is highly depressing: "He hated going back to himself as he would have hated putting on a shabby suit of clothes, a grease-spotted, unpressed suit of clothes that had not been very good even when it was new" (164). He becomes upset at catching sight of himself in the mirror: "He looked as if he were trying to convey the emotions of fear and shock by his posture and his expression and *because the way he looked was involuntary and real*, he became suddenly twice as frightened" (164, my italics). It should be remembered that Tom enjoys mirrors when he is practicing a role before them. At this point, Tom arrives at his second major revelation— that "Tom Ripley" is like "Dickie Greenleaf"; it is a role and he controls the performance of it: "It was senseless to be despondent, anyway, even as Tom Ripley . . . Hadn't he learned something from these last months? If you wanted to be cheerful, or melancholic, or wistful, or thoughtful, or courteous, you simply had to act those things with every gesture" (165). Settling into the role of Tom Ripley, he finds enjoyment in hamming it up: "He began to feel happy even in his dreary role as Thomas Ripley. He took a pleasure in it, overdoing almost the old Tom Ripley reticence with strangers, the inferiority in every duck of his head and wistful, sidelong glance" (166). Later, Tom sets himself off from the lighter-haired Dickie by dyeing his hair "so that it would be even darker than his normal hair" (170). Tom even pulls off the tour de force of successfully playing Tom to the same policemen to whom he had earlier played Dickie.

It is not surprising that Tom "had wanted to be an actor" (35) since the main thematic pattern in *The Talented Mr. Ripley* is Tom's confirmation in the belief that acting creates reality. At this point, a distinction is necessary. It is possible to construe a determinate identity for Tom in terms of two culturally talismanic terms: "homosexual" and "schizophrenic." The reader has doubtless picked up intimations of these identities simply in the quotes I've given, especially the one in which Tom, playing Dickie to the mirror, justifies himself to an imaginary Marge. "You were interfering between Tom and me—No, not that!" *That* obviously refers to homosexual attachment, and we may suspect that Tom doth protest too much. Both earlier and later, Tom shows notable anxiety about being perceived as effeminate or homosexual and, in the scene where Dickie finds Tom playacting in Dickie's clothes, Tom is accused to his face of being "queer" (70). In what is so far the latest in the Ripley series, *The Boy Who Followed Ripley*, Tom dresses in drag partly as a disguise but more just for the experience. Most suggestive of all, Freddie Miles, before it dawns on him that Tom is impersonating Dickie Greenleaf, suspects that Tom's presence in what is supposedly Dickie's apartment wearing Dickie's clothes and jewelry must indicate a homosexual relation between them. After murdering Freddie, Tom thinks, "how sad, stupid, clumsy, dangerous and unnecessary his death had been, and how brutally unfair to Freddie. Of course, one could loath Freddie, too. A selfish, stupid bastard who had sneered at one of his best friends—Dickie certainly was one of his best friends—just because he suspected him of sexual deviation. Tom laughed at that phrase 'sexual deviation.' Where was the sex? Where was the deviation? He looked at Freddie and said low and bitterly: 'Freddie Miles, you're a victim of your own dirty mind'" (127).

The above passage also can be read as evincing Tom's schizophrenic tendencies. Tom's indignation at Freddie's suspicions seems curiously displaced. After all, Tom has *murdered* Dickie, surely rather more unfriendly an act than sneering, however unjustly, at supposedly deviant tendencies in him. Equally odd is that Tom, when he returns to his Ripley identity, feels free of guilt for Freddie's murder: "Being Tom Ripley had one compensation at least: it relieved his mind of guilt for the stupid, unnecessary murder of Freddie Miles" (166). This is because Tom was being Dickie at that time. Later, when Marge asks Tom where he had been that winter—we know, of course, that he spent it playing Dickie—Tom suffers a slight identity slippage: "'Well not with Tom, I mean, not with Dickie,' he said laughing, flustered at his slip of the tongue" (193).

But to anchor Tom's identity in latent homosexuality and schizophrenia is to read against the clear indications in Highsmith's novel that Tom's strength is in his indeterminacy of identity, in an emptiness of self that allows the superior performance of roles, eventuating in Tom's finest performance—the role of himself.[36] So my answer to the question I raised at the beginning of this section, the question of who Tom is—why we are interested in him and care about him—is that we are interested in and care about Tom precisely because he is not anybody. It is this negative capability that exempts Tom from detection and exposure. Along, that is, with the author's sympathy for what Tom isn't. Ripley's nonessentiality, his lack of a determinate identity, is the making of him. It is his talent, his vocation, and we may recall that, as Falstaff pointed out, "'Tis no sin for a man to labour in his vocation." Ripley's interest is, in fact, paradigmatic; he refers back to the trickster archetype while traversing the narrow field of postmodern identity, beginning as a sleazy version of David Riesman's other-directed man and developing into a sinister version of Robert Jay Lifton's protean man,[37] a player with his own and others' destinies.

Tom's transformation begins with his other-directed need "to make Dickie like him" (47), progresses to imitating Dickie, playing Dickie, and finally to the protean triumph of playing himself. The central feature of protean man, Lifton notes, is the "repeated, autonomously willed death and rebirth of the self," associated with the theme of "fatherlessness."[38] Tom, whose parents conveniently died in his early childhood, leaving him to the care of an aunt he detests, has carried the protean tendency to its logical extreme, reflecting at one point, "this was the real annihilation of his past and of himself, Tom Ripley, who was made up of that past and his rebirth as a completely new person" (110). Divested of past and parentage, Tom is remarkably free of the conventional constraints of superego, again matching Lifton's definition of protean man: "What has actually disappeared . . . is the *classical* superego, the internalization of clearly defined criteria of right and wrong transmitted within a particular culture by parents to their children."[39] Alisdair McIntyre, in a less sanguine view of protean man than Lifton, could have been describing Highsmith's creation: "The self thus conceived, utterly distinct on the one hand from its social embodiments and lacking on the other any rational history of its own, may seem to have a certain abstract and ghostly character."[40] One recalls Iago, whose motto is "I am not what I am."

Tom's sexual anxieties, then, can be best explained as compounding a conventional enough shame at a socially derogatory label (the novel was published in 1956) with an emergent protean man's dislike of getting fixed in *any* identity. In accord with Diderot's paradox of the actor, Tom is able to be anyone or anything only by way of being detached from the acts and identities he performs. Marge may well be on the right track when she comments in a letter to Dickie—which Tom in his Dickie role actually receives and reads—"All right, he may not be queer. He's just nothing, which is worse" (106). In the later books, we find Tom happily married to a lady as amoral and as relatively passionless as himself. And though Tom's self-detachment may be taken as schizophrenic, it is questionable whether he is any more so than other literary adumbrations or fulfillments of the protean self—say, for a short list, Gide's Lafcadio, Mann's Felix Krull, and Barth's Jacob Horner ("In a sense, I am Jacob Horner"), among others. In all these characters, as in Tom, indeterminacy of identity seems, as Lifton argues, less a dysfunction than a survival mechanism. Even when most absorbed in his role of Dickie, Tom never completely loses himself in his role:

> He felt alone, yet not at all lonely. It was very much like the feeling
> on Christmas Eve in Paris, a feeling that everyone was watching ·
> him, as if he had an audience made up of the entire world, a feeling
> that kept him on his mettle, because to make a mistake would be
> catastrophic. Yet he felt absolutely confident he would not make a
> mistake. It gave his existence a peculiar, delicious atmosphere of pu-
> rity, like that, Tom thought, which a fine actor probably feels when
> he plays an important role on a stage with the conviction that the
> role he is playing could not be played better by anyone else. He was
> himself and yet not himself. He felt blameless and free, despite the
> fact that he consciously controlled every move he made. (118)

Finally, within the conventions of the crime novel, Tom's survival and triumph is an evident authorial endorsement. The structure of Highsmith's book is built on the tension between Tom's potential exposure and punishment and his actual evasion and exemption. The novel begins with Tom's fear of arrest, and throughout the novel Tom vacillates between fear of "nemesis" (140) and confidence in luck: "Something always turned up. That was Tom's philosophy" (12). After his murder of Freddie, Tom imagines all the possibilities of disaster he must face in carrying a dead body down several flights of stairs; he "imagined it all with such intensity, writhing upstairs in his apartment, that to have descended all the stairs without a single one of his imaginings happening made him feel that he was gliding down under a magical protection of some kind, with ease in spite of the mass on his shoulder" (128). His magical protector is, of course, Highsmith, a protection she extends on condition that Tom play his roles audaciously and with a kind of artistic lightness. Tom's initial blunder with Dickie is to have come on too seriously, heavily: "Tom cursed himself for having been so heavy-handed and so humorless today. Nothing he took desperately seriously ever worked out. He'd found that out years ago" (47). (Note, again, the paradox of the actor.) Tom's *virtù* is his joy in risk taking: "Risks were what made the whole thing fun" (154).

Highsmith deliberately and shamelessly evades the conventional morality of crime and punishment. Toward the end of the novel she presents us with a barrage of signs that Tom has pushed his luck too far, has risked too much, that nemesis is finally, if a bit belatedly, approaching. Tom "considered that he had been lucky beyond reason," speculating that "something was going to happen now . . . and it couldn't be good. His luck had held just too long" (244). Certainly this is the way it ought to be and in the film version of *The Talented Mr. Ripley*, René Clement's *Plein Soleil* (*Purple Noon* is the American title), Tom is exposed at the end as Dickie's body literally surfaces. In *Plotting and Writing Suspense Fiction* Highsmith comments that it "makes a book altogether more eligible for television and movie sales if the criminal is caught, punished, and made to feel awful at the end."[41] So Tom's exemption is a thoroughly calculated flouting of moral and literary expectations, a play against genre since even in the relatively subversive crime genre a murderer-protagonist *usually* ends up being hoist with his own petard. Simone Trevanny in *Ripley's Game* stands in for readers shocked by any play with, evasion of, or undercutting of such expectation, though Highsmith rather unfairly characterizes Simone as hysterical and unreasonable for reacting with predictable shock and outrage to the bodies she keeps finding Tom stacking like cordwood. Highsmith can, however, turn back the accusation of immorality on more conventional writers and readers: "The public wants to see the law triumph, or at least the general public does, though at the same time the public likes brutality. The brutality must be on the right side, however. Sleuth-heroes can be brutal, sexually unscrupulous, kickers of women, and still be popular heroes, because they are chasing something worse than themselves, presumably."[42] Tom Ripley, it is true, has never achieved the popularity of Mike Hammer.

Still, he does all right for himself and Highsmith does all right by him. At the conclusion of *The Talented Mr. Ripley*, Tom has gotten off clear from two murders and found his forged will accepted with almost magical ease. It should not be too surprising that Highsmith's ending resembles that of Gide's *Lafcadio's Journey*, in which by a chain of extraordinary coincidences Lafcadio escapes the consequences of the gratuitous murder he has committed. Both endings imply a quasi-providential endorsement of the protagonists' actions with the respective authors in the role of deus ex machina. The deity is, of course, Proteus. Both these novels adumbrate a long reign for this usurper deity, an appropriate modern replacement for Zeus with his obsolescent baggage of nemesis and superego. In the last lines of *The Talented Mr. Ripley*, we see Tom instructing a taxi driver, "To a hotel, please . . . Il meglio albergo. Il meglio, il meglio!" (249).

Jim Thompson

No one has yet taken the possibilities of the crime novel farther than Jim Thompson. A French critic awards him a kind of literary croix de guerre: "le plus noir, le plus amer, le plus pessimiste de tous les auteurs des romans policiers américains."[43] This is exact but leaves out an essential feature; as Barry Gifford comments, Thompson has a gift for creating protagonists "possessing what can only be described as the most bizarre senses of humor in the annals of crime fiction."[44]

He not only presses tough-guy conventions to a surrealistic extreme but infiltrates them so as to sabotage them from within, sending them up and blowing them up. I shall examine two especially extremist Thompson novels: *The Getaway* (1959) and *Pop. 1280* I direct the reader to R. V. Cassill's classic essay, one which makes further commentary superfluous.[45]

I shall begin by questioning the notion that Thompson is that rare bird, the consistent nihilist. Of course, Thompson exploits the literary possibilities of negation and is fascinated with the concept of nihilism. But hardly more so than many classic American writers from Melville on. Or should one go back to Jonathan Edwards?[46] But though a *Newsweek* review of Thompson's *The Nothing Man* as exhibiting an "incipient case of cirrhosis of the soul" is apt, the conclusion that Thompson's fiction shows "the absence of any moral center at all" and that "whatever order obtains at the end of one of his stories is a writer's order, not a moralist's" is mistaken.[47] There is in Thompson a tacit moral sense that displaces the dubious moral "center." Moreover, a "writer's order" is *always* the order a writer ends up with, though this comes not out of the blue but from a complex negotiation with moral convention and moral tradition. Though compared with the pervasive nastiness of Thompson's world, Chandler's mean streets seem like Sunnybrook Farm, Thompson is no nihilist. Which is not to deny that the force of Thompson's fiction comes from skating along the razor's edge in a way that does, in fact, draw blood. But this is itself a national tradition, as American as apple pie.

The Getaway

Unfortunately, Sam Peckinpah's film version of this is far better known than the novel. Though by a brilliant director, this film subtracts from the novel at every level, beginning with the casting of Steve McQueen as the novel's Doc McCoy.[48] An effective actor in his own kind of roles, McQueen's tight-lipped intensity is the antithesis of the novel's genial protagonist, a character type rather like Drouet in Dreiser's *Sister Carrie* for whom a somewhat toned-down Robert Preston would have been ideal:

> Doc McCoy's breakfast had cooled before he could get rid of Charlie, the night clerk. But he ate it with an enjoyment which may or may not have been as real as it was apparent. It was hard to tell with Doc: to know whether he actually did like something or someone as well as he seemed to. Nor is it likely that Doc himself knew. Agreeability was his stock in trade. He had soaked up so much of it that everything he touched seemed roseately transformed. (15–16)

What underlies this affable appearance is not hatred or resentment but the absence of affect of the classic Cleckley psychopath. Doc does not have to dislike people to kill them. His partner is Carol, a kind of Marian the Librarian, rescued from small-town spinsterhood by the magnetic Doc but now as predatory and dangerous as he. A kind of taken-for-granted American affability is seen from a different perspective, its psychopathic potential foregrounded.

In the first part of the novel we see Doc and Carol in a series of hiding places from the law. These places accumulate allegorical implications until we see that Doc and Carol have been constructing their own space and this is Hell. Their first refuge is a cave, with two one-person niches, invisible because its entrance is below the water line. The two, then, are in the same predicament but isolated from each other, an exact structural analogue to a relationship between two committed egoists. Carol is driven to the real meaning of what it is to be oneself alone:

> It was like being in a coffin, she thought. A dimly lit, well-ventilated
> coffin. It wasn't uncomfortable; not yet at least. Merely confining. As
> long as one was content to remain in it, and did not try to get out . . .
>   Abruptly, she cut off the thought. (91, Thompson's ellipsis)

She had been told to take sleeping pills, as Doc does, and only by a
last-minute frantic resort to them does she survive. This is Pascalian
psychology: the prison of self can only be endured by way of nar-
cotics. Their next hiding place is a haystack-size mound of manure:
"It was partly dug out, roofed over with boards which were in turn
covered over with manure. Facing away from the house, the entrance
was covered with a piece of canvas which was smeared with cow
dung, dried now but apparently applied when wet" (97). Here, at
least, they have togetherness: "Doc politely held the canvas door
aside, and waited for Carol to precede him" (97). (Is there a more bizarre instance of conventional manners in American literature?)
Naked within the manure pile, Doc foregrounds the allegorical implication: "'Which would you say was the funniest?' he whispered.
'Me or the symbolism of the situation?'" (97). Revolting as this shelter is, Carol finds it less disorienting than the cave, even attempting
to make love. But this does not work out:

> Head tilted to one side, she gave him an impish look. Then, leaning
> forward suddenly, she took his bristled face in her hands and . . .
>   A soggy mass struck her on the forehead, slid down across her
> face. She sat back abruptly, scrubbing and brushing at herself.
> "Gaah!" she spat disgustedly, nose wrinkled. "Ugh! of all the filthy,
> messy . . ."
>   "Now, that was a shame," Doc said. "It's the heat, I suppose. It
> softens this stuff up and . . ." (98, Thompson's ellipses)

Peckinpah's film leaves out the cave and manure-pile scenes and
ends with Doc and Carol's successful flight into Mexico. But the
novel takes them onto an outlaw city in the interior:

> The tiny area where El Rey is uncrowned king appears on no maps
> and, for very practical reasons, it has no official existence. This has
> led to the rumor that the place actually does not exist, that it is only
> an illusory haven conjured up in the minds of the wicked. And since
> no one with a good reputation for truth and veracity has ever re-
> turned from it . . .
>   Well, you see?
>   But it is there, all right. (105, Thompson's ellipsis)

The kingdom of El Rey would seem almost heavenly compared with
the cave and the manure pile. Everything there is first class and at
reasonable prices. But there is a catch. The fugitives in the kingdom

have no economic resources beyond the flat sum of their loot. So the
reasonable prices of first-class items begin to eat away at this sum.
The fugitives deposit their sum in a bank since it will otherwise certainly be stolen. But this bank operates under curious though logical
principles; it charges interest *on* deposits, a percentage rate in inverse ratio to the balance "reaching a murderous twenty five percent
on amounts of fifty thousand and under" (106). But austerity is not
an option for keeping the account healthy since there are stiff charges
for falling under a fixed sum of monthly withdrawals. Most immi-
grants to the kingdom come in couples and pool their resources into
a joint account to keep up the balance. But since the sum must
inevitably shrink toward the point where it can sustain only one
person, "well, the outcome depends on which of the two is the
shrewder, the more cold-blooded or requires the least sleep" (107).
Naturally there are bitter complaints to which El Rey retorts "with
biting and ironic parables" (107). It is clear what kingdom El Rey is
ruler of; a Dante critic notes that "the devil is irony incarnate"[49]
and El Rey is the very devil: "People curse him. They call him the
devil, and accuse him of thinking he is God. And El Rey will nod to
either charge. 'But is there a difference, señor? Where the difference
between punishment and reward when one gets only what he asks
for?'" (107). In the twenty-eighth canto of Dante's *Inferno* Bertran de
Born admits the logic of his punishment: "Cosí s'osserva in me lo
contrapasso." Thompson's sinners, like Dante's, are simply fixed in
a symbolic version of the self they chose. As the still arrogant Ca-
paneus tells Dante, "Qual io fui vivo, tal son morto."[50] The "contrapasso" in El Rey's kingdom is an essentialization of the zero-sum
game played by those whose gains were taken from others, whether
by force or fraud. The kingdom simply literalizes this principle:

El Rey does only what he has to. His criminal sanctuary is a big
improvement over most. He does not kill you for your loot. He gives
you value for your money. He runs a first-class place, and he could
not do so if you were allowed to be miserly. Nor can he permit you
to linger on when your money is gone. There would be no room for
newcomers if he did; and allowed to accumulate, you and your kind
would soon take over. You would be in his place, and he would be in
yours . . . And he knows this. He and his native subjects know it. It
explains their delight in irony, in symbolism; in constantly holding
up a mirror to you so that you must see yourself as you are, and as
they see you. (111, my ellipsis)

The principle reaches its apogee in the village Doc comes upon
while walking in the hills: "The one street was attractively cob-

blestoned; the buildings were freshly whitewashed. Drifting to him on the breeze came the smell of roasting peppery meat" (108). When Doc finds that the village is a kind of cooperative, the inhabitants contributing their labor to its upkeep in lieu of money, he suggests to the village carabinero that he might move there but is told he is not yet eligible. The village, in fact, is where those must go who have run out of money in the city. Its most peculiar feature is that neither food nor drink is on sale since there is no money to buy with. As the carabinero tells Doc, "Nothing is brought from the city. Nothing but the people themselves" (109). Doc has a realization:

> *That smell that filled the air. The odor of peppery, roasting flesh. Peppers could be had anywhere, for the picking, the asking, but the meat . . .*
> "Quite fitting, eh señor? And such an easy transition. One need only live literally as he has always done figuratively." (109)

The novel ends with Doc and Carol, mutually aware of their plans to murder each other, drinking a toast to their "getaway" (115).

Pop. 1280

The irony of Thompson's *The Getaway* is that Doc and Carol didn't need to go through their ordeal to find El Rey's kingdom because they had it within them all along. For that matter, why cross the Rio Grande?

One wonders whether Joel and Ethan Koen's original screenplay of *Blood Simple* (1983) was influenced by Thompson's fiction? The opening voice-over monologue of the private detective (played with a wheezingly sublime nastiness by M. Emmet Walsh) almost out-Thompsons Thompson:

> The world is full of complainers. The fact is nothing comes with a guarantee. And I don't care if you're the Pope of Rome, the President of the United States, the man of the year, something can all . . . go wrong. And go ahead, you know, complain, tell your problems to your neighbor, ask for help and watch him fly. Now in Russia they got it mapped out so that everyone pulls for everyone else. That's the theory, anyway. But what I know about is Texas. Down here, you're on your own.

Later this character hands his client a set of photographs of the client's wife and her boyfriend in bed with the tactful remark, "I know where you can get these framed." And when the client shows up for a meeting with his finger in a splint, broken by his wife when he attempted to abduct and rape her, the detective cheerily greets him with the remark, "Stick your finger up the wrong person's ass?" The detective then tells how his friend, Creighton, managed to get both hands in casts, provoking this sensitive condolence: "I hope your wife really loves you because for the next five weeks you're not going to be able to wipe your own goddamn ass. That's a test isn't it? A test of true love?"

Texans didn't invent obscenity and scatology (though they would have been mighty proud), but there is a characteristic Texas idiom of what Robert M. Adams nicely terms "dysphuism."[51] This is the exact reverse of the pretentiously elegant language of euphuism, with its own dictionary, Ken Weaver's *Texas Crude*, which memorializes such phrases as "I don't care if it harelips the Governor," "he just can't do *anything* without stepping on his dick," "try that and you are in a world of shit," and, finally, a succinct expression of Texas folk ideology: "You can wish in one hand and shit in the other and see which one fills up first."[52]

A philosophy of sorts shows in this lexicon, its first premise being that the most valid phenomenological starting point for a general theory of the nature of things is to reduce everything to its lowest common physical denominator. While expressing an ontology, the lexicon can become a weapon in a rhetorical challenge where put-on segues into gross-out. The extraordinary first-person killer of *Pop. 1280* could be taken as an *expansum ad absurdum* of the motifs of unreliable narration, seductive point of view, and open-ended, decentered irony, an overdetermination of those tendencies that Wayne Booth in *The Rhetoric of Fiction* found so morally questionable. Booth saw Céline's *Voyage au bout de la nuit* as a corrupting book, one with a "sympathy for evil."[53] Whatever one makes of Booth's conclusions, his questions are apt and Thompson does remind one of Céline. Is what fascinates us in *Pop. 1280* its sympathy for the devil?

Nick Corey of *Pop. 1280* may be the most unnerving first-person killer in the crime novel genre. Obscene, scatological, blasphemous, malicious, murderous, probably crazy, he is also an intelligent, ironic buffoon, a satanic trickster whose clownish posturings do not quite conceal inner anguish. He is the kind of narrator, along with Lou Ford in *The Killer Inside Me*, who makes readers wonder about a writer. What manner of man could create such a *monstre sacré*? Jim Thompson's agent, Jerry Bick, describes him as a man of "perfect integrity. He was absolutely the most honest, generous, gentle man I have ever known." He remembers Thompson as "the kind of man who would agree to write a letter to you for nothing, and then takes eight days slaving over it." How could such a man create so absurd a world, delineating it with a kind of horror comedy? But who else, in fact? Bick notes, "He was sensitive, even nervous. He was like a child, he couldn't bear the realities of everyday life."[54] This blend of a sense of the contradictions and cruelties of life, disgust for hypocrisy, and an awareness of the gap between ideal and real is the formula for the creation of an irony that by creatively matching the terror of life maintains control in the face of it.

Ursula Brumm in *American Thought and Religious Typology* compellingly analyzes the protagonist of *Pop. 1280:* "He is a man with a damaged psyche. He has not only fallen out of the divine world order, he also doubts, the passion of his accusations notwithstanding, that its evils are capable of rational explanation . . . Being motivated by this abysmal despair of the divine world order, which leads to a psychological compulsion with no escape, makes [him] more modern than the demonic heroes of Romanticism, who do evil because they are inexplicably fascinated by evil itself . . . He is the man enraged by the contradictions in the divine world order . . ."[55]

Except this is about Captain Ahab. It fits Thompson's protagonist point for point, though he seems anything but a head-on metaphysical rebel, having made a comfortable accommodation to the state of things:

> Well, sir, I should have been sitting pretty, just about as pretty as a man could sit. Here I was, the high sheriff of Potts County, and I was drawing almost two thousand dollars a year [the novel is set sometime before 1918]—not to mention what I could pick up on the side . . . I guess you could say Kingdom Come was really here as far as I was concerned. I had it made, and it looked like I could go on having it made—being high sheriff of Potts County—as long as I minded my own business and didn't arrest no one unless I just couldn't get out of it and they didn't amount to nothin'. (365)

But there are complications both with Nick's relation to his world and our relation to Nick:

> And yet I was worried, I had so many troubles that I was worried plumb sick.
> I'd sit down to a meal of maybe half a dozen pork chops and a few fried eggs and a pan of hot biscuits with grits and gravy, and I couldn't eat it. Not all of it. I'd start worrying about those problems of mine, and the next thing you knew I was getting up from the table with food still left on my plate.
> It was the same way with sleeping. You might say I didn't really get no sleep at all. I'd climb in bed, thinking this was one night I was

> bound to sleep, but I wouldn't. It'd be maybe twenty or thirty
> minutes before I could doze off. And then, no more than eight or
> nine hours later, I'd wake up. Wide awake. And I couldn't go back to
> sleep, frazzled and wore out as I was. (365)

How are we to take Nick's comments on food and sleep? Is he really
that dumb? If ironic, at whom or what is the irony directed? At himself, his own exaggerated gluttony and sloth? Or at a moderately fas-
tidious reader, as possibly in another passage: "I got out of bed that
morning, and I shaved and took a bath even if it was only Monday
and I'd washed real good the Saturday before" (366).

Perhaps he really is the buffoon that people, his wife especially,
take him for. One of his troubles is that the two town pimps have
been playing practical jokes on him, "not showing me no respect at
all like you'd naturally expect pimps to show a sheriff, even if he was
shaking 'em down for a little money" (370). And his nonperformance
is a little too little even for the undemanding folks of Potts County:
". . . I'd begun to suspect lately that people weren't quite satisfied
with me. That they expected me to do a little something instead of
just grinning and joking and looking the other way" (370). He decides to visit Ken Lacey, a sheriff of an adjoining county, to ask advice. Ken introduces him to his deputy, Buck, at the beginning of a
scene in which it is clear that someone is putting someone on:

> "This here Buck is the smartest deputy I got," Ken said, as we all had
> a drink . . .
> Buck said all he'd ever done was just to try to do his duty, and Ken
> said, "No, sir, he was smart."
> "Like old Nick here. That's why he's sheriff of the forty-seventh
> largest county in the state."
> "Yeah?" Buck said. "I didn't know they was but forty-seven coun-
> ties in the state."
> "Pre-zackly!" Ken said, sort of frowning at him. (377)

The book's title derives from Nick's comment that a road sign just
outside his county seat of Pottsville reads: "Pop. 1280 . . . Twelve
hundred and eighty souls" (377). This begins a debate in which Ken
argues, "That twelve hundred and eighty would be countin' niggers—them Yankee lawmakers force us to count 'em—and niggers
ain't got no souls" (379). The conversation gets progressively grosser
until finally Ken and Buck treat Nick to a practical demonstration of
pimp-control by kicking him out the door. Twice, since he bends
over *again*. This time he lands hard on his elbow and Ken, pretend-
ing concern, asks where he is hurt. Nick's response is revelatory:

"I'm not positive," I said. "It could be either the *radius* or the *ulna.*"
  Buck gave me a sudden sharp look out from under his hatbrim.
Sort of like I'd just walked into the room and he was seeing me for
the first time. But of course Ken didn't notice anything. Ken had so
much on his mind, I reckon, helping poor stupid fellas like me, that
he maybe didn't notice a lot of things. (382)

Ken's idea is to retaliate with something twice as hurtful as the
original provocation or you merely end up with a standoff. He gives
Nick some benevolent advice:

"So I'll tell you what to do about them pimps. The next time they
even look like they're goin' to sass you, you just kick 'em in the balls
as hard as you can."
  "Huh?" I said. "But—but don't it hurt awful bad?"
  "Pshaw, 'course it don't hurt. Not if you're wearin' a good pair o'
boots without no holes in 'em." (383)

At this point Buck intervenes, claiming that actually Ken would
be harder yet on such types—he would "just yank out his pissolver
and shoot 'em right in their sassy mouths." When Ken agrees, Nick
decides that "It looked like I'd got what I came for, and it was getting
kind of late by then. So I thanked Ken for his advice, and stood up"
(383). Buck accompanies Nick to the station; "We were getting along
real fine, just like I thought we might, and we had a lot of things to
say to each other" (384).
  By this point we know who is *ultimately* putting on whom. Buck
realizes from Nick's vocabulary that he is not the fool he pretends to
be and gives Nick what he came for by manipulating Ken into advis-
ing the pimps' murder. Nick and Buck are getting along real fine because Nick is arranging to frame Ken for murder and Buck wants
Ken's job. So Potts County politics is more byzantine than it seemed,
even having a foreign policy. Buck caught on to Nick precisely because of the attribute that Ken later cites as proof that Buck is "a
low-down maniac": "I mean I caught him reading a book . . . Yes, sir,
I caught him red-handed. Oh, he claimed he was only lookin' at the
pitchers, but I knew he was lyin'" (390). This exploits an ambiguity
in a still-current Texas phrase:

"He's read a book."
  1. He has academic pretensions, and no common sense. Said sar-
castically. "He can't change a tire but he's read a book."
  2. He really is smart. Said with deference. "That guy with the
glasses on; he's a good hand, and he's read a book. Wish I had six
more just like him."[56]

Buck, like Nick, has read a book.

In pillowtalk with the schoolmistress, Amy, Nick explains why he talks as he does: grammar and logic are not in demand in Potts County. The role of buffoon is protective coloration. When in Potts County . . . His policy as sheriff is to let people be. Nick has not always felt this way; his excoriating cynicism derives from an underlying *horror mundi:*

> There were the helpless little girls, cryin' when their own daddies crawled into bed with 'em. There were the men beating their wives, the women screamin' for mercy. There were the kids wettin' the beds from fear and nervousness, and their mothers dosin' 'em with red pepper for punishment. There were the haggard faces, drained white from hookworm and blotched with scurvy. There was the near-starvation, the never-bein' full, the debts that always outrun the credits. There was the how-we-gonna-eat, how-we-gonna-sleep, how-we-gonna-cover-our-poor-bare-asses thinkin'. The kind of thinkin' that when you ain't doing nothing else but that, why you're better off dead. Because that's the emptiness thinkin' and you're already dead inside, and all you'll do is spread the stink and the terror, the weepin' and wailin', the torture, the starvation, the shame of your deadness. Your emptiness. (482)

Thompson plants a psychological explanation for Nick's malaise in his relation with a father who hated him from the moment his mother died in bearing him. But in relation to Nick's growing murderousness (four personal and two he set up) it seems inadequate. Another father is accused: "I shuddered, thinking how wonderful was our Creator to create such downright hideous things in the world, so that something like murder didn't seem at all bad by comparison. Yea, verily, it was indeed merciful and wonderful of Him" (482). Nick has decided that if you can't fight Him, join Him. As he explains to George Barnes, the operative from the Talkington Detective Agency, hired by the family of one of the two pimps Nick murdered, he has cast himself as the Messiah Potts County deserves:

> "I guess mostly what I mean is that there can't be no personal hell because there ain't no personal sins. They're all public, George, we all share in the other fellas' and the other fellas all share in ours. Or maybe I mean this, George, that I'm the Savior himself, Christ on the Cross come right here to Potts County, because God knows I was needed here, an' I'm goin' around doing kindly deeds—so that people will know they got nothing to fear, and if they're worried about hell they don't have to dig for it." (471)

Barnes himself as a Talkington (read Pinkerton) operative is an example of the inverted actuality of law and order:

"So you're with the Talkington Agency," I said. "Why, god-dang if I
ain't heard a lot about you people! Let's see now, you broke up that
big railroad strike, didn't you?"
    "That's right. . . . The railroad strike was one of our jobs."
    "Now, by golly, that really took nerve," I said. "Them railroad
workers throwin' chunks of coal at you an' splashin' you with water,
and you fellas without nothin' to defend yourself with except shot-
guns an' automatic rifles! Yes, sir, god-dang it, I really got to hand it
to you!" (467)

Later Nick explains to his *other* girlfriend, Rose, why he does not
feel responsible for their adultery, his murder of her husband, and
his tricking her into killing his own wife:

"Not a speck," I said. "Just because I put temptation in front of
people, it don't mean they got to pick it up."
    "I asked you a question, damn you! Who planned those murders?
Who tells a lie every time he draws a breath? Who the hell is it that's
been fornicating with me, and God knows how many others?"
    "Oh, well," I said. "It don't count when I do those things."
    "It don't count! What the hell do you mean?"
    I said I mean I was just doing my job, followin' the holy precepts
laid down in the Bible. "It's what I'm supposed to do, you know, to
punish the heck out of people for bein' people. To coax 'em into re-
vealin' theirselves, an' then kick the crap out of 'em. And it's a god-
danged hard job, Rose, honey, and I figure that if I can get a little
pleasure in the process of trappin' folks I'm mighty well entitled
to it."
    Rose stared at me, frowning.
    "What is this?" she said. "What kind of nutty talk is that?"
    "Well, now, I guess it does sound kind of nutty," I said, "but that
ain't hardly no ways my fault. By rights, I should be rompin' on the
high an' the mighty, the folks that really run this country. But I ain't
allowed to touch them, so I've got to make up for it by being twice as
hard on the white trash an' Negroes, and people like you that let
their brains sink down to their butts because they couldn't find no
place else to use them. Yes, sir, I'm laborin' in the Lord's vineyard,
and if I can't reach up high, I got to work all the harder on the low-
hangin' vines. For the Lord loveth a willin' worker, Rose; He liketh
to see a man bustin' his ass during workin' hours. And I got them
hours cut way, way down with eatin' and sleepin' but I can't eat and
sleep all the time." (487)

The last sentence explains Nick's initial gluttony and sloth as his
temporary evasion of his mission to further God's injustice in Potts
County:

I yawned and stretched. I sure was needing some sleep, but I guess
I'm always in need of food. Because my labors were mighty ones—ol'
Hercules didn't know what hard work was—and what is there to do

but eat and sleep? And when you're eatin' and sleepin' you don't have
to fret about things that you can't do nothing about. And what else is
there to do but laugh and joke . . . how else can you bear up under
the unbearable?
It was a cinch that cryin' didn't do no good. I'd tried that before in
my agony—I'd cried out as loud as a fella could cry—an' it hadn't
done no good at all. (474)

De profundis clamavi.

Standard psychological explanations are not adequate to Nick's
irony and despair. His condition answers better to what might be
called theological psychoanalysis (on the analogy with existential
psychoanalysis). Seeing no real possibility of *caritas* or justice in his
world, Nick has made an ironic concession to its basic evil. He is
doing what any other sheriff does, the difference being that in naming it accurately, he bares the device. Clearly, he is God's agent to
enforce cosmic irony in Potts County. The doctrine according to
Nick has an ironic consistency, even to its version of the golden rule,
atonement, and vocation: "Because it was all so clear to me, Christ
knew it was clear: love one another and don't screw no one unless
they're bending over, and forgive us our trespasses because we may
be a minority of one. For God's sake, *for God's sake*—why else had I
been put here in Potts County, and why else did I stay here? Why
else, who else, what else but Christ Almighty would put up with
it?" (494). Buck, to whom he tries to explain this, is dubious:

"Prob'ly got yourself mixed up with that other fella," he said.
"The one with the same front initial."
"That's right, Buck!" I said. "That's right! I'm both don't you see?
The fella and the one that does the betrayin' all in one man!" (493)

Nick has two "front" initials, N for Nick and C for Corey; he sees
himself as uniting Old Nick and Christ in a single principle. If
Christ stopped at Eboli what could He make of Potts County? So
Nick was called.
He plays his satanic role with a certain relish; when Rose accuses
him of enjoying her distress he responds: "Not really . . . It's just
part of my job, you know, to gloat over folks in trouble" (488). Theo-
logically considered, Nick is a play on the archetype of the scourge
of God, who serves as the instrument of God's wrath against a community without thereby escaping reprobation for his own sins of
anger and pride. We have by now seen a blackly comic providence
operate in *A Hell of a Woman* and *The Getaway.* Roy Battenhouse
argues an orthodox outcome to Marlowe's *Tamburlaine,* the most
obvious instance of the scourge theme, in that Marlowe "expected

his audience to understand Tamburlaine's tragedy as an instance of the unwitting self-destruction God assigns his presumptuous Scourges."[57] I do not think it strains *Pop. 1280* any more than Battenhouse strains the ending of *Tamburlaine* (whose protagonist dies of fever after his venture at Malthusian population control) to construct an orthodox reading of the novel in terms of theological psychoanalysis: Nick, unable to hear an answer to his cry from the depths, retreats into engrossment with this world at its most material, devoting himself to Gluttony and Sloth, really forms of a deeper Sloth, a spiritual inertia yielding to Despair. But forced out of this protective retreat, Nick believes himself called to become the Scourge of Potts County (somewhat in the register of "the Scunge of Corsica"), thereby turning from the sins of the flesh to the sins of the spirit: Anger and especially Pride, carried to its extreme in Nick's conflation of the roles of Christ and Satan and appropriation of these to himself. His evident misery is the inherent punishment of this presumptuousness.

But while all the above is, I believe, clearly implied in the novel, there are too many contradictions and inconsistencies to provide reassuring moral closure. Nick's misery is more than slightly offset by his obvious enjoyment of his malice and he is by no means clearly punished for his blasphemies. In fact, we are not quite certain how much Thompson sees them as blasphemies. Sin may be self-punishing in Thompson's home-brew variations on Dante's *Inferno*, but Nick's role seems closer to El Rey, the ironic explicator of the process, the master of ceremonies at the Inferno Club, than its prisoner, Doc McCoy. Having learned from Ken, Nick inflicts far more punition than he receives. The novel concludes with Nick's apparently irresolvable dilemma: two characters are in a position to expose him if he does not meet their irreconcilable demands. Perhaps this implies his impending defeat. The novel's final passage is Nick's exclamation to Buck, one of the characters coercing him: "So here it is, Buck, here's my decision. I thought and I thought and then I thought some more, and finally I came to a decision. I decided I didn't no more know what to do than if I was just another lousy human being!" (494). But his dilemma seemed equally irresolvable in the first chapter of the novel, which ends with this reflection:

> So I thought and I thought and then I thought some more. And finally I came to a decision.
> I decided I didn't know what the heck to do. (365)

He did, in fact, work it out. And seductive narrator that he is, are we sure we wish for his downfall or fully dissent from his irony and cynicism? The absurdity of Nick's world is not offset, as in *A Hell of a Woman*, by clues that its protagonist has misconstructed it. Yet this world is based not on the writer's disregard of central values but his intense, anguished, comic, thwarted grasp after them, Superego running wild, having appropriated the anarchic comic energy of Id, a Presbyterian conscience that, having lost doctrinal support, turns to irony as an instrument of discord with things as they are.

Meredith Brody notes the difficulty of transferring a Thompson story to film. Even *Série Noire*, a fine film that "adheres to the plot of . . . A Hell of a Woman* with Gallic strictness" cannot handle the double narrative of the novel's conclusion.[58] But Brody admits the perfection of the film version of *Pop. 1280*, Bertrand Tavernier's *Coup de Torchon* (*Clean Slate*, 1981). This eerily brilliant movie stays extraordinarily close to Thompson's novel, some of its dialogue straight translation into French and all of it finely translating the novel's tone and feel. Tavernier's equivalent of West Texas around 1918, eloquently described by Nick as "just about as close to the asshole of creation as you can get without having a finger snapped off" (489), is French West Africa in 1938, perhaps a libel on the latter.

Blood Simple ends much in the spirit of *Pop. 1280*. The loathsome detective, having murdered the husband and lover of the female protagonist, pursues her through the rooms of her apartment, though all she sees of him is his gloved hand. She doesn't know for sure that her husband, Marty, is dead and thinks it is Marty who is pursuing her. In the film's last moments she shoots the detective through a door he is opening and he collapses backward into the adjacent room. She *still* has not seen him and, hearing him stir, she says defiantly, "I'm not afraid of you, Marty." The detective laughs and laughs and laughs. Then, with his dying breath, he replies: "Well, ma'am, if I see him I'll sure give him the message."

Georges Simenon: "there are no criminals." (Courtesy Roger-Viollet)

Margaret Millar: "a puzzle really of persons." (© Hal Boucher Photo)

Patricia Highsmith: "one of the true masters of crime." (Courtesy Diogenes Verlag AG)

Jim Thompson: "a man of 'perfect integrity.'" (Courtesy Alberta Thompson)

Coda

IT WOULD REASSURE me no end to conclude this study with a definitive aesthetic, political, and moral evaluation of the genre of crime fiction. But this could only falsify a genre the central convention of which is deviancy, sometimes deviance from a sense of closure. Marxist critics such as Ernest Mandel and Stephen Knight have plausibly analyzed the manner in which the conventions of the detective novel, not excluding the hard-boiled American variation, accredit the political and economic status quo.[1] I can find no such neat correlation in the crime novel. Certainly Shelley Smith for one is a moral traditionalist, but I fail to see how this discredits her perceptions. It is arguable that the privately motivated nature of crimes in the genre divert us from more important public wrongs. But I can only despair of a reader, especially a critic, who supposes any form of murder to be trivial.

Against the American tough-guy mode of crime novel a different objection can be raised. No one could pretend that these books reassure us about the American night that frequently swallows up their characters. The argument here would be that the isolated and hopeless struggle of the protagonist becomes a left-handed acknowledgment of the futility of resistance, inspiring not a desire to communally seek justice but merely a resigned, if bitter, concession to fatality. This was essentially Sartre's case against Faulkner, a humanistic French response to the American pull toward nihilism.[2] But Sartre's own commitment to commitment led him to some extremely dubious *engagements*.[3]

Perhaps then I could turn to negation as my ground of evaluation, grading writers on a scale of dissonance, the best those who achieve an absolute dissidence of dissent. But I can find no such reliable absolute and if my texts very nearly find a common ground in the disturbance they cause, the modes of this disturbance are disturbingly variable. What is disturbing in Smith *is* her traditionalism, deployed in response to the dogmas of modern liberalism, while Jim Thompson's almost Calvinistic moral ferocity can be misread as nihilism; indeed, it is *less* unnerving when so read, easier to back off from.

So without a well-formed critical pot to parse in, I can only resort to something more provisional. So without claiming a universal aesthetic or even ethical relevance for them, I shall quote a number of Kafka aphorisms that seem to be correlative to the themes of this chapter and this study. Of course, since these were allegedly recorded by Gustav Janouch from conversations, we have no absolute assurance of their authenticity:

> One cannot break one's chains when there are not chains to be seen. One's imprisonment is therefore organized as a perfectly ordinary, not over-comfortable daily life. Everything looks as if it were made of solid, lasting stuff. But on the contrary it is a life in which one is falling toward the abyss. It isn't visible. But if one closes one's eyes, one can hear its rush and roar.

> Our superhuman greed and vanity, the hubris of our will to power. We struggle to achieve values which are not really values at all, in order to destroy things on which our whole existence as human beings depends. Therein lies a confusion which drags us into the mire and destroys us.

> One look out the window will show the world to you. Where are the people going? What do they want? We no longer recognize the metaphysical order of things. In spite of all the noise, everyone is dumb and isolated within himself. The interrelation of objective and personal values doesn't function any more. We live not in a ruined but a bewildered world. Everything creaks and rattles like the rigging of an unseaworthy sailing ship.

> Mankind can only become a grey, formless, and therefore nameless mass through a fall from the Law which gives it form. But in that case there is no above and below anymore; life is levelled out into

mere existence; there is no struggle, no drama, only the consumption of matter, decay. But that is not the world of the Bible and of Jewry.[4]

I do not claim my writers meet these standards. Few if any writers, mainstream or even canonized, do. But I find them *thinkable* within these terms. And not despite but because of their negotiation with convention. This has been my argument throughout.

Notes

Introduction

1. The term *crime novel* is problematic in that many critics use it as synonymous with *detective story, mystery,* and *thriller.* Moreover, some critics who recognize the distinctively oppositional genre that is my subject call it *suspense novel* or *inverted detective novel.* But *crime novel* is used most often to describe the kind of novel I shall be examining, while *suspense novel* can be another name for *spy novel,* and *inverted detective novel* is used almost exclusively to describe English rather than American crime novels.

2. Alastair Fowler, *Kinds of Literature,* p. 38.

3. Ibid.

4. Ibid., p. 31.

5. Italo Calvino, "Readers, Writers and Literary Machines," *New York Times Book Review,* September 7, 1986, p. 30.

6. Ibid., p. 36.

7. Thelma M. Smith and Ward W. Miner, *Transatlantic Migration: The Contemporary American Novel in France,* p. 69. Also see Jean-Paul Sartre, "American Novelists in French Eyes," *Atlantic* 178 (August 1946): 114–118.

8. Steven Mailloux, *Interpretive Conventions,* p. 139.

9. Charles Eric Reeves, "'Conveniency to Nature': Literary Art and Arbitrariness," *PMLA* 101 (October 1986): 801.

10. Blake Morrison, "Love and Betrayal in the Mist," *Times Literary Supplement*, April 11, 1986, p. 381.

11. For this distinction see Michael Colarcurcio, "The Symbolic and the Symptomatic: D. H. Lawrence in Recent American Criticism," *American Quarterly* 27 (October 1975): 486–501.

12. Some outstanding examples are Edward Anderson, *Thieves Like Us* (1937); Carolyn Banks, *The Girls on the Row* (1984); Nicholas Blake, *The Beast Must Die* (1938); Stanley Ellin, *Mirror Mirror on the Wall* (1972); Helen Eustis, *The Horizontal Man* (1946) and *The Fool Killer* (1954); Celia Fremlin, *The Trouble Makers* (1963) and *Prisoner's Base* (1967); David Goodis, *Down There* (1956); C. W. Grafton, *Beyond a Reasonable Doubt* (1950); William Lindsay Gresham, *Nightmare Alley* (1946); W. L. Heath, *Ill Wind* (1957); Dorothy Hughes, *Ride the Pink Horse* (1946) and *In a Lonely Place* (1947); Sebastien Japrisot, *A Trap for Cinderella* (1979); Walter Tyrer, *Such Friends Are Dangerous* (1954).

13. For an account of the metaphysical detective story see Michael Holquist, "Whodunit and Other Questions: Metaphysical Detective Stories in Postwar Fiction," in *The Poetics of Murder*, ed. Glenn W. Most and William W. Stowe; Patricia Merrivale, "The Flaunting of Artifice in Vladimir Nabokov and Jorge Luis Borges," *Wisconsin Studies in Contemporary Literature* 8 (Spring 1967); Frank Kermode, "Novel and Narrative," in *The Poetics of Murder*, ed. Most and Stowe.

1. The Crime Novel: Guilt and Menace

1. See Walter L. Reed, *An Exemplary History of the Novel*, and Robert Scholes and Robert Kellogg, *The Nature of Narrative*.

2. Frederic Jameson, *The Political Unconscious*, pp. 141, 145, 126.

3. Fowler, *Kinds of Literature*, p. 175.

4. Julian Symons, *Bloody Murder: From the Detective Story to the Crime Novel*, pp. 162–164.

5. "Interview with P. D. James," in Diana Cooper-Clark, *Designs of Darkness: Interviews with Detective Novelists*, pp. 20–21.

6. Abraham Kaplan, "The Aesthetics of the Popular Arts," in *Popular Arts: A Critical Reader*, ed. Irving Deer and Harriet A. Deer, p. 336.

7. Jacques Barzun, *The Delights of Detection*, p. 18.

8. Brophy, along with P. D. James, is one of the few critics who defines the crime novel in a manner parallel to my own. But, though her analysis is brilliant, she acknowledges only Simenon and Highsmith as first-rate performers in the genre. See Brigid Brophy, *Don't Never Forget*, pp. 150–151. Similarly, in a perceptive essay on Margaret Millar, John M. Reilly gets everything right except for taking devices to be *sui generis* that are actually *criminis generis*. See Reilly, "Margaret Millar," in *Ten Women of Mystery*, ed. Earl F. Bargannier. Glenn Most, in one of the best structural analyses of the detective form, sees "mysteries in which the narrator is the murder-

er . . . or the hero is" as "only deformations of the expected conventions and must be understood as such; that is their point." See Most, "The Hippocratic Smile," in *The Poetics of Murder*, ed. Most and Stowe, p. 364. In fact, such conventions add up to a deviant genre.

9. John Cawelti, *Adventure, Mystery, and Romance*, p. 92.

10. Brophy, *Don't Never Forget*, p. 141.

11. Nancy Wingate, "Getting Away with Murder: An Analysis," *Journal of Popular Culture* 12 (Spring 1979): 598.

12. Brophy, *Don't Never Forget*, p. 140.

13. Reginald Hill, "Scuttlings and Skewerings," *Times Literary Supplement*, April 25, 1986, p. 454.

14. Cawelti, *Adventure, Mystery, and Romance*, p. 96. Auden's classic essay is collected in his *The Dyer's Hand*.

15. Tzvetan Todorov, "The Typology of Detective Fiction," in *The Poetics of Prose*, p. 51.

16. See Peter L. Berger and Thomas A. Luckmann, *The Social Construction of Reality*.

17. James Sandoe, "Dagger of the Mind," in *The Art of the Mystery Story*, ed. Howard Haycraft, p. 260.

18. That readers forced Doyle to resurrect Holmes from Reichenbach Falls proves the force of this expectation. Recently, however, Nicholas Freeling not only killed off a series detective but had his widow solve the crime.

19. See F. Tennyson Jesse, *Murder and Its Motives*, pp. 150–151; and Georges Simenon, *When I Was Old*, tr. Helen Eustis, p. 190. Simenon's translator, Helen Eustis, is herself a formidable crime writer, one of many I had to pass over in this book. See especially *The Fool Killer*.

20. Brophy, *Don't Never Forget*, p. 154.

21. George Grella, "The Formal Detective Novel," in *Detective Fiction*, ed. Robin W. Winks; George Grella, "Murder and the Mean Streets: The Hard-Boiled Detective Novel," in *Detective Fiction: Crime and Compromise*, ed. Dick Allen and David Chacko; and Cawelti, *Adventure, Mystery, and Romance*.

22. Grella, "The Formal Detective Novel," p. 101.

23. Jerry Palmer points out that there is deduction even in Mickey Spillane. See *Thrillers*, p. 102.

24. Cawelti, *Adventure, Mystery, and Romance*, p. 88.

25. William James, *Principles of Psychology*, vol. 1, p. 442.

26. William W. Stowe, "From Semiotics to Hermeneutics: Modes of Detection in Doyle and Chandler," in *The Poetics of Murder*, ed. Most and Stowe, p. 368.

27. See Frederic Jameson, *The Prison House of Language*.

28. Dashiell Hammett, *The Maltese Falcon*, p. 107.

29. Stephen Knight, *Form and Ideology in Crime Fiction*, p. 147.

30. James McLaren Ross, *Memoirs of the Forties*, pp. 78–79.

31. Julian Symons, "Out of the Thin Man's Shadow," *Times Literary Supplement*, March 14, 1986, p. 266.

32. Symons, *Bloody Murder,* p. 207.

33. David Nokes, "The Brimstone Voice," *Times Literary Supplement,* December 26, 1986, p. 1450.

34. Ibid.

2. Deviant Impulses: Incest and Doubling

1. Nathanael West, "Some Notes on Miss L.," in *Nathanael West: Twentieth Century Views,* ed. Jay Martin, pp. 66–67.

2. Erich Heller, "Conversation on *The Magic Mountain,*" in *Thomas Mann,* ed. Henry Hatfield, p. 85.

3. Sigmund Freud, *Beyond the Pleasure Principle,* tr. James Strachey, p. 39.

4. Ibid., pp. 44–45.

5. Sigmund Freud, "A Special Type of Choice of Object Made by Men," in *On Creativity and the Unconscious,* p. 165.

6. Ibid., pp. 166–167.

7. Quoted in Peter Brooks, "Freud's Masterplot," *Reading for the Plot,* p. 106.

8. Sigmund Freud, "The Most Prevalent Form of Degradation in Erotic Life," in *On Creativity and the Unconscious,* p. 173.

9. Brooks, "Freud's Masterplot," p. 109.

10. Sigmund Freud, "The 'Uncanny,'" in *On Creativity and the Unconscious,* p. 157.

11. Robert Graves, *The Greek Myths,* pp. 125, 38.

12. W. H. Mendel, "Schizophrenia," in *Encyclopedia of Psychology,* ed. Raymond J. Corsini, vol. 3, p. 267.

13. Ibid.

14. Ibid.

15. Some of these writers predate R. D. Laing, and there is no evidence that he influenced the others, but the parallel is evident. Note Laing's recent ferocious comment on *DSM III* (*The Diagnostic and Statistical Manual of the American Psychiatric Association, Third Edition*):

> *DSM III* imputes to a person that his or her feelings, thoughts, impulses, actions, are not his or her own. They are not integral aspects of him/her as a responsible, interesting, thinking, feeling, acting person, but they are products of a mentally disordered process. The patient is not a person suffering from measles. He, she, the person is a patient suffering from his/her own thoughts, feelings, impulses, actions. The fact that many persons feel that their thoughts are taken away from them is named a bizarre delusion of persecution.
>
> The act of taking away, in theory, and in practice by "treatment," a person's thoughts, feelings, actions, is not named as bizarre persecution, but as a theoretical diagnosis and psychiatric treatment. The fact that you feel persecuted by such treatment means that you need more treatment not to feel persecuted by the treatment that is persecuting you. (*DSM III* has a name "psychosis" for a mental disorder it computes on to people who have a very

different sense of reality from the minds behind *DSM III*, but no name, no concept, no description, of that state of mind which it manifests in naming someone psychotic.)

See R. D. Laing, "God and Psychiatry," *Times Literary Supplement*, May 23, 1986, p. 559.

16. John Dryden, "The Secular Masque," in *The Pilgrim, Poems and Fables of John Dryden*, pp. 838–839.

3. Ontological Insecurities: Time and Space in the American Crime Novel

1. Auden, "The Guilty Vicarage," pp. 150–151.
2. Grella, "Murder and the Mean Streets," pp. 428, 411–412. See also Richard Chase, *The American Novel and Its Tradition.*
3. See Raymond Chandler, "The Simple Art of Murder," in *Pearls Are a Nuisance*, p. 198.
4. Raymond Chandler, *Selected Letters of Raymond Chandler*, ed. Frank McShane, pp. 90, 114.
5. Grella, "Murder and the Mean Streets," p. 418.
6. Maurice Merleau-Ponty, *The Phenomenology of Perception*, tr. Colin Smith, p. xiii.
7. Ibid., p. 360.
8. Ibid., p. 342.
9. Ibid., pp. 109, 287.
10. Ibid., pp. 290, 286.
11. Ludwig Binswanger, "The Existential Analysis School of Thought," tr. Ernest Angel, in *Existence*, ed. Rollo May, Ernest Angel, and Henri F. Ellenberger, pp. 194–195.
12. Quoted in Alain Silver, "The Dark Corner," in *Film Noir: An Encyclopedic Reference to the American Style*, ed. Alain Silver and Elizabeth Ward, p. 82.
13. Merleau-Ponty, *The Phenomenology of Perception*, pp. 353, 355.
14. For personal sources of Woolrich's malaise, see Terry Curtis Fox, "City Knights," *Film Comment* 20 (September–October 1984): 37, 36; and Francis M. Nevins, Jr., introduction to *Deadline at Dawn*, by Cornell Woolrich, pp. ix, xiv. Nevins is working on a biography.
15. Merleau-Ponty, *The Phenomenology of Perception*, pp. 25, 283–284.
16. Chandler, *Selected Letters*, pp. 372–373.
17. See E. R. Hageman, "Focus on *You Play the Black and the Red Comes Up*: 'No Bet,'" in *Tough Guy Writers of the Thirties*, ed. David Madden, pp. 164–165.
18. Edmund Wilson, "The Boys in the Back Room," in *A Literary Chronicle 1920–1950*, p. 217.
19. See Hageman, "Focus on *You Play the Black*," p. 165; and David

Feinberg, introduction to *You Play the Black and the Red Comes Up,* by Eric Knight, pp. vi–vii.

20. See Bertrand Russell, *A History of Western Philosophy,* p. 831: "Suppose I say 'The golden mountain does not exist,' and suppose you ask 'What is it that does not exist?' It would seem that, if I say 'It is the golden mountain,' I am attributing some sort of existence to it. Obviously I am not making the same statement as if I said, 'The round square does not exist.' This seemed to imply that the golden mountain is one thing and the round square is another although neither exists." Russell's solution:

> Thus "The golden mountain does not exist" means:
> "There is no entity C such that 'x is golden and mountainous' is true when x is c but not otherwise."
> With this definition the puzzle as to what is meant when we say 'The golden mountain does not exist' disappears. . . .
> This clears up two millennia of muddle-headedness about 'existence,' beginning with Plato's Theoaetetus.

It may be cleared up for Russell but not for Kenneth Burke, who sees the negative as "a peculiarly linguistic resource" and suggests that "There might even be a sense in which we could derive the linguistic faculty itself from the ability to use the Negative *qua* Negative." He proposes that *"The essential distinction between the verbal and nonverbal is in the fact that language adds the peculiar possibility of the Negative."* See Kenneth Burke, *Language as Symbolic Action,* pp. 419–420.

21. The novel was completed in 1940 but not published until 1967. Flann O'Brien (Brian O'Nolan) is best known for the Joycean *At Swim-Two-Birds.*

4. Devil or Angel: Fatal Passion in the American Crime Novel

1. Performed by The Clovers. Copyright © 1963 UNICHAPPELL Music, Inc. All rights reserved. Used by permission.

2. Cawelti, *Adventure, Mystery, and Romance,* pp. 167–168.

3. Leslie Fiedler, *Love and Death in the American Novel,* emphasizes misogyny as a characteristic of the American romance.

4. Denis de Rougemont, *Love in the Western World,* tr. Montgomery Belgion, p. 8.

5. See Geoffrey O'Brien, *Hardboiled America,* p. 74; David Madden, *James M. Cain,* p. 104; and, especially, Peter Porter, "A Scene of Verismo," *Times Literary Supplement,* September 5, 1986, p. 976: "But it is not really a case of admiring the way Visconti brings an American story of adultery and murder to life in a quintessentially Italian landscape. The plot, after all, is strongly reminiscent of *Cavallieria rusticana* and Cain's characters are archetypal enough to turn up in any impoverished community."

6. O'Brien, *Hardboiled America,* p. 73.

7. James M. Cain, preface to *Three of a Kind,* p. xiv.

8. Foster Hirsch, *Film Noir: The Dark Side of the Screen*, p. 38.

9. Ivan Moffat, "On the Fourth Floor of Paramount: Interview with Billy Wilder," in *The World of Raymond Chandler*, ed. Miriam Gross, pp. 48–49.

10. Janey Place, "Woman in Film Noir," in *Women in Film Noir*, ed. E. Ann Kaplan, p. 38.

11. See Joseph Kruppa, *Darkness Visible: Style and Substance in Film Noir*, forthcoming.

12. Place, "Woman in Film Noir," p. 48.

13. Richard Dyer, "Resistance through Charisma: Rita Hayworth and *Gilda*," in *Women in Film Noir*, ed. Kaplan, p. 91.

14. Place, "Woman in Film Noir," p. 43.

15. Christine Gledhill, "*Klute* 1: A Contemporary Film Noir and Feminist Criticism," in *Women in Film Noir*, ed. Kaplan, p. 15.

16. William S. Baring-Gould and Ceil Baring-Gould, *The Annotated Mother Goose*, p. 127.

17. Jeffrey Burton Russell, *Mephistopheles: The Devil in the Modern World*, p. 144.

18. Quoted in W. D. Snodgrass, "Crime for Punishment: The Mare-Beating Episode," in *Crime and Punishment, and The Critics*, ed. Edward Wasiolek, p. 98.

19. Mary Midgley, *Wickedness*, pp. 62–63, 155.

20. A good French film, Alain Corneau's *Série Noire*, was made from Thompson's novel, with Patrick DeWaere's hyperactive performance giving a twist to the protagonist that impinges on us quite as discomfitingly as the novel's whining narrator. One scene splendidly adds to the novel: the protagonist parks his car in an isolated industrial wasteland—the edge of the city—and does an impromptu dance, flapping about in his loose black raincoat like an underfed crow, an image both of alienation and of the awkward, violent energy it inspires. Recently, in response to feminism, tough private eyes have begun to exhibit more benevolent sentiments, some, like Robert Parker's Spenser, evolving into a rather dubious form of male feminist, some becoming sensitive to a fault. Meanwhile, women writers are producing some wonderfully tough female private detectives.

5. Pale Criminals and Murderees: The Problem of Justice in the English Crime Novel

1. Friedrich Nietzsche, *Thus Spoke Zarathustra*, in *The Portable Nietzsche*, tr. Walter Kaufman, pp. 150–151.

2. Jesse, *Murder and Its Motives*, pp. 60–62.

3. See Susan Jacoby, *Wild Justice*; and Midgley, *Wickedness*, for strongly argued justifications of traditional concepts of moral responsibility and retribution.

4. Eric R. Watson, ed., *Trial of George Joseph Smith*, Notable British Trials, pp. 33, 58, 33.

5. Quoted in Jacoby, *Wild Justice,* p. 66.
6. See Peter Ackroyd, *T. S. Eliot,* p. 143, for an account of Eliot's participation in the judicial lynching with his January 1923 letter to the *Daily Mail* commending its editorial cry for Thompson's blood. If only indirectly, Eliot got the wish of his protagonist, Sweeney, to "do a girl in."
7. Filson B. Young, ed., *Trial of Frederick Bywaters and Edith Thompson,* Notable British Trials, p. xxx.
8. Ibid., p. xxv.
9. Ibid., pp. xiv–xvi.
10. Ibid., pp. xxvi, xxvii.
11. Quoted in Joanna Glenbrander, *A Portrait of Fryn,* p. 190.
12. Young observes that if Thompson and Bywaters "had belonged to another class, where people have leisure and freedom, we should never have heard of them except, perhaps, in the Divorce Court" (*Trial of Frederick Bywaters and Edith Thompson,* pp. xxx–xxxi).
13. Quoted in Glenbrander, *A Portrait of Fryn,* p. 167.
14. See D. T. Lukken, "Psychopathic Personality," in *Encyclopedia of Psychology,* ed. Corsini, vol. 3, pp. 165–166.
15. Ibid., p. 167.

6. Civilization and Its Discontents: Simenon, Millar, Highsmith, and Thompson

1. Joseph Conrad to Cunninghame Graham, quoted in John Lucas, review of *The Collected Letters of Joseph Conrad,* vol. 2, ed. Frederick R. Karl and Laurence Davies, *Times Literary Supplement,* August 29, 1986, p. 931.
2. Brophy, *Don't Never Forget,* p. 148.
3. Quoted in J. Stuart Whitely, "Simenon: The Shadow and the Self," in *The Mystery and Detective Annual, 1973,* ed. Donald K. Adams, p. 224.
4. Ibid., p. 225.
5. Ibid., pp. 224–225.
6. Lucille Frackman Becker, *Georges Simenon,* p. 80.
7. Ibid., p. 60.
8. Quoted from *Maigret aux assises* in ibid., p. 47.
9. Quoted from Simenon's *The Time of Anais* in Claude Mauriac, *The New Literature,* tr. Samuel I. Stone, p. 145.
10. Quoted in Whitely, "Simenon," p. 224.
11. Quoted in Gavin Lambert, *The Dangerous Edge,* p. 176.
12. Simenon, *When I Was Old,* p. 113.
13. See Anne Richter, *Georges Simenon et l'homme désintégré.*
14. Mauriac, *The New Literature,* p. 135.
15. Whitely, "Simenon," p. 236.
16. Lambert, *The Dangerous Edge,* p. 200.
17. Jacques Dubois, "Simenon et la déviance," *Littérature* 1 (February 1971): 70.

18. Georges Simenon, *The Novel of Man*, tr. Bernard Frechtman, pp. 57–58.

19. Maurice Richardson, "Simenon and Highsmith: Into the Criminal's Head," in *Crime Writers*, ed. H. R. F. Keating, p. 103.

20. Gilbert Sigaux, "Lire Simenon," in *Simenon*, ed. François Lacassin and Gilbert Sigaux, pp. 15–16.

21. One of Simenon's finest novels, this is not currently available in English though there is an out-of-print Penguin translation, *Newhaven-Dieppe*. In any case, this novel especially suffers in translation.

22. Quoted in "Georges Simenon," in *Writers at Work*, First Series, ed. Malcolm Cowley, p. 158.

23. Dubois, "Simenon et la déviance," p. 64, notes a recurrent pattern of a Simenon protagonist who breaks with "ses habitudes, ses fonctions et les normes de son milieu," proceeds to complete rupture "consacré par un crime," and ends with an "impression de néant," but "toutefois, le héros a conquis, en cours d'expérience, une sorte de lucidité et il a dressé un bilan de soi." He cites Kees but not Maloin as examples.

24. "Interview with Margaret Millar," in Cooper-Clark, *Designs of Darkness*, p. 71.

25. "Interview with Patricia Highsmith," in ibid., p. 162.

26. Graham Greene, foreword to *Eleven*, by Patricia Highsmith, p. 9.

27. In Holly-Jane Rahlens, "Patricia Highsmith im Gesprach mit Holly-Jane Rahlens," Highsmith gives a detailed account of a childhood nightmare which closely resembles Clarence's dream. This is in Franz Cavagelli and Fritz Senn, eds., *Uber Patricia Highsmith*. I am indebted to Bernd Wachter, a fellow criminal scholar, for not only bringing this book to my attention but sending it to me.

28. Peter Handke sees Highsmith's central metaphor as that of a private world war. See "Die privaten Weltkriege der Patricia Highsmith," in ibid., p. 150.

29. Patricia Highsmith, *Plotting and Writing Suspense Fiction*, pp. 50–51.

30. "South Bank Show," London Weekend Television, November 17, 1982.

31. Highsmith, *Plotting and Writing Suspense Fiction*, pp. 69, 90.

32. In the Rahlens interview she guesses: "vielleicht sechs [wenn ich sie genau zahlte]." See Rahlens, "Patricia Highsmith im Gesprach," p. 170.

33. "Patricia Highsmith," *The New Review* (August 1977): 33.

34. "South Bank Show."

35. Rahlens, "Patricia Highsmith im Gesprach," p. 170.

36. "Patricia Highsmith," *The New Review*, p. 34: "Ripley's supposed to be not exactly totally masculine. Not that he's homosexual either."

37. See David Riesman, with Nathan Glazer and Reuel Denney, *The Lonely Crowd*; Robert Jay Lifton, "Protean Man," in *History and Human Survival*, pp. 311–331.

38. Lifton, "Protean Man," p. 321.

39. Ibid., pp. 321–322.
40. Alisdair McIntyre, *After Virtue*, p. 31.
41. Highsmith, *Plotting and Writing Suspense Fiction*, p. 50.
42. Ibid., pp. 50–51. Highsmith, in fact, had reservations about Clément's film: "Réné Clément, qui adapté la premiere aventure de Ripley . . . a eu raison de confier le role à Alain Delon, qui était magnifique. Mais il a tort d'ajouter . . . une fin morale." Quoted in Noelle Loriot, "Trois jours avec Patricia Highsmith," *L'Express*, June 2–8, 1979, p. 173.
43. Noel Simisolo, "Notes sur le film noir," *Cinéma* 223 (July 1977): 102.
44. Barry Gifford, "The Godless World of Jim Thompson," in *A Hell of a Woman*, by Jim Thompson, p. vi.
45. R. V. Cassill, "*The Killer Inside Me:* Fear, Purgation, and the Sophoclean Light," in *Tough Guy Writers of the Thirties*, ed. David Madden.
46. See Terence Martin, "The Negative Structures of American Literature," *American Literature* 57 (March 1985): 1–22. See also Harold Bloom's argument that from Emerson's time to ours "American authors either are in his [Emerson's] tradition, or in a countertradition originating in opposition to him." Two traditions emerge: "Place everything upon the nakedness of the American self, and you open every imaginative possibility from self-deification to absolute nihilism." See Harold Bloom, "Mr. America," *New York Review of Books*, November 25, 1984, pp. 19, 24. Nick Corey's characterization, as will be seen, plays on both possibilities.
47. Peter S. Prescott, "The Cirrhosis of the Soul," *Newsweek*, November 17, 1986, p. 90.
48. Though a friend of Peckinpah's, Thompson disliked the film. See Meredith Brody, "Killer Instinct: Jim Thompson," in Terry Curtis Fox, "City Knights," *Film Comment* 20 (September–October 1984): 46.
49. John D. Sinclair, translator and editor, *Dante's Inferno*, p. 344.
50. Ibid., pp. 352, 182.
51. Robert M. Adams, *Bad Mouth*, p. 24.
52. See Ken Weaver, *Texas Crude*. The phrases illustrating the lexicon items are my own, derived from overheard discourse. Though the state in which *Pop. 1280* is set is nowhere specified and could be Oklahoma, somehow I see it as Texas.
53. Wayne Booth, *The Rhetoric of Fiction*, pp. 383–384, 185.
54. Quoted in Roderick Thorp, introduction to *Hard Core*, by Jim Thompson, pp. x, vii, x.
55. Ursula Brumm, *American Thought and Religious Typology*, p. 180.
56. Weaver, *Texas Crude*, p. 40.
57. Roy W. Battenhouse, "Tamburlaine, The 'Scourge of God,'" in *Christopher Marlowe's Tamburlaine*, ed. Irving Ribner, p. 200.
58. Brody, "Killer Instinct," pp. 46–47.

Coda

1. Knight, *Form and Ideology in Crime Fiction;* and Ernest Mandel, *Delightful Murder.* For a dissent from Knight's Marxist interpretation, see Robin Winks, *Modus Operandi*, pp. 112–115.

2. Jean-Paul Sartre, "Time in Faulkner: The Sound and the Fury," in *Faulkner: Three Decades of Criticism*, ed. Frederic J. Hoffman and Olga W. Vickery, pp. 225–232. Sartre sees Faulkner as typifying, however brilliantly, a capitalist culture in his lack of political hope in the future: "You won't recognize in yourself the Faulknerian man, a creature deprived of potentiality and explained only by what he was . . . Man is not the sum of what he has, but the totality of what he does not yet have, of what he could have. And if we are thus immersed in the future, is not the irrational brutality of the present diminished?" It would be interesting to see how Sartre's question in his 1939 essay might have been answered by someone in the Gulag. Of course, Sartre's objections to Faulkner would apply a fortiori to many of the American crime novels I have described.

3. See John Weightman, "Summing Up Sartre," *New York Review of Books*, August 13, 1987, pp. 42–46, for a devastating account of Sartre's political expediency and casuistry, his totalitarian tendencies, and his sometime embrace of Stalinism.

4. Gustav Janouch, *Conversations with Kafka,* tr. Goronwy Rees, pp. 53–54, 73–74, 103, 172.

Bibliography

Primary Works

Bardin, John Franklin. *The Deadly Percheron.* 1946. Reprint. In *The John Franklin Bardin Omnibus.* Harmondsworth: Penguin, 1976.

———. *Devil Take the Blue-Tail Fly.* 1948. Reprint. In *Omnibus.*

———. *The Last of Philip Banter.* 1947. In *Omnibus.*

Behm, Marc. *The Eye of the Beholder.* New York: Ballantine, 1981.

Brown, Fredric. *Night of the Jabberwock.* 1949. Reprint. In *Four Novels by Fredric Brown.* London: Black Box Thrillers, Zomba Books, 1983.

———. *The Screaming Mimi.* 1950. Reprint. In *Four Novels.*

Cain, James M. *Double Indemnity.* 1936. Reprint. In *Three of a Kind.* New York: Knopf, 1944.

———. *The Postman Always Rings Twice.* 1934. Reprint. New York: Vintage, 1978.

Caspary, Vera. *Laura.* Garden City: Sundial, 1944.

Chamberlain, Ann. *The Tall Dark Man.* 1955. Reprint. Chicago: Academy Chicago, 1986.

Chandler, Raymond. *The Big Sleep.* 1939. Reprint. New York: Ballantine Books, 1971.

———. *Farewell, My Lovely.* 1940. Reprint. New York: Vintage Books, 1976.

———. *The Little Sister.* 1949. Reprint. New York: Ballantine Books, 1971.

———. *The Long Goodbye.* 1953. Reprint. New York: Ballantine Books, 1971.

Fearing, Kenneth. *The Big Clock.* 1946. Reprint. New York: Harper and Row, 1980.

Grierson, Edward. *Reputation for a Song.* 1952. Reprint. Harmondsworth: Penguin, 1986.

Hamilton, Patrick. *Hangover Square or The Man with Two Minds: A Story of Darkest Earl's Court in the Year 1939.* London: Constable, 1941.

Hammett, Dashiell. *The Maltese Falcon.* 1930. Reprint. New York: Vintage Books, 1972.

———. *Red Harvest.* 1929. Reprint. New York: Vintage Books, 1972.

Highsmith, Patricia. *A Dog's Ransom.* 1972. Reprint. Harmondsworth: Penguin, 1975.

———. *Ripley's Game.* 1974. Reprint. New York: Pyramid, 1976.

———. *The Talented Mr. Ripley.* 1956. Reprint. Harmondsworth: Penguin, 1976.

Hull, Richard. *The Murder of My Aunt.* 1934. Reprint. New York: International Polygonics, 1979.

Iles, Francis. *Before the Fact.* 1932. Reprint. New York: Dell, 1958.

———. *Malice Aforethought.* 1931. Reprint. London: Pan Books, 1979.

Jesse, F. Tennyson. *A Pin to See the Peepshow.* New York: St. Martin's, 1934.

Knight, Eric. *You Play the Black and the Red Comes Up.* 1938. Reprint. Berkeley: Black Lizard, 1980.

Lowndes, Marie Belloc. *The Lodger.* 1913. Reprint. New York: Avon, 1971.

McCabe, Cameron. *The Face on the Cutting-Room Floor.* 1937. Harmondsworth: Penguin, 1986.

McCoy, Horace. *Kiss Tomorrow Goodbye.* 1948. Reprint. In *Four Novels by Horace McCoy.* London: Black Box Thrillers, Zomba Books, 1983.

Millar, Margaret. *Beast in View.* 1955. Reprint. New York: Bantam, 1966.

———. *Beyond This Point Are Monsters.* 1970. Reprint. New York: Avon, 1974.

———. *Mermaid.* New York: William Morrow, 1982.

———. *A Stranger in My Grave.* 1960. Reprint. New York: Avon, 1973.

O'Brien, Flann. *The Third Policeman.* New York: Walker, 1967.

Onions, Oliver. *In Accordance with the Evidence.* 1912. Reprint. London: Chatto and Windus, 1968.

Potter, Dennis. *The Singing Detective.* London: Faber and Faber, 1986.

Raymond, Ernest. *We, the Accused.* 1935. Reprint. Harmondsworth: Penguin, 1983.

Rogers, Joel Townsley. *The Red Right Hand.* 1945. Reprint. New York: Carroll and Graf, 1983.

Ross, James. *They Don't Dance Much.* 1940. Reprint. New York: Popular Library, 1975.

Simenon, Georges. *L'homme de Londres.* 1933. Reprint. Paris: Presses Pocket, 1976.

———. *The Man Who Watched the Trains Go By.* Tr. Stuart Gilbert. London: George Routledge and Sons, 1942.

Smith, Shelley. *The Cellar at No. 5.* 1954. Reprint. Chicago: Academy, 1985.
———. *The Crooked Man.* New York: Harper, 1952.
Spillane, Mickey. *I the Jury.* 1947. Reprint. New York: New American Library, 1954.
Symons, Julian. *The Color of Murder.* 1957. Reprint. New York: Harper and Row, 1978.
———. *The Man Who Killed Himself.* 1967. Reprint. In *The Julian Symons Omnibus.* Harmondsworth: Penguin, 1977.
———. *The Man Whose Dreams Came True.* 1968. Reprint. In *Omnibus.*
Thompson, Jim. *The Getaway.* 1959. Reprint. In *Four Novels by Jim Thompson.* London: Black Box Thrillers, Zomba Books, 1983.
———. *A Hell of a Woman.* 1954. Reprint. Berkeley: Black Lizard, 1984.
———. *Pop. 1280.* 1964. Reprint. In *Four Novels.*
Woolrich, Cornell. *The Black Angel.* 1943. Reprint. New York: Ballantine, 1982.
———. *The Black Curtain.* 1941. Reprint. New York: Ballantine, 1982.
———. *The Black Path of Fear.* 1944. Reprint. New York: Ballantine, 1982.
———. *The Bride Wore Black.* 1940. Reprint. New York: Ballantine, 1984.
———. *I Married a Dead Man.* 1948. Reprint. New York: Ballantine, 1982.
———. *Night Has a Thousand Eyes.* 1945. Reprint. New York: Ballantine, 1982.
———. *Phantom Lady.* 1942. Reprint. New York: Ballantine, 1982.
———. *Rendezvous in Black.* 1948. Reprint. New York: Ballantine, 1982.

Secondary Works

Ackroyd, Peter. *T. S. Eliot.* New York: Simon and Schuster, 1984.
Adams, Robert M. *Bad Mouth.* Berkeley: University of California Press, 1977.
Auden, W. H. "The Guilty Vicarage." In *The Dyer's Hand.* New York: Vintage Books, 1968.
Baring-Gould, William S., and Ceil Baring-Gould. *The Annotated Mother Goose.* New York: Clarkson N. Potter, 1962.
Barzun, Jacques. *The Delights of Detection.* New York: Criterion Books, 1961.
Battenhouse, Roy W. "Tamburlaine, The Scourge of God." In *Christopher Marlowe's Tamburlaine,* ed. Irving Ribner. Indianapolis: Odyssey Press, 1974.
Becker, Lucille Frackman. *Georges Simenon.* Boston: Twayne, 1977.
Berger, Peter L., and Thomas A. Luckmann. *The Social Construction of Reality.* Garden City, N.Y.: Anchor, 1967.
Binswanger, Ludwig. "The Existential Analysis School of Thought," tr. Ernest Angel. In *Existence,* ed. Rollo May, Ernest Angel, and Henri F. Ellenberger. New York: Basic Books, 1958.

Bloom, Harold. "Mr. America." *The New York Review of Books*, November 25, 1984.

Booth, Wayne. *The Rhetoric of Fiction*. Chicago: University of Chicago Press, 1961.

Brody, Meredith. "Killer Instinct: Jim Thompson." In Terry Curtis Fox, "City Knights." *Film Comment* 20 (September–October 1984).

Brooks, Peter. "Freud's Masterplot." In *Reading for the Plot*. New York: A. A. Knopf, 1984.

Brophy, Brigid. *Don't Never Forget*. New York: Holt, Rinehart and Winston, 1966.

Brumm, Ursula. *American Thought and Religious Typology*. New Brunswick: Rutgers University Press, 1970.

Burke, Kenneth. *Language as Symbolic Action*. Berkeley: University of California Press, 1966.

Cain, James M. Preface to *Three of a Kind*. New York: Knopf, 1944.

Calvino, Italo. "Readers, Writers and Literary Machines." *New York Times Book Review*, September 7, 1986.

Cassill, R. V. "*The Killer Inside Me:* Fear, Purgation, and the Sophoclean Light." In *Tough Guy Writers of the Thirties*, ed. David Madden. Carbondale: University of Southern Illinois Press, 1968.

Cawelti, John. *Adventure, Mystery, and Romance*. Chicago: University of Chicago Press, 1976.

Chandler, Raymond. *Selected Letters of Raymond Chandler*. Ed. Frank McShane. New York: Columbia University Press, 1981.

———. "The Simple Art of Murder." In *Pearls Are a Nuisance*. Harmondsworth, Middlesex: Penguin, 1964.

Chase, Richard. *The American Novel and Its Tradition*. Garden City, N.Y.: Doubleday, 1975.

Cleckley, Hervey. *The Mask of Sanity*. St. Louis: C. V. Mosby Co., 1955.

Colarcurcio, Michael. "The Symbolic and the Symptomatic: D. H. Lawrence in Recent American Criticism." *American Quarterly* 27 (October 1975).

Collins, Carvel. "Interview with Georges Simenon." In *Writers at Work*. First Series, ed. Malcolm Cowley. Harmondsworth, Middlesex: Penguin, 1977.

Cooper-Clark, Diana. *Designs of Darkness: Interviews with Detective Novelists*. Bowling Green, Ohio: Bowling Green State University Press, 1983.

Cowley, Malcolm, ed. *Writers at Work*. First Series. Harmondsworth, Middlesex: Penguin, 1977.

Cavagelli, Franz, and Fritz Senn, eds. *Uber Patricia Highsmith*. Zurich: Diogenes, 1980.

Dante. *Inferno*. Ed. John D. Sinclair. New York: Oxford University Press, 1961.

de Rougemont, Denis. *Love in the Western World*. Tr. Montgomery Belgion. Garden City, N.Y.: Doubleday, 1957. Originally published as *L'Amour et l'occident* (1939).

Dryden, John. "The Secular Masque." In *The Pilgrim, Poems and Fables of John Dryden.* London: Oxford University Press, 1962.

Dubois, Jacques. "Simenon et la déviance." *Literature 1* (February 1971).

Dyer, Richard. "Resistance through Charisma: Rita Hayworth and *Gilda.*" In *Women in Film Noir.* Ed. E. Ann Kaplan. London: British Film Institute, 1981.

Feinburg, David. Introduction to *You Play the Black and the Red Comes Up,* by Eric Knight. Berkeley: Black Lizard Books, 1980.

Fiedler, Leslie. *Love and Death in the American Novel.* Briarcliff Manor, N.Y.: Stein and Day, 1982.

Fowler, Alastair. *Kinds of Literature.* Cambridge, Mass.: Harvard University Press, 1982.

Fox, Terry Curtis. "City Knights." *Film Comment* 20 (September–October 1984).

Freud, Sigmund. *Beyond the Pleasure Principle.* Tr. James Strachey. New York: Bantam Books, 1959.

Freud, Sigmund. *On Creativity and the Unconscious.* New York: Harper and Brothers, 1958. Originally published as *Collected Papers,* vol. 4. London: Hogarth Press, 1925.

Gifford, Barry. "The Godless World of Jim Thompson." In *A Hell of a Woman,* by Jim Thompson. Berkeley: Black Lizard, 1984.

Gledhill, Christine. "*Klute* 1: A Contemporary Film Noir and Feminist Criticism." In *Women in Film Noir.* Ed. E. Ann Kaplan. London: British Film Institute, 1981.

Glenbrander, Joanna. *A Portrait of Fryn.* London: Andre Deutsch, 1984.

Graves, Robert. *The Greek Myths.* New York: George Braziller, 1957.

Greene, Graham. Foreword to *Eleven,* by Patricia Highsmith. Harmondsworth, Middlesex: Penguin, 1972.

Grella, George. "The Formal Detective Novel." In *Detective Fiction.* Ed. Robin W. Winks. Englewood Cliffs, N.J.: Prentice-Hall, 1980.

———. "Murder and the Mean Streets: The Hard-Boiled Detective Novel." In *Detective Fiction: Crime and Compromise.* Ed. Dick Allen and David Chacko. New York: Harcourt Brace Jovanovich, 1974.

Hageman, E. R. "Focus on *You Play the Black and the Red Comes Up:* 'No Bet.'" In *Tough Guy Writers of the Thirties.* Ed. David Madden. Carbondale: University of Southern Illinois Press, 1968.

Handke, Peter. "Die privaten Weltkriege der Patricia Highsmith." In *Uber Patricia Highsmith.* Ed. Franz Cavigelli and Fritz Senn. Zurich: Diogenes, 1980.

Heller, Erich. "Conversation on *The Magic Mountain.*" In *Thomas Mann.* Ed. Henry Hatfield. Englewood Cliffs, N.J.: Prentice-Hall, 1964.

Highsmith, Patricia. *Plotting and Writing Suspense Fiction.* Boston: The Writer Inc., 1966.

Hill, Reginald. "Scuttlings and Skewerings." *Times Literary Supplement,* April 25, 1986.

Hirsch, Foster. *Film Noir: The Dark Side of the Screen.* New York: Da Capa Press, 1981.

Holquist, Michael. "Whodunit and Other Questions: Metaphysical Detective Stories in Postwar Fiction." In *The Poetics of Murder*. Ed. Glenn W. Most and William W. Stowe. San Diego: Harcourt Brace Jovanovich, 1983.

Jacoby, Susan. *Wild Justice*. New York: Harper and Row, 1983.

James, William. *Principles of Psychology*. Vol. 1. 1890. Reprint. New York: Dover, 1950.

Jameson, Frederic. *The Political Unconscious*. Ithaca: Cornell University Press, 1981.

————. *The Prison House of Language*. Princeton: Princeton University Press, 1972.

Janouch, Gustav. *Conversations with Kafka*. Tr. Goronwy Rees. 2d ed. London: Andrew Deutsch, 1968.

Jesse, F. Tennyson. *Murder and Its Motives*. 1924. Reprint. London: George G. Harrap and Co., 1952.

Kaplan, Abraham. "The Aesthetics of the Popular Arts." In *Popular Arts: A Critical Reader*. Ed. Irving Deer and Harriet A. Deer. New York: Charles Scribner's Sons, 1967.

Kaplan, E. Ann, ed. *Women in Film Noir*. London: British Film Institute, 1981.

Kermode, Frank. "Novel and Narrative." In *The Poetics of Murder*. Ed. Glenn Most and William Stowe. San Diego: Harcourt Brace Jovanovich, 1983.

Knight, Stephen. *Form and Ideology in Crime Fiction*. Bloomington: Indiana University Press, 1980.

Laing, R. D. "God and Psychiatry." *Times Literary Supplement*, May 23, 1986.

Lambert, Gavin. *The Dangerous Edge*. London: Barrie and Jenkins, 1975.

Lifton, Robert Jay. "Protean Man." In *History and Human Survival*. New York: Vintage, 1971.

Loriot, Noelle. "Trois jours avec Patricia Highsmith." *L'Express*, June 2–8, 1979.

Lucas, John. Review of *The Collected Letters of Joseph Conrad*. Vol. 2. Ed. Frederick R. Karl and Laurence Davies. *Times Literary Supplement*, August 29, 1986.

Lykken, D. T. "Psychopathic Personality." In *Encyclopedia of Psychology*. Vol. 3. Ed. Raymond J. Corsini. New York: John Wiley and Sons, 1984.

Madden, David. *James M. Cain*. New York: Twayne, 1970.

————, ed. *Tough Guy Writers of the Thirties*. Carbondale: University of Southern Illinois Press, 1968.

Mailloux, Steven. *Interpretive Conventions*. Ithaca: Cornell University Press, 1982.

Mandel, Ernest. *Delightful Murder*. London: Pluto Press, 1984.

Martin, Terence. "The Negative Structures of American Literature." *American Literature* 57 (March 1985).

Mauriac, Claude. *The New Literature*. Tr. Samuel I. Stone. New York: George Braziller, 1959.

McIntyre, Alisdair. *After Virtue.* Notre Dame: Notre Dame Press, 1981.

Mendel, W. H. "Schizophrenia." In *Encyclopedia of Psychology.* Vol. 3. Ed. Raymond J. Corsini. New York: John Wiley and Sons, 1984.

Merleau-Ponty, Maurice. *The Phenomenology of Perception.* Tr. Colin Smith. London: Routledge and Kegan Paul, 1962.

Merrivale, Patricia. "The Flaunting of Artifice in Vladimir Nabokov and Jorge Luis Borges." *Wisconsin Studies in Contemporary Literature* 8 (Spring 1967).

Midgley, Mary. *Wickedness.* London: Routledge and Kegan Paul, 1984.

Moffat, Ivan. "On the Fourth Floor of Paramount: Interview with Billy Wilder." In *The World of Raymond Chandler.* Ed. Miriam Gross. London: Weidenfeld and Nicholson, 1977.

Morrison, Blake. "Love and Betrayal in the Mist." *Times Literary Supplement,* April 11, 1986.

Most, Glenn. "The Hippocratic Smile." In *The Poetics of Murder.* Ed. Glenn Most and William Stowe. San Diego: Harcourt Brace Jovanovich, 1983.

————, and William Stowe, eds. *The Poetics of Murder.* San Diego: Harcourt Brace Jovanovich, 1983.

Nevins, Francis M., Jr. Introduction to *Deadline at Dawn,* by Cornell Woolrich. 1944. Reprint. New York: Ballantine, 1983.

Nietzsche, Friedrich. *Thus Spoke Zarathustra.* In *The Portable Nietzsche.* Tr. Walter Kaufman. Viking Press: New York, 1954.

Nokes, David. "The Brimstone Voice." *Times Literary Supplement,* December 26, 1986.

O'Brien, Geoffrey. *Hardboiled America.* New York: Van Nostrand Reinhold, 1981.

Palmer, Jerry. *Thrillers.* London: Edward Arnold, 1978.

"Patricia Highsmith." *The New Review* 4 (August 1977).

Place, Janey. "Woman in Film Noir." In *Women in Film Noir.* Ed. E. Ann Kaplan. London: British Film Institute, 1981.

Porter, Peter. "A Scene of Verismo." *Times Literary Supplement,* September 5, 1986.

Prescott, Peter S. "The Cirrhosis of the Soul." *Newsweek,* November 17, 1986.

Rahlens, Holly-Jane. "Patricia Highsmith im Gesprach mit Holly-Jane Rahlens." In *Uber Patricia Highsmith.* Ed. Franz Cavagelli and Fritz Senn. Zurich: Diogenes, 1980.

Reed, Walter L. *An Exemplary History of the Novel.* Chicago: University of Chicago Press, 1981.

Reeves, Charles Eric. "'Conveniency to Nature': Literary Art and Arbitrariness." *PMLA* 101 (October 1986).

Reilly, John M. "Margaret Millar." In *Ten Women of Mystery.* Ed. Earl F. Bargannier. Bowling Green, Ohio: Bowling Green State University Press, 1981.

Richardson, Maurice. "Simenon and Highsmith: Into the Criminal's Head." In *Crime Writers.* Ed. H. R. F. Keating. London: BBC, 1978.

Richter, Anne. *Georges Simenon et l'homme désintégré*. Brussells: La Renaissance du livre, 1964.

Riesman, David, with Nathan Glazer and Reuel Denney. *The Lonely Crowd*. Garden City, N.Y.: Doubleday, 1953.

Ross, James McLaren. *Memoirs of the Forties*. 1965. Reprint. Harmondsworth, Middlesex: Penguin, 1984.

Russell, Bertrand. *A History of Western Philosophy*. New York: Simon & Schuster, 1945.

Russell, Jeffrey Burton. *Mephistopheles: The Devil in the Modern World*. Ithaca: Cornell University Press, 1986.

Sandoe, James. "Dagger of the Mind." In *The Art of the Mystery Story*. Ed. Howard Haycraft. New York: Simon and Schuster, 1946.

Sartre, Jean-Paul. "American Novelists in French Eyes." *Atlantic* 178 (August 1946).

————. "Time in Faulkner: The Sound and the Fury." In *Faulkner: Three Decades of Criticism*. Ed. Frederic J. Hoffman and Olga W. Vickery. Lansing: Michigan State University Press, 1960.

Scholes, Robert, and Robert Kellogg. *The Nature of Narrative*. London: Oxford University Press, 1966.

Sigaux, Gilbert. "Lire Simenon." In *Simenon*. Ed. François Lacassin and Gilbert Sigaux. Paris: Plon, 1973.

Silver, Alain. "The Dark Corner." In *Film Noir: An Encyclopedic Reference to the American Style*. Ed. Alain Silver and Elizabeth Ward. Woodstock, N.Y.: Overlook Press, 1979.

Simenon, Georges. *The Novel of Man*. Tr. Bernard Frechtman. New York: Harcourt Brace World, 1964.

————. *When I Was Old*. Tr. Helen Eustis. New York: Harcourt Brace Jovanovich, 1970.

Simisolo, Noel. "Notes sur le film noir." *Cinema* 223 (July 1977).

Sinclair, John D., tr. and ed. *Dante's Inferno*. New York: Oxford University Press, 1961.

Smith, Thelma M., and Ward W. Miner. *Transatlantic Migration: The Contemporary American Novel in France*. Durham, N.C.: Duke University Press, 1955.

Snodgrass, W. D. "Crime for Punishment: The Mare-Beating Episode." In *Crime and Punishment and The Critics*. Ed. Edward Wasiolek. San Francisco: Wadsworth, 1961.

Stowe, William W. "From Semiotics to Hermeneutics: Modes of Detection in Doyle and Chandler." In *The Poetics of Murder*. Ed. Glenn Most and William Stowe. San Diego: Harcourt Brace Jovanovich, 1983.

Symons, Julian. *Bloody Murder: From the Detective Story to the Crime Novel*. Rev. ed. New York: Viking, 1985.

————. "Out of the Thin Man's Shadow." *Times Literary Supplement*, March 14, 1986.

Thorp, Roderick. Introduction to *Hard Core*, by Jim Thompson. New York: Donald I. Fine, 1986.

Todorov, Tzvetan. "The Typology of Detective Fiction." In *The Poetics of Prose*. Ithaca: Cornell University Press, 1977.

Watson, Eric R., ed. *Trial of George Joseph Smith*. Notable British Trials. Edinburgh: William Hodge and Co., n.d.

Weaver, Ken. *Texas Crude*. New York: E. P. Dutton, 1984.

Weightman, John. "Summing Up Sartre." *New York Review of Books*, August 13, 1987.

West, Nathanael. "Some Notes on Miss L." In *Nathanael West: Twentieth Century Views*. Ed. Jay Martin. Englewood Cliffs, N.J.: Prentice-Hall, 1971.

Whitely, J. Stuart. "Simenon: The Shadow and the Self." In *The Mystery and Detective Annual, 1973*. Ed. Donald K. Adams. Beverly Hills: Donald Adams, 1974.

Wilson, Edmund. "The Boys in the Back Room." In *A Literary Chronicle 1920–1950*. Garden City, N.Y.: Doubleday Anchor Books, 1952.

Wingate, Nancy. "Getting Away with Murder: An Analysis." *Journal of Popular Culture* 12 (Spring 1979).

Winks, Robin. *Modus Operandi*. Boston: David R. Godine, 1982.

Young, Filson B., ed., *Trial of Frederick Bywaters and Edith Thompson*. Notable British Trials. Edinburgh: William Hodge and Co., 1923.

Index